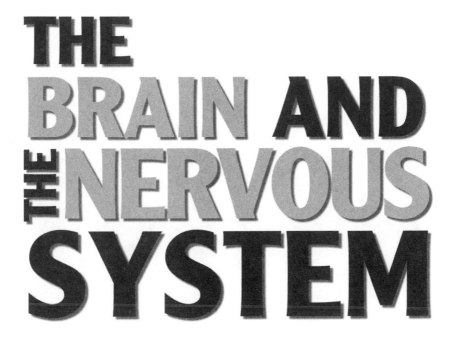

THE BRAIN AND THE NERVOUS SYSTEM

THE HUMAN BODY

THE BRAIN AND THE NERVOUS SYSTEM

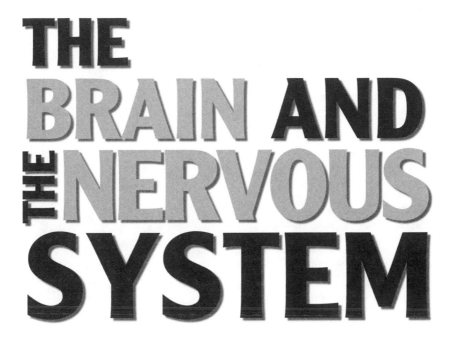

EDITED BY KARA ROGERS, SENIOR EDITOR, BIOMEDICAL SCIENCES

Britannica®
Educational Publishing

IN ASSOCIATION WITH

ROSEN
EDUCATIONAL SERVICES

Published in 2011 by Britannica Educational Publishing
(a trademark of Encyclopædia Britannica, Inc.)
in association with Rosen Educational Services, LLC
29 East 21st Street, New York, NY 10010.

Distributed exclusively by Rosen Educational Services.
For a listing of additional Britannica Educational Publishing titles, call toll free (800) 237-9932.

First Edition

Britannica Educational Publishing
Michael I. Levy: Executive Editor
J.E. Luebering: Senior Manager
Marilyn L. Barton: Senior Coordinator, Production Control
Steven Bosco: Director, Editorial Technologies
Lisa S. Braucher: Senior Producer and Data Editor
Yvette Charboneau: Senior Copy Editor
Kathy Nakamura: Manager, Media Acquisition
Kara Rogers: Senior Editor, Biomedical Sciences

Rosen Educational Services
Alexandra Hanson-Harding: Senior Editor
Nelson Sá: Art Director
Cindy Reiman: Photography Manager
Matthew Cauli: Designer, Cover Design
Introduction by Don Rauf

Library of Congress Cataloging-in-Publication Data

The brain and the nervous system / edited by Kara Rogers.
    p. cm. — (The human body)
"In association with Britannica Educational Publishing, Rosen Educational services."
Includes bibliographical references and index.
ISBN 978-1-61530-136-2 (library binding)
1. Nervous system—Popular works. 2. Brain—Popular works. I. Rogers, Kara.
QP355.2.B725 2011
612.8—dc22

                                                            2010004639

Manufactured in the United States of America

On the cover: The human brain makes up only 2 percent of peoples' total body weight.
© *www.istockphoto.com / Sebastian Kaulitzki*

Introduction: This image shows a longitudinal section of the human torso showing the autonomic nervous system. *3DClinic/Getty Images*

On pages 19, 50, 85, 112, 142, 167, 201, 233, 266, 268, 271, 275: © www.istockphoto.com / Stephen Kirklys

CONTENTS

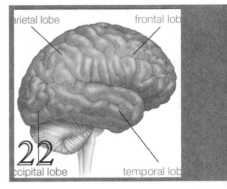

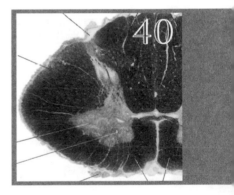

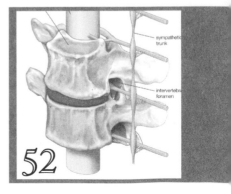

INTRODUCTION

The smell of fresh baked chocolate-chip cookies. The pain from stubbing a toe. The enjoyment of watching a movie in a theatre. All the sensory details that one absorbs in life travel along the body's own information superhighway called the nervous system. Composed of central and peripheral components, with the brain as the command centre, the nervous system is responsible for the body's most fundamental activities. Nerves, which are made up of bundles of fibres, deliver impulses to various parts of the body, including the brain. The brain translates the information delivered by the impulses, which then enables the person to react. The pan is hot—put it down fast. The traffic light is red—hit the brakes. The brain tells the body how to react based on all the information delivered through the nervous system. Every movement a person makes depends on the nervous system, as do thoughts and communication. In this volume, readers are introduced to the body's incredible information processing mechanisms and are presented with an opportunity to learn about the intricate system around which the field of neuroscience has developed.

The most basic unit of the nervous system is the nerve cell, also called a neuron. Neurons consist of three parts: a dendrite, a cell body, and an axon, all of which function to transmit information in the form of electrical impulses or signals. Dendrites receive the signals, which then move to the cell body and travel until they reach the end of an axon, or nerve fibre. The signal then crosses a gap (synapse) between the axon and the next dendrite, changing into a chemical signal called a neurotransmitter to bridge the gap. To transmit information through the neurons, the body relies on special cells called receptors. Receptors receive information from both external and internal environments and play an important role in converting this information into electrical impulses. Receptors in the nose, for example, react to molecules in the air and then pass along the smell details through the nerves and along to the brain. Nasal receptor cells are classified as exteroceptive, as are receptors for sight, hearing, touch, and taste. Interoceptive sensors receive signals from inside the body and convey information about internal conditions, such as when the bladder is full or when blood pressure is high. Proprioceptors are stimulated by movements of parts of the body, such as the limbs.

Together, the brain and the spinal cord form what is known as the central nervous system. Though weighing in at a mere 0.9 to 1.4 kilograms (about 2 to 3 pounds), the human brain has an immense capacity to process, retain, and deliver information to the rest of the body. Contained in a protective compartment known as the skull, it consists of billions of neurons. It is comprised of three main sections: the cerebrum, the brainstem, and the cerebellum.

The biggest part of the brain, the cerebrum, has two hemispheres, which consist of two different types of tissue: gray matter and white matter. Because each hemisphere handles distinct functions, the hemispheres are two different sizes. For example, for most people, language ability is in the left hemisphere. The left side also appears to be dominant for math and logic, whereas the right side may be dominant for spatial abilities, face recognition, visual imagery, and music.

The cerebral cortex, made of gray matter, is the thin wrinkled outer layer of the cerebrum. The folding, in effect, creates hills (called gyri) and valleys (called sulci). The number of wrinkles and ridges on the brain may correspond to intelligence on the species level. For example, humans and monkeys, which are capable of complex activities such as reasoning and language, have many ridges compared to mice and rats, which have smooth brains and appear to lack the cognitive abilities known to primates.

The cortex is divided into distinct areas called lobes, which control specific activities. The frontal lobes of the cerebrum handle thinking, intelligence, memory, speech, and movement. The temporal lobes take care of hearing, taste, and smell. The occipital lobe functions in sight, and the parietal lobes manage touch. Many of the processes handled by the various lobes, however, are highly integrated, often requiring the participation of multiple regions of the brain to be interpreted completely.

Beneath the cortex rests the white matter, which is composed of nerve fibres (axons) encased in whitish myelin sheaths that relay information between the cerebral cortex and the rest of the body. The gray matter is really the thinking, active part of the brain (like a hard drive in a computer), while the white matter serves as the wiring. However, the architecture of the white matter is also vital to a person's intelligence, and its function may be enhanced by learning new skills and by challenging the brain.

The second major part of the brain is the brainstem, which is the connection between the brain and spinal cord. The brainstem regulates all primary bodily functions, such as breathing, heartbeat, blood circulation, and digestion. All essential functions that every animal must have but does not need to think about are taken care of by the brainstem.

Several sections make up the brainstem, including: the midbrain on top (for head and eye movement and shutting off stimuli during sleep); the pons in the middle (for sleep functions, such as rapid eye movement); the medulla oblongata on the bottom (providing the connection to the spinal cord, relaying motor skills, and the centre for breathing and heart beat control, as well as coughing, swallowing, and vomiting); the thalamus (regulating alertness and attention); and the hypothalamus (for maintaining a range of bodily activity and behaviour).

The third major section of the brain is called the cerebellum. Literally meaning "little cerebrum," this part of the brain is in charge of movements, balance, and coordination. (Lance Armstrong has his cerebellum to thank for being able to handle his bicycle with such agility.) In some ways, the cerebellum is the brain's autopilot and coordinates muscles and nerves to respond appropriately. A person has the ability to walk or turn a page or scratch an itch because of the function of the cerebellum.

Running down from the brainstem and located inside the spine, the spinal cord serves as the main highway along which the body's nerves deliver information and receive directions from the brain. Different sensations are communicated to the brain along the spinal cord in distinct tracts. For example, sensations of pain and temperature run along the ascending spinothalamic tracts to the thalamus. Voluntary motor stimuli are carried along the descending corticospinal tracts from the brainstem to the spinal cord.

These tracts of communication connect the spinal cord to the peripheral nervous system, which consists of all the neural tissue outside the central nervous system. One aspect of the peripheral nervous system is the autonomic nervous system, which further breaks down into the sympathetic and parasympathetic nervous systems. As a whole, the autonomic nervous system is responsible for the body's involuntary activity. The sympathetic system generally handles the heart's responses to activity and stimuli—for example, if a person runs, the heart beats faster. When the body is active or under stress, sympathetic nerves constrict blood vessels throughout the body, sending more blood to the heart. Parasympathetic nerves do the opposite—dilating blood vessels to slow down the heart. They also regulate the activity of the glands throughout the body.

Pathways in the peripheral nervous system that occur in the tissues of the head connect directly to the brainstem and therefore bypass the spinal cord altogether. For example, the optic nerve (vision), the olfactory nerve (smell), the vestibulocochlear nerve (hearing and balance), the glossopharyngeal nerve (taste), and the facial nerve (facial expressions) are all examples of cranial nerves that form connections between muscles and sense organs of the head and the brain. Alongside the spinal nerves, or those nerves in the spinal cord, the cranial nerves directly control the most basic functions of the body, including those of the respiratory and cardiovascular systems.

The human body is able to move because of coordination between the various parts of the nervous system. Reflexes are the central nervous system's immediate and automatic responses to a stimulus. To make sure the nervous system is in working order, doctors often check the knee-jerk reflex by tapping the knee with a small hammer. If the person's nervous system is working appropriately, the patient typically gives an involuntary small kick. The vestibular system regulates other essential aspects of movement, such as maintaining balance and equilibrium. Most people take these abilities for granted, but balance and equilibrium involve a neural coordination of inner ear, eyes, muscles, joints, feet, and gravity receptors on the skin, to name a few parts in play. The nerves in this system also adjust blood pressure and limb positions to maintain equilibrium and balance.

Nerves are essential to perception and sensation, and the human nervous system is specially designed for experiencing these functions on a sophisticated level. In the act of seeing, humans tend to group things and see the whole (or gestalt) rather than a collection of individual items. In a picture made of dots, people tend to see the whole picture. These ways of perceiving and sensing illustrate the remarkable complexity of the brain.

The brain is also incredibly adaptive, and its ability to act and react to many different and changing circumstances is referred to as neuroplasticity. This quality gives people the ability to learn new information and adjust to new conditions. Because of its plasticity, the brain can rebuild damage from trauma and disease. Healthy brain cells near an injured area of the brain can take on the functions of the damaged part of the brain. Sometimes a brain that has suffered trauma can figure out a new approach by reorganizing preexisting neuronal networks in a process called compensatory masquerade.

As remarkable as the brain is at compensating and finding ways to "heal," there are also many ailments that can damage the brain and spinal cord. The function of these tissues may be impaired as a result of external forces or internal abnormalities. Neurobiological abnormalities affect the physical makeup of the brain and nervous system and can result in developmental and behavioral disorders. Some of these disorders start at a very young age or in the womb. For example, neural tube defects result from the failure of the neural tube structure to close during the embryonic stage. In a healthy embryo, this structure eventually closes to form the central nervous system. The most common neural tube defect is spina bifida. Symptoms vary but can include partial or total paralysis. Cerebral palsy is another neurological disorder in which paralysis results from abnormal development in the brain. While the disease has no cure, treatments can help patients perform everyday activities.

Other neurobiological diseases include pervasive developmental disorders (PDDs), such as autism and Asperger syndrome, and mental disorders. PDDs affect the ways in which individuals interact and communicate with others as well as the activities in which they engage. For example, people with autism often have limited language abilities and interests and cannot develop sustained relationships with peers. Though the causes are uncertain, many of the symptoms can be controlled. Mental disorders such as depression, schizophrenia, obsessive-compulsive disorder, and attention-deficit/hyperactivity disorder are sometimes correlated with chemical imbalances in the brain. However, as with PDDs, the causes of mental disorders are often unknown, and treatment typically involves management of the symptoms.

Neurodegenerative disorders often affect the brain or nervous system later in life and are frequently caused by genetic factors or infection. The memory loss typically associated with aging is often indicative of dementia, which entails an irreversible and progressive destruction of nerve cells and brain tissue. Alzheimer disease is a particular type of dementia that is characterized not only by memory loss but also by the increasing inability to function alone. When neurons in the brain that are responsible for voluntary movement begin to deteriorate, individuals lose control of their arms and legs, as is the case with Parkinson disease. Other neurological disorders include epilepsy, marked by excessive electrical activity in the brain, which results in seizures, and meningitis, a communicable disease that attacks the meninges, or membranes that cover the brain and spinal cord.

A host of other diseases or afflictions can damage the central nervous system as well. The destruction of the myelin sheath around the nerve fibres in the brain, spinal cord, and optic nerves results in multiple sclerosis. Amyotrophic lateral sclerosis (ALS), or Lou Gehrig disease, destroys neurons that control movement.

Every year advances are being made in brain research and in the treatment of brain and nervous system disorders; however, many of the mysteries of the remarkable human brain and nervous system have yet to be discovered. The intricacies of the nervous system make it both highly adaptable and highly susceptible to damage on a number of levels, and the brain's versatility and capacity to develop is in many ways unparalleled by any other part of the body. To better understand these abilities, however, careful study is required. Thus, only with further research can the strengths and weaknesses of the human brain and nervous system become more fully known.

CHAPTER 1

THE CENTRAL
NERVOUS SYSTEM

The human nervous system functions as a high-speed anatomical and physiological unit. It controls the body's movements, and through its ability to receive, process, and transmit information in the form of chemical and electrical signals, it can adjust and fine-tune its control. The integration of chemical and electrical signaling pathways in the brain provides us with cognitive abilities, such as perception, thought, memory, and emotion. The human nervous system can be divided into two main parts: the central nervous system and the peripheral nervous system. The central nervous system consists of the brain and spinal cord, while the peripheral system consists of all the neural (nerve) tracts that lie outside these central tissues and connect to the rest of the body.

The brain and spinal cord are both derived from the neural tube, a structure found in embryos. Both are surrounded by protective membranes called the meninges, and both float in a crystal-clear cerebrospinal fluid. The brain is encased in a bony vault, the neurocranium, while the cylindrical and elongated spinal cord lies in the vertebral canal, which is formed by successive vertebrae connected by dense ligaments.

THE BRAIN

The brain essentially serves as the body's information processing centre. It receives signals from sensory neurons (nerve cell bodies and their axons and dendrites) in the central and peripheral nervous systems, and in response it generates and sends new signals that instruct the corresponding parts of the body to move or react in some way. It also integrates signals received from the body with signals from adjacent areas of the brain, giving rise to perception and consciousness.

The brain weighs about 1,500 grams (3 pounds) and constitutes about 2 percent of total body weight. It consists of three major divisions: (1) the massive paired hemispheres of the cerebrum, (2) the brainstem, consisting of the thalamus, hypothalamus, epithalamus, subthalamus, midbrain, pons, and medulla oblongata, and (3) the cerebellum.

CEREBRUM

The cerebrum is the largest, uppermost portion of the brain. It is involved with sensory integration, control of voluntary movement, and higher intellectual functions, such as speech and abstract thought. There are two cerebral hemispheres—one on the left and one on the right side of the brain. The outer layer of each of these duplicate cerebral hemispheres is composed of a convoluted (wrinkled) outer layer of gray matter, called the cerebral cortex.

Beneath the cerebral cortex is an inner core of white matter, which is composed of a special kind of nerve fibre called myelinated commissural nerve fibres. Nerve fibres, or axons, are long, thin strands of tissue that project from a nerve cell and carry electrical impulses to and from the brain. These fibres connect the two cerebral hemispheres via a thick band of white matter called the corpus callosum. Other fibres, called association fibres, connect different regions of a single hemisphere. Myelinated fibres (myelin is a fatty white material that forms a sheath around some nerve fibres) projecting to and from the cerebral cortex form a concentrated fan-shaped band, known as the internal capsule. The internal capsule consists of an anterior (forward) limb and a larger posterior limb and is abruptly curved, with the apex directed toward the centre of the brain; the junction is called the genu. The cerebrum also contains the basal ganglia, a mass of nerve fibre that helps to initiate and control matters of movement.

The cerebral hemispheres are partially separated from each other by a deep groove called the longitudinal fissure. At the base of the longitudinal fissure lies the corpus callosum, which provides a communication link between corresponding regions of the cerebral hemispheres.

Each cerebral hemisphere supplies motor function to the opposite, or contralateral, side of the body from which it receives sensory input. In other words, the left hemisphere controls the right half of the body, and vice versa. Each hemisphere also receives impulses conveying the senses of touch and vision, largely from the contralateral half of the body, while auditory input comes from both sides. Pathways conveying the senses of smell and taste to the cerebral cortex are ipsilateral (they do not cross to the opposite hemisphere).

In spite of this arrangement, the cerebral hemispheres are not functionally equal. In each individual, one hemisphere is dominant. The dominant hemisphere controls language, mathematical and analytical functions, and handedness. The nondominant hemisphere controls simple spatial concepts, recognition of faces, some auditory aspects, and emotion.

Lobes of the Cerebral Cortex

The cerebral cortex is highly convoluted. The crest of a single convolution is known as a gyrus, and the fissure between two gyri is known as a sulcus. Sulci and gyri form a more or less constant pattern, on the basis of which the

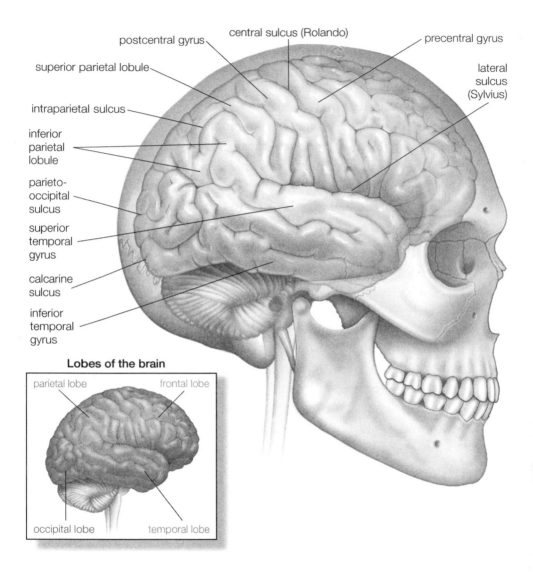

Lateral (side) view of the right cerebral hemisphere of the human brain, shown in situ within the skull. A number of convolutions (called gyri) and fissures (called sulci) in the surface define four lobes—the parietal, frontal, temporal, and occipital—that contain major functional areas of the brain. Encyclopædia Britannica, Inc.

surface of each cerebral hemisphere is commonly divided into four lobes: (1) frontal, (2) parietal, (3) temporal, and (4) occipital. Two major sulci located on the lateral, or side, surface of each hemisphere distinguish these lobes. The first one, the central sulcus, or fissure of Rolando, separates the frontal and parietal lobes. The second one, the deeper lateral sulcus, or fissure of Sylvius, forms the boundary between the temporal lobe and the frontal and parietal lobes.

The frontal lobe, the largest of the four cerebral lobes, lies rostral to the central sulcus (toward the nose from the sulcus). One important structure in the frontal lobe is the precentral gyrus, which constitutes the primary motor (motion) region of the brain. When parts of the gyrus are electrically stimulated in conscious patients who are under local anesthesia, they produce localized movements on the opposite side of the body that are interpreted by the patients as voluntary. Injury to parts of the precentral gyrus results in paralysis on the contralateral half of the body. Parts of the inferior frontal lobe constitute the Broca area, a region involved with speech.

The parietal lobe, which lies behind, or posterior, to the central sulcus, is divided into three parts: (1) the postcentral gyrus, (2) the superior parietal lobule, and (3) the inferior parietal lobule. The postcentral gyrus receives sensory input from the contralateral half of the body. The sequential representation is the same as in the primary motor area. Sensations from the head are represented in inferior (lower) parts of the gyrus and impulses from the lower extremities are represented in superior portions. The superior parietal lobule, located caudal to (below and behind) the postcentral gyrus, lies above the intraparietal sulcus. This lobule is regarded as an association cortex, an area that is not involved in either sensory or motor processing, although part of the superior parietal lobule may be concerned with motor function. The inferior parietal lobule (composed of the angular and supramarginal gyri) is a cortical—i.e; outer layer—region involved with the integration of multiple sensory signals.

In both the parietal and frontal lobes, each primary sensory or motor area is close to, or surrounded by, a smaller secondary area. The primary sensory area receives input only from the thalamus, while the secondary sensory area receives input from the thalamus, the primary sensory area, or both. The motor areas receive input from the thalamus as well as the sensory areas of the cerebral cortex.

The temporal lobe, which is below the lateral sulcus, fills the middle fossa, or hollow area, of the skull. The outer surface of the temporal lobe is an association area made up of the superior, middle, and inferior temporal gyri. An association area is a part of the cerebral cortex that is connected to both cerebral hemispheres and which helps link parts of the brain that are concerned with motor and sensory function. Near the margin of the lateral sulcus, two transverse (lying across) temporal gyri constitute the primary auditory area of the brain. The sensation of hearing is represented here in a tonotopic fashion—that is, with different frequencies of sound represented on different parts of the auditory area. The transverse gyri are surrounded by a less finely tuned secondary auditory area. A medial, or inner, protrusion near the underside, or ventral surface of the temporal lobe, known as the uncus, constitutes a large part of the primary olfactory area, concerning the sense of smell.

The occipital lobe, important to vision, lies toward the back of the brain, behind the parieto-occipital sulcus. The parieto-occipital sulcus joins another sulcus, the calcarine sulcus, in a Y-shaped formation. Cortex—a special kind of gray matter that makes up the outer layer of the cerebrum—on both banks of the calcarine sulcus constitutes the primary visual area, which receives input from the contralateral visual field via an information-carrying nerve fibre system called optic radiation. The visual field is represented near the calcarine sulcus with upper quadrants of the visual field laid out along the lower bank of the sulcus and lower quadrants of the visual field represented on the upper bank.

Aside from the four major cerebral lobes there are two other lobes worth noting. The insular lobe, or central lobe, is an invaginated (folded back in upon itself) triangular area on the medial surface of the lateral sulcus. Not visible from the surface of the cerebrum, it can be seen in the intact brain only by separating the frontal and parietal lobes from the temporal lobe. The insular lobe is thought to be involved in sensory and motor visceral functions as well as taste perception.

The limbic lobe is located on the medial margin (or limbus) of each hemisphere. Composed of adjacent portions of the frontal, parietal, and temporal lobes that surround the corpus callosum, the limbic lobe is involved with autonomic (involuntary) and related somatic (body) behavioral activities. The limbic lobe receives input from thalamic nuclei. A nucleus is a structure in the brain made up of a group of neurons. The thalamic nuclei, made up of neurons in the thalamus, are connected with and relay information from parts of the brain such as the hypothalamus. These neurons are also connected to the hippocampal formation.

Cerebral Ventricles

The hippocampal formation is located within one of the cerebral ventricles, cavities deep within the white matter of the cerebral hemispheres. These cavities, which are filled with cerebrospinal fluid, form the ventricular system. They include a pair of C-shaped lateral ventricles with anterior, inferior, and posterior "horns" protruding into the frontal, temporal, and occipital lobes, respectively. Most of the clear cerebrospinal fluid that flows both in the brain and the spinal column is produced in the ventricles, and about 70 percent of it is secreted by the choroid plexus, a collection of blood vessels in the walls of the lateral ventricles. The fluid drains via interventricular foramina, or openings, into a slitlike third ventricle, which, situated along the midline of the brain, separates the symmetrical halves of the thalamus and hypothalamus. From there the fluid passes through the cerebral aqueduct in the midbrain and into the fourth ventricle in the hindbrain. Openings in the fourth ventricle permit cerebrospinal fluid to enter certain regions called subarachnoid spaces surrounding both the brain and the spinal cord.

Basal Ganglia

Deep within the cerebral hemispheres, large gray masses of nerve cells, called nuclei, form components of the basal ganglia. Four basal ganglia can be distinguished: (1) the caudate nucleus, (2) the putamen, (3) the globus pallidus, and (4) the amygdala. Phylogenetically, the amygdala was the first to evolve and is the oldest of the basal ganglia.

The caudate nucleus and the putamen have similar cellular compositions, cytochemical features, and functions but slightly different connections. The putamen lies deep within the cortex of the insular lobe, while the caudate nucleus has a C-shaped configuration that parallels the lateral ventricle. The head of the caudate nucleus protrudes into the anterior horn of the lateral ventricle, the body lies above and lateral to the thalamus, and the tail is in the roof of the inferior horn of the lateral ventricle. The tail of the caudate nucleus ends in relationship to the amygdaloid nuclear complex , which lies in the temporal lobe beneath the cortex of the uncus.

There are an enormous number of neurons within the caudate nucleus and putamen; they are of two basic types: spiny and aspiny. Spiny striatal neurons are medium-size cells with radiating dendrites (small projections) that are studded with spines. The long, slender axons of these cells project beyond the caudate nucleus and putamen's boundaries. All nerves providing input to these two kinds of

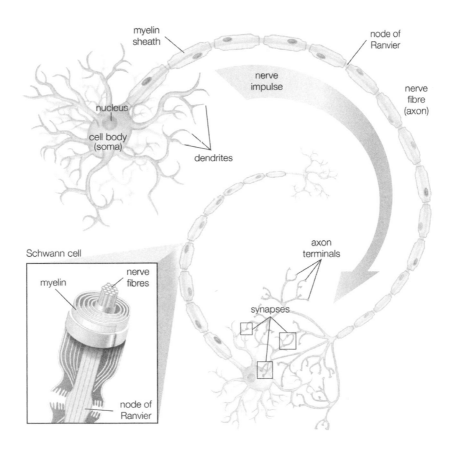

The structural features of a motor neuron include the cell body, the nerve fibre (or axon), and the dendrites. 2002 Encyclopædia Britannica, Inc

basal ganglia terminate upon the dendrites of spiny striatal neurons. All output is via axons of the same neurons. Chemically, spiny striatal neurons are heterogeneous; that is, most contain more than one neurotransmitter (a chemical that moves nerve impulses). One kind of neurotransmitter, Gamma-aminobutyric acid (GABA) is the primary neurotransmitter contained in spiny striatal neurons. Other neurotransmitters found in spiny striatal neurons include substance P and enkephalin.

Aspiny striatal neurons have smooth dendrites and short axons confined to the caudate nucleus or putamen. Small aspiny striatal neurons secrete GABA, neuropeptide Y, somatostatin, or some combination of these. The largest aspiny neurons are evenly distributed neurons that also secrete neurotransmitters and are important in maintaining the balance of GABA and yet another kind of neurotransmitter called dopamine.

Because the caudate nucleus and putamen receive varied and diverse inputs from multiple sources that utilize different neurotransmitters, they are regarded as the receptive component of the corpus striatum (a unit of basal ganglia made up of the caudate nucleus, putamen, and globus pallidus). Most input originates from regions of the cerebral cortex, via connecting fibres called corticostriate fibres which contain the excitatory neurotransmitter glutamate. In addition, afferent fibres (which carry impulses to a nerve centre in the spinal cord or brain) project to the caudate nucleus or the putamen. These afferent fibres originate from a large nucleus located in the midbrain called the substantia nigra or from intralaminar thalamic nuclei. Neurons in the substantia nigra are known to synthesize dopamine, but the neurotransmitter secreted by thalamostriate neurons has not been identified. All striatal afferent systems terminate, or end, in patchy areas called strisomes; areas not receiving terminals are called the matrix. Spiny striatal neurons containing GABA, substance P, and enkephalin project in a specific pattern onto the globus pallidus and the substantia nigra.

The pattern is as follows: The globus pallidus, consisting of two cytologically (cellularly) similar wedge-shaped segments, the lateral and the medial, lies between the putamen and the internal capsule. Striatopallidal fibres from the caudate nucleus and putamen converge on the globus pallidus like spokes of a wheel. Both segments of the pallidum receive GABAergic terminals, but in addition the medial segment receives substance P fibres, and the lateral segment receives enkephalinergic projections. The output of the entire corpus striatum arises from GABAergic cells in the medial pallidal segment and in the substantia nigra, both of which receive fibres from the striatum. GABAergic cells in the medial pallidal segment and the substantia nigra project to different nuclei in the thalamus; these in turn influence distinct regions of the cerebral cortex involved with motor function. The lateral segment of the globus pallidus, on the other hand, projects almost exclusively to the subthalamic nucleus, from which it receives reciprocal input. No part of the corpus striatum projects fibres to spinal levels.

When basal ganglia don't function properly, pathological processes result. These processes, involving the corpus striatum and related nuclei, are associated with a variety of specific diseases characterized by abnormal involuntary movements (collectively referred to as dyskinesia) and significant alterations of muscle tone. Parkinson disease and Huntington disease are among the more prevalent syndromes; each is associated with deficiencies in the synthesis of particular neurotransmitters.

The amygdala, located in the temporal lobe, is an almond-shaped nucleus underlying the uncus. Although it

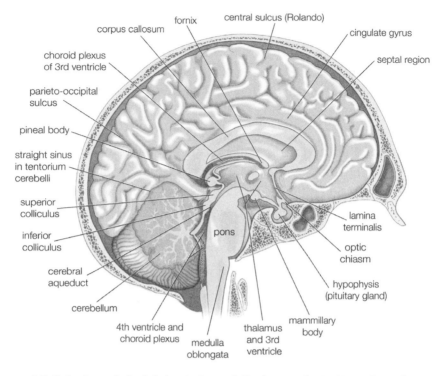

corpus callosum

fornix

central sulcus (Rolando)

cingulate gyrus

choroid plexus
of 3rd ventricle

septal region

parieto-occipital
sulcus

pineal body

straight sinus
in tentorium
cerebelli

superior
colliculus

inferior
colliculus

cerebral
aqueduct

cerebellum

pons

lamina
terminalis

optic
chiasm

hypophysis
(pituitary gland)

4th ventricle and
choroid plexus

medulla
oblongata

thalamus
and 3rd
ventricle

mammillary
body

Medial view of the left hemisphere of the human brain. Encyclopædia
Britannica, Inc.

receives olfactory inputs, the amygdala plays no role in the
perception of smell. This nucleus also has reciprocal connections with the hypothalamus, the basal forebrain, and
regions of the cerebral cortex. It plays important roles in
visceral, endocrine, and cognitive functions related to
motivational behaviour.

BRAINSTEM

The brainstem is made up of all the unpaired structures
that connect the cerebrum with the spinal cord. Most
rostral (forward) in the brainstem are structures often
collectively referred to as the diencephalon. These

structures are the epithalamus, the thalamus, the hypothalamus, and the subthalamus. Directly beneath the diencephalon is the midbrain, or mesencephalon, and beneath the midbrain are the pons and medulla oblongata, often referred to as the hindbrain.

Epithalamus

The epithalamus is represented mainly by the pineal gland, which lies in the midline posterior and dorsal to (in the back of) the third ventricle. This gland synthesizes melatonin and enzymes sensitive to daylight. Rhythmic changes in the activity of the pineal gland in response to daylight suggest that the gland serves as a biological clock.

Thalamus

The thalamus has long been regarded as the key to understanding the organization of the central nervous system. It is involved in the relay and distribution of most, but not all, sensory and motor signals to specific regions of the cerebral cortex. Sensory signals generated in all types of receptors are projected via complex pathways to specific relay nuclei in the thalamus, where they are segregated and systematically organized. The relay nuclei in turn supply the primary and secondary sensory areas of the cerebral cortex. Sensory input to thalamic nuclei is contralateral for the sensory and visual systems, bilateral and contralateral for the auditory system, and ipsilateral for the gustatory and olfactory systems.

The sensory relay nuclei of the thalamus, collectively known as the ventrobasal complex, receive input from the medial lemniscus (originating in the part of the brainstem called the medulla oblongata). The medial lemniscus is a collection of nerve fibres that sends messages between the spinal cord and the thalamus. The sensory relay nuclei also receive input from spinothalamic tracts, and from the trigeminal nerve. Fibres within these ascending tracts that terminate in the central core of the ventrobasal complex receive input from deep sensory receptors, while fibres projecting onto the outer shell receive input from cutaneous (skin) receptors. This segregation of deep and superficial sensation is preserved in projections of the ventrobasal complex to the primary sensory area of the cerebral cortex.

The metathalamus is concerned with vision and hearing. It is composed of the medial and lateral geniculate bodies, or nuclei. The lateral geniculate body is a kind of visual relay station that conveys messages to nerve cells. Fibres of the optic nerve end in the lateral geniculate body, which consists of six cellular laminae, or layers, folded into a horseshoe configuration. Each lamina represents a complete map of the contralateral visual hemifield. Cells in all layers of the lateral geniculate body project via optic radiation to the visual areas of the cerebral cortex. Another neural structure, the medial geniculate body, receives auditory impulses from the inferior colliculus of the midbrain and relays them to the auditory areas of the temporal lobe. Only the ventral nucleus of the medial geniculate body is laminated and tonotopically organized; this part projects to the primary auditory area and is finely tuned. Other subdivisions of the medial geniculate body project to the belt of secondary auditory cortex surrounding the primary area.

Most output from the cerebellum projects to specific thalamic relay nuclei in a pattern similar to that for sensory input. The thalamic relay nuclei in turn provide input to the primary motor area of the frontal lobe. This system appears to provide coordinating and controlling influences that result in the appropriate force, sequence, and direction of voluntary motor activities. Output from the corpus striatum, on the other hand, is relayed by thalamic nuclei that have access to the supplementary and premotor areas. The supplementary motor area, located on the medial aspect of the hemisphere, exerts modifying influences upon the primary motor area and appears to be involved in programming skilled motor sequences. The premotor area, rostral to the primary motor area, plays a role in sensorially guided movements.

Other major thalamic nuclei include the anterior nuclear group, the mediodorsal nucleus, and the pulvinar. The anterior nuclear group receives input from the hypothalamus and projects upon parts of the limbic lobe (i.e., the cingulate gyrus). The mediodorsal nucleus, part of the medial nuclear group, has reciprocal connections with large parts of the frontal lobe rostral to the motor areas. The pulvinar is a posterior nuclear complex that, along with the mediodorsal nucleus, has projections to association areas of the cortex.

Output ascending from the reticular formation of the brainstem is relayed to the cerebral cortex by intralaminar thalamic nuclei, which are located in laminae separating the medial and ventrolateral thalamic nuclei. This ascending system is involved with arousal mechanisms, maintaining alertness, and directing attention to sensory events.

Hypothalamus

The hypothalamus lies below the thalamus in the walls and floor of the third ventricle. It is divided into medial and lateral groups by a curved bundle of axons called the fornix, which originate in the hippocampal formation and project to two round masses of gray matter on the underside of the brain that are part of the limbic system called the mammillary bodies. The hypothalamus controls major endocrine functions by secreting hormones (i.e., oxytocin and vasopressin) that induce smooth muscle contractions of the reproductive, digestive, and excretory systems; other neurosecretory neurons convey hormone-releasing factors (e.g., growth hormone, corticosteroids, thyrotropic hormone, and gonadotropic hormone) via a vascular portal system (i.e., through the blood) to the adenohypophysis, a portion of the pituitary gland. Specific regions of the hypothalamus are also involved with the control of sympathetic (such as pupil dilation) and parasympathetic (such as salivation) activities, temperature regulation, food intake, the reproductive cycle, and emotional expression and behaviour.

Subthalamus

The subthalamus is represented mainly by the subthalamic nucleus, a lens-shaped structure lying behind and to the sides of the hypothalamus and on the dorsal surface of the internal capsule. The subthalamic region is traversed by fibres related to the globus pallidus. Discrete lesions of the subthalmic nucleus produce hemiballismus, a violent form of dyskinesia in which the limbs are involuntarily flung about.

Midbrain

The midbrain (mesencephalon) contains the nuclear complex of the oculomotor nerve as well as the trochlear nucleus; these cranial nerves innervate (or activate) muscles that move the eye and control the shape of the lens and the diameter of the pupil. In addition, between the midbrain reticular formation and the crus cerebri is a large pigmented nucleus called the substantia nigra. The substantia nigra consists of two parts, the pars reticulata and the pars compacta.

Cells of the pars compacta contain the dark pigment melanin; these cells synthesize dopamine and project to either the caudate nucleus or the putamen. By inhibiting the action of large aspiny striatal neurons in the caudate nucleus and the putamen, the dopaminergic cells of the pars compacta influence the output of the neurotransmitter GABA from spiny striatal neurons. The spiny neurons in turn project to the cells of the pars reticulata, which, by projecting fibres to the thalamus, are part of the output system of the corpus striatum.

At the caudal (rear) midbrain, crossed fibres of the superior cerebellar peduncle (the major output system of the cerebellum) surround and partially terminate in a large centrally located structure known as the red nucleus. Most crossed ascending fibres of this bundle project to thalamic nuclei, which have access to the primary motor cortex. A smaller number of fibres synapse, or pass a nerve impulse from one neuron to another, on large cells in caudal regions of the red nucleus; these give rise to the crossed fibres of the rubrospinal tract.

The roof plate of the midbrain is formed by two paired rounded swellings, the superior and inferior colliculi. The superior colliculus receives input from the retina and the visual cortex and participates in a variety of visual reflexes, particularly the tracking of objects in the contralateral visual field. The inferior colliculus receives both crossed and uncrossed auditory fibres and projects upon the medial geniculate body, the auditory relay nucleus of the thalamus.

Pons

The pons (metencephalon) consists of two parts: the tegmentum, a phylogenetically older part that contains the reticular formation, and the pontine nuclei, a larger part composed of masses of neurons that lie among large bundles of longitudinal and transverse nerve fibres.

Fibres originating from neurons in the cerebral cortex terminate upon the pontine nuclei, which in turn project to the opposite hemisphere of the cerebellum. These massive crossed fibres, called crus cerebri, form the middle cerebellar peduncle and serve as the bridge that connects each cerebral hemisphere with the opposite half of the cerebellum. The fibres originating from the cerebral cortex constitute the corticopontine tract.

The reticular formation (an inner core of gray matter found in the midbrain, pons, and medulla oblongata) of the pontine tegmentum contains multiple cell groups that influence motor function. It also contains the nuclei of several cranial nerves. The facial nerve and the two components of the vestibulocochlear nerve (which serves the organs of equilibrium and of hearing), for example, emerge from and enter the brainstem at the junction of the pons, medulla, and cerebellum. In addition, motor nuclei of the trigeminal nerve (which serves in facial sensation and motor control) lie in the upper pons. Long ascending and descending tracts that connect the brain to the spinal cord are located on the periphery of the pons.

Medulla Oblongata

The medulla oblongata (myelencephalon), the most caudal segment of the brainstem, appears as a conical expansion of the spinal cord. The roof plate of both the pons and the medulla is formed by the cerebellum and a membrane containing a cellular layer called the choroid plexus, located in the fourth ventricle. Cerebrospinal fluid entering the fourth ventricle from the cerebral aqueduct passes into the cisterna magna, a subarachnoid space surrounding the medulla and the cerebellum, via openings in the lateral recesses in the midline of the ventricle.

At the transition of the medulla to the spinal cord, there are two major decussations, or crossings, of nerve fibres. The corticospinal decussation is the site at which 90 percent of the fibres of the medullary pyramids cross and enter a part of the spinal cord called the dorsolateral funiculus. Signals conveyed by this tract provide the basis for voluntary motor function on the opposite side of the body. In the other decussation, two groups of ascending sensory fibres in parts of the spinal cord called the fasciculus gracilis and the fasciculus cuneatus terminate upon large nuclear masses on the back, or dorsal, surface of the medulla. Known as the nuclei gracilis and cuneatus, these masses give rise to fibres that decussate above the corticospinal tract and form the major ascending sensory pathway known as the medial lemniscus that is present in all brainstem levels. The medial lemniscus projects upon the sensory relay nuclei of the thalamus.

The medulla contains nuclei associated with the hypoglossal, accessory, vagus, and glossopharyngeal cranial nerves. In addition, it contains portions of the vestibular nuclear complex, parts of the trigeminal nuclear complex involved with pain and thermal sense, and solitary nuclei related to the vagus, glossopharyngeal, and facial nerves that subserve the sense of taste.

CEREBELLUM

The cerebellum ("little brain") overlies the posterior aspect of the pons and medulla oblongata and fills the greater part of the posterior fossa of the skull. This distinctive part of the brain is derived from the rhombic lips, thickenings along the margins of the embryonic hindbrain. It consists of two paired lateral lobes, or hemispheres, and a midline portion known as the vermis. The cerebellar cortex appears very different from the cerebral cortex in that it consists of small leaflike laminae called folia. The cerebellum consists of a surface cortex of gray matter and a core of white matter containing four paired intrinsic (i.e., deep) nuclei: the dentate, globose, emboliform, and

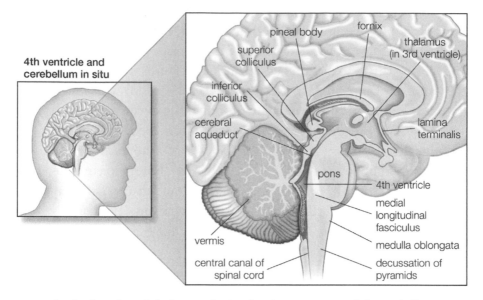

Sagittal section of the human brain, showing structures of the cerebellum, brainstem, and cerebral ventricles. Encyclopædia Britannica, Inc.

fastigial. Three paired fibre bundles—the superior, middle, and inferior peduncles—connect the cerebellum with the midbrain, pons, and medulla, respectively.

On an embryological basis the cerebellum is divided into three parts: (1) the archicerebellum, related primarily to the vestibular system, (2) the paleocerebellum, or anterior lobe, involved with control of muscle tone, and (3) the neocerebellum, known as the posterior lobe. Receiving input from the cerebral hemispheres via the middle cerebellar peduncle, the neocerebellum is the part most concerned with coordination of voluntary motor function.

The three layers of the cerebellar cortex are an outer synaptic layer (also called the molecular layer), an intermediate discharge layer (the Purkinje layer), and an inner receptive layer (the granular layer). Sensory input from all sorts of receptors is conveyed to specific regions of the receptive layer, which consists of enormous numbers of small nerve cells (hence the name granular) that project axons into the synaptic layer. There the axons excite the dendrites of the Purkinje cells, which in turn project axons to portions of the four intrinsic nuclei and upon dorsal portions of the lateral vestibular nucleus. Because most Purkinje cells are GABAergic and therefore exert strong inhibitory influences upon the cells that receive their terminals, all sensory input into the cerebellum results in inhibitory impulses being exerted upon the deep cerebellar nuclei and parts of the vestibular nucleus. Cells of all deep cerebellar nuclei, on the other hand, are excitatory (secreting the neurotransmitter glutamate) and project upon parts of the thalamus, red nucleus, vestibular nuclei, and reticular formation.

The cerebellum thus functions as a kind of computer, providing a quick and clear response to sensory signals. It plays no role in sensory perception, but it exerts profound influences upon equilibrium, muscle tone, and the coordination of voluntary motor function. Because the input and output pathways both cross, a lesion of a lateral part of the cerebellum will have an ipsilateral effect on coordination.

THE SPINAL CORD

The spinal cord is an elongated cylindrical structure, about 45 cm (18 inches) long, that extends from the medulla oblongata to a level between the first and second lumbar vertebrae of the backbone. The terminal part of the spinal cord is called the conus medullaris.

The spinal cord is composed of long tracts of myelinated nerve fibres (known as white matter) arranged around the periphery of a symmetrical butterfly-shaped cellular matrix of gray matter. The gray matter contains

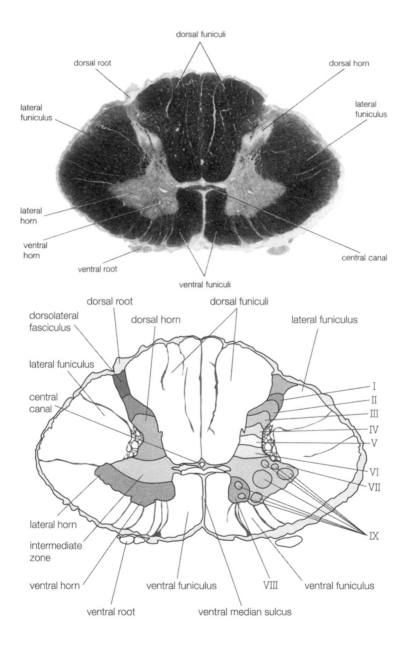

Two views of a cross section of the lower cervical segment of the spinal cord.
(Top) *Photograph, with the white matter stained dark.* (Bottom) *Schematic drawing, showing cytoarchitectural lamination.* From D.E. Haines, *Neuroanatomy: An Atlas of Structures, Sections, and Systems*, 3rd ed. (1991), Urban & Schwarzenberg Encyclopædia Britannica, Inc.

cell bodies, unmyelinated motor neuron fibres, and interneurons connecting either the two sides of the cord or the dorsal and ventral ganglia. Many interneurons have short axons distributed locally, but some have axons that extend for several spinal segments. Some interneurons may modulate or change the character of signals, while others play key roles in transmission and in patterned reflexes.

The gray matter forms three pairs of horns throughout most of the spinal cord: (1) the dorsal horns, composed of sensory neurons, (2) the lateral horns, well defined in thoracic segments and composed of visceral neurons, and (3) the ventral horns, composed of motor neurons. The white matter forming the ascending and descending spinal tracts is grouped in three paired funiculi, or sectors: the dorsal or posterior funiculi, lying between the dorsal horns; the lateral funiculi, lying on each side of the spinal cord between the dorsal-root entry zones and the emergence of the ventral nerve roots; and the ventral funiculi, lying between the ventral median sulcus and each ventral-root zone.

Associated with local regions of the spinal cord and imposing on it an external segmentation are 31 pairs of spinal nerves, each of which receives and furnishes one dorsal and one ventral root. On this basis the spinal cord is divided into the following segments: 8 cervical (C), 12 thoracic (T), 5 lumbar (L), 5 sacral (S), and 1 coccygeal (Coc). Spinal nerve roots emerge via intervertebral foramina; lumbar and sacral spinal roots, descending for some distance within the subarachnoid space before reaching the appropriate foramina, produce a group of nerve roots at the conus medullaris known as the cauda equina. Two enlargements of the spinal cord are evident: (1) a cervical enlargement (C_5 through T_1), which provides innervation for the upper extremities, and (2) a lumbosacral enlargement (L_1 through S_2), which innervates the lower extremities.

CELLULAR LAMINAE

The gray matter of the spinal cord is composed of nine distinct cellular layers, or laminae, traditionally indicated by Roman numerals. Laminae I to V, forming the dorsal horns, receive sensory input. Lamina VII forms the intermediate zone at the base of all horns. Lamina IX is composed of clusters of large alpha motor neurons, which innervate striated muscle, and small gamma motor neurons, which innervate contractile elements of the muscle spindle. Axons of both alpha and gamma motor neurons emerge via the ventral roots. Laminae VII and VIII have variable configurations, and lamina VI is present only in the cervical and lumbosacral enlargements. In addition, cells surrounding the central canal of the spinal cord form an area often referred to as lamina X.

All primary sensory neurons that enter the spinal cord originate in ganglia that are located in openings in the vertebral column called the intervertebral foramina. Peripheral processes of the nerve cells in these ganglia convey sensation from various receptors, and central processes of the same cells enter the spinal cord as bundles of nerve filaments. Fibres conveying specific forms of sensation follow separate pathways. Impulses involved with pain and noxious stimuli largely end in laminae I and II, while impulses associated with tactile sense end in lamina IV or on processes of cells in that lamina. Signals from stretch receptors (i.e., muscle spindles and tendon organs) end in parts of laminae V, VI, and VII; collaterals of these fibres associated with the stretch reflex project into lamina IX.

Virtually all parts of the spinal gray matter contain interneurons, which connect various cell groups. Many interneurons have short axons distributed locally, but some have axons that extend for several spinal segments. Some interneurons may modulate or change the character of signals, while others play key roles in transmission and in patterned reflexes.

ASCENDING SPINAL TRACTS

Information detected by sensory receptors in the periphery is transmitted along ascending neuronal tracts in the spinal cord. These ascending tracts, located in the white matter of the spinal cord, arise either from cells of spinal ganglia or from intrinsic neurons within the gray matter that receive primary sensory input.

Dorsal Column

The largest ascending tracts, the fasciculi gracilis and cuneatus, arise from spinal ganglion cells and ascend in the dorsal funiculus to the medulla oblongata. The fasciculus gracilis receives fibres from ganglia below thoracic 6, while spinal ganglia from higher segments of the spinal cord project fibres into the fasciculus cuneatus. The fasciculi terminate upon the nuclei gracilis and cuneatus, large nuclear masses in the medulla. Cells of these nuclei give rise to fibres that cross completely and form the medial lemniscus; the medial lemniscus in turn projects to the ventrobasal nuclear complex of the thalamus. By this pathway, the medial lemniscal system conveys signals associated with tactile, pressure, and kinesthetic (or positional) sense to sensory areas of the cerebral cortex.

Spinothalamic Tracts

Fibres concerned with pain, thermal sense, and light touch enter the lateral-root entry zone and then ascend or descend near the periphery of the spinal cord before entering superficial laminae of the dorsal horn—largely parts of laminae I, IV, and V. Cells in these laminae then give rise to fibres of the two spinothalamic tracts. Those fibres crossing in the ventral white commissure (ventral to the central canal) form the lateral spinothalamic tract, which, ascending in the ventral part of the lateral funiculus, conveys signals related to pain and thermal sense. The anterior spinothalamic tract arises from fibres that cross the midline in the same fashion but ascend more anteriorly in the spinal cord; these fibres convey impulses related to light touch. At medullary levels the two spinothalamic tracts merge and cannot be distinguished as separate entities. Many of the fibres, or collaterals, of the spinothalamic tracts terminate upon cell groups in the reticular formation, while the principal tracts convey sensory impulses to relay nuclei in the thalamus.

Spinocerebellar Tracts

Impulses from stretch receptors are carried by fibres that synapse upon cells in deep laminae of the dorsal horn or in lamina VII. The posterior spinocerebellar tract arises from the dorsal nucleus of Clarke and ascends peripherally in the dorsal part of the lateral funiculus. The anterior spinocerebellar tract ascends on the ventral margin of the lateral funiculus. Both tracts transmit signals to portions of the anterior lobe of the cerebellum and are involved in mechanisms that automatically regulate muscle tone without reaching consciousness.

DESCENDING SPINAL TRACTS

Tracts descending to the spinal cord are involved with voluntary motor function, muscle tone, reflexes and equilibrium, visceral innervation, and modulation of ascending sensory signals. The largest, the corticospinal tract, originates in broad regions of the cerebral cortex. Smaller descending tracts, which include the rubrospinal tract, the vestibulospinal tract, and the reticulospinal tract, originate in nuclei in the midbrain, pons, and medulla oblongata. Most of these brainstem nuclei themselves receive input from the cerebral cortex, the cerebellar cortex, deep nuclei of the cerebellum, or some combination of these.

In addition, autonomic tracts, which descend from various nuclei in the brainstem to preganglionic sympathetic and parasympathetic neurons in the spinal cord, constitute a vital link between the centres that regulate visceral functions and the nerve cells that actually effect changes.

Corticospinal Tract

The corticospinal tract originates from pyramid-shaped cells in the premotor, primary motor, and primary sensory cortex and is involved in skilled voluntary activity. Containing about one million fibres, it forms a significant part of the posterior limb of the internal capsule and is a major constituent of the crus cerebri in the midbrain. As the fibres emerge from the pons, they form compact bundles on the ventral surface of the medulla, known as the medullary pyramids. In the lower medulla about 90 percent of the fibres of the corticospinal tract decussate and descend in the dorsolateral funiculus of the spinal cord. Of the fibres that do not cross in the medulla, approximately 8 percent cross in cervical spinal segments. As the tract descends, fibres and collaterals branch off at all segmental levels, synapsing upon interneurons in lamina VII and upon motor neurons in lamina IX. Approximately 50 percent of the corticospinal fibres terminate within cervical segments.

At birth, few of the fibres of the corticospinal tract are myelinated; myelination takes place during the first year after birth, along with the acquisition of motor skills. Because the tract passes through, or close to, nearly every

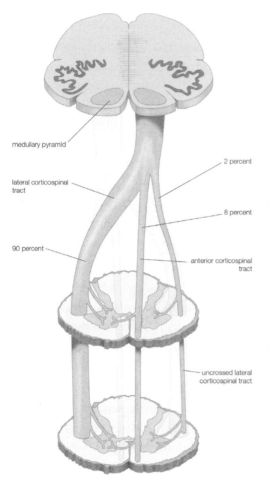

major division of the neuraxis, it is vulnerable to vascular and other kinds of lesions. A relatively small lesion in the posterior limb of the internal capsule, for example, may result in contralateral hemiparesis, which is characterized by weakness, spasticity, greatly increased deep tendon reflexes, and certain abnormal reflexes.

The decussation of the medullary pyramids and the formation of the corticospinal tract in the spinal cord. Encyclopædia Britannica, Inc.

Rubrospinal Tract

The rubrospinal tract arises from cells in the caudal part of the red nucleus, an encapsulated cell group in the midbrain tegmentum. Fibres of this tract decussate at midbrain levels, descend in the lateral funiculus of the spinal cord (overlapping ventral parts of the corticospinal tract), enter the spinal gray matter, and terminate on interneurons in lamina VII. Through these crossed rubrospinal projections, the red nucleus exerts a facilitating influence on flexor alpha motor neurons and a reciprocal inhibiting influence on extensor alpha motor neurons. Because cells of the red nucleus receive input from the motor cortex (via corticorubral projections) and from globose and emboliform nuclei of the cerebellum (via the superior cerebellar peduncle), the rubrospinal tract effectively brings flexor muscle tone under the control of these two regions of the brain.

Vestibulospinal Tract

The vestibulospinal tract originates from cells of the lateral vestibular nucleus, which lies in the floor of the fourth ventricle. Fibres of this tract descend the length of the spinal cord in the ventral and lateral funiculi without crossing, enter laminae VIII and IX of the anterior horn, and terminate upon both alpha and gamma motor neurons, which innervate ordinary muscle fibres and fibres of the muscle spindle. Cells of the lateral vestibular nucleus receive facilitating impulses from labyrinthine receptors in the utricle of the inner ear and from fastigial nuclei in the cerebellum. In addition, inhibitory influences upon these cells are conveyed by direct projections from Purkinje cells in the anterior lobe of the cerebellum. Thus, the vestibulospinal tract mediates the influences of the vestibular end organ and the cerebellum upon extensor muscle tone.

A smaller number of vestibular projections, originating from the medial and inferior vestibular nuclei, descend ipsilaterally in the medial longitudinal fasciculus only to cervical levels. These fibres exert excitatory and inhibitory effects upon cervical motor neurons.

Reticulospinal Tracts

The reticulospinal tracts arise from relatively large but restricted regions of the reticular formation of the pons and medulla oblongata—the same cells that project ascending processes to intralaminar thalamic nuclei and are important in the maintenance of alertness and the conscious state. The pontine reticulospinal tract arises from groups of cells in the pontine reticular formation, descends ipsilaterally as the largest component of the medial longitudinal fasciculus, and terminates among cells in laminae VII and VIII. Fibres of this tract exert facilitating influences upon voluntary movements, muscle tone, and a variety of spinal reflexes. The medullary reticulospinal tract, originating from reticular neurons on both sides of the median raphe, descends in the ventral part of the lateral funiculus and terminates at all spinal levels upon cells in laminae VII and IX. The medullary reticulospinal tract inhibits the same motor activities that are facilitated by the pontine reticulospinal tract. Both tracts receive input from regions of the motor cortex.

Autonomic Tracts

Descending fibres involved with visceral and autonomic activities emanate from groups of cells at various levels of the brainstem. For example, hypothalamic nuclei project to visceral nuclei in both the medulla oblongata and the spinal cord; in the spinal cord these projections terminate upon cells of the intermediolateral cell column in thoracic, lumbar, and sacral segments. Preganglionic parasympathetic neurons originating in the oculomotor nuclear complex in the midbrain project not only to the ciliary ganglion but also directly to spinal levels. Some of these fibres reach lumbar segments of the spinal cord, most of them terminating in parts of laminae I and V.

Pigmented cells in the isthmus, an area of the rostral pons, form a blackish-blue region known as the locus ceruleus; these cells distribute the neurotransmitter norepinephrine to the brain and spinal cord. Fibres from the locus ceruleus descend to spinal levels without crossing and are distributed to terminals in the anterior horn, the intermediate zone, and the dorsal horn. Other cell groups that either release or are activated by norepinephrine in the pons, near the motor nucleus of the facial nerve, project uncrossed noradrenergic fibres that terminate in the intermediolateral cell column (in lamina VII of the lateral horn). Postganglionic sympathetic neurons associated with this system have direct effects upon the cardiovascular system. Cells in the nucleus of the solitary tract project crossed fibres to the phrenic nerve nucleus (in cervical segments three through five), which controls the diaphragm, the intermediate zone, and the anterior horn at thoracic levels (the chest area); these innervate respiratory muscles.

CHAPTER 2

THE PERIPHERAL AND AUTONOMIC NERVOUS SYSTEMS

The peripheral nervous system is a channel for the relay of sensory and motor impulses between the central nervous system on one hand and the body surface, skeletal muscles, and internal organs on the other hand. It is composed of (1) spinal nerves, (2) cranial nerves, and (3) certain parts of the autonomic nervous system. The autonomic nervous system is the part of the nervous system that controls and regulates the internal organs without any conscious recognition or effort. It is made up of two antagonistic (opposing) sets of neuronal tracts, known as the sympathetic and parasympathetic nervous systems, as well as a third neuronal network, known as the enteric nervous system, which involves the digestive organs.

THE PERIPHERAL NERVOUS SYSTEM

As in the central nervous system, peripheral nervous pathways are made up of neurons and synapses, the points at which one neuron communicates with the next. The structures commonly known as nerves (or by such names as roots, rami, trunks, and branches) are composed of orderly arrangements of the axonal and dendritic processes of many nerve cell bodies.

The cell bodies of peripheral neurons are often found grouped into clusters called ganglia. On the basis of the type of nerve cell bodies found in ganglia, they may be classified as either sensory or motor. Sensory ganglia are oval swellings located on the dorsal roots of spinal nerves and on the roots of certain cranial nerves. The sensory neurons making up these ganglia are unipolar. Shaped much like a golf ball on a tee, they have round or slightly oval cell bodies with concentrically located nuclei. Unipolar neurons contain a single nerve fibre that undergoes a T-shaped bifurcation, one branch going to the periphery and the other entering the brain or spinal cord. There are no synaptic contacts between neurons in a sensory ganglion.

Motor ganglia are associated with neurons of the autonomic nervous system, the part of the nervous system that controls and regulates the internal organs. Many motor ganglia are located in the sympathetic trunks, two long chains of ganglia stretching along each side of the vertebral column from the base of the skull to the coccyx at the bottom of the back; these are referred to as paravertebral ganglia. Prevertebral motor ganglia are located near internal organs innervated by their projecting fibres, while terminal ganglia are found on the surfaces or within the walls of the target organs themselves. Motor ganglia have multipolar cell bodies, which means they have irregular shapes and eccentrically located nuclei and which project several dendritic and axonal processes (projections). Fibres originating from the brain or spinal cord, called preganglionic fibres, enter motor ganglia, where they synapse on multipolar cell bodies. These postganglionic cells, in turn, send their processes to visceral structures (internal organs).

SPINAL NERVES

Sensory input from the body surface, from joint, tendon, and muscle receptors, and from internal organs passes

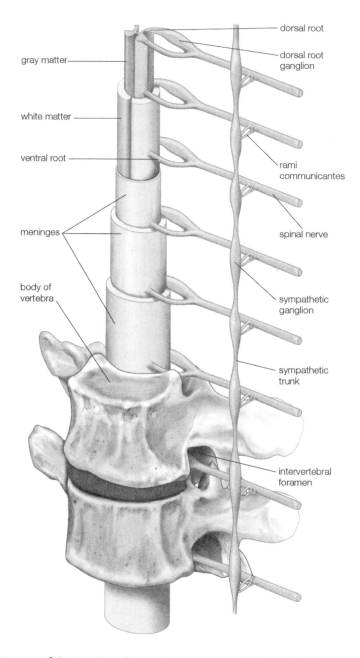

Diagram of the spinal cord, vertebrae, and sympathetic trunk (shown on one side only). Dorsal rami of the spinal nerves are not shown. Encyclopædia Britannica, Inc.

centrally through the dorsal roots of the spinal cord. Fibres from motor cells in the spinal cord exit via the ventral roots and course to their peripheral targets (autonomic ganglia or skeletal muscle). Each spinal nerve is formed by the joining of a dorsal root and a ventral root, and it is the basic structural and functional unit of the peripheral nervous system.

Structural Components of Spinal Nerves

As was mentioned in the first chapter of this book, there are 31 pairs of spinal nerves; in descending order from the most rostral end of the spinal cord, there are 8 cervical (designated C_1–C_8), 12 thoracic (T_1–T_{12}), 5 lumbar (L_1–L_5), 5 sacral (S_1–S_5), and 1 coccygeal (Coc_1). Each spinal nerve exits the vertebral canal through an opening called the intervertebral foramen. The first spinal nerve (C_1) exits the vertebral canal between the skull and the first cervical vertebra; consequently, spinal nerves C_1–C_7 exit above the correspondingly numbered vertebrae. Spinal nerve C_8, however, exits between the 7th cervical and first thoracic vertebrae, so that, beginning with T_1, all other spinal nerves exit below their corresponding vertebrae.

Just outside the intervertebral foramen, two branches, known as the gray and white rami communicantes, connect each spinal nerve with the sympathetic trunk. These rami, along with the sympathetic trunk and more distal ganglia, are involved with the innervation of visceral structures. In addition, small meningeal branches leave each spinal nerve and gray ramus and reenter the vertebral canal, where they innervate the dura mater (the outermost of the meninges) and blood vessels.

More peripherally, each spinal nerve divides into ventral and dorsal rami. All dorsal rami (with the exception of those from C_1, S_4, S_5, and Coc_1) have medial and lateral

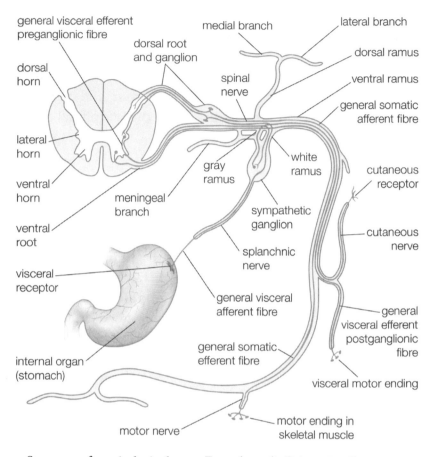

Structures of a typical spinal nerve. Encyclopædia Britannica, Inc.

branches, which innervate deep back muscles and overlying skin. The medial and lateral branches of the dorsal rami of spinal nerves C_2-C_8 supply both the muscles and the skin of the neck. Those of T_1-T_6 are mostly cutaneous (supplying only the skin), while those from T_7-T_{12} are mainly muscular. Dorsal rami from L_1-L_3 have both sensory and motor fibres, while those from L_4-L_5 are only muscular. Dorsal rami of S_1-S_3 may also be divided into medial and lateral branches, serving deep muscles of the lower back as well as cutaneous areas of the lower buttocks and perianal area. Undivided dorsal rami from S_4, S_5, and Coc_1 also send cutaneous branches to the gluteal and perianal regions.

Ventral rami of the spinal nerves carry sensory and motor fibres for the innervation of the muscles, joints, and skin of the lateral and ventral body walls and the extremities. Both dorsal and ventral rami also contain autonomic fibres.

Functional Types of Spinal Nerves

Because spinal nerves contain both sensory fibres (from the dorsal roots) and motor fibres (from the ventral roots), they are known as mixed nerves. When individual fibres of a spinal nerve are identified by their specific function, they may be categorized as one of four types: (1) general somatic afferent, (2) general visceral afferent, (3) general somatic efferent, and (4) general visceral efferent. The term *somatic* refers to the body wall (broadly defined to include skeletal muscles as well as the surface of the skin), and *visceral* refers to structures composed of smooth muscle, cardiac muscle, glandular epithelium, or a combination of these. Efferent fibres carry motor information to skeletal muscle and to autonomic ganglia (and then to visceral structures), and afferent fibres carry sensory information from them.

General somatic afferent receptors are sensitive to pain, thermal sensation, touch and pressure, and changes in the position of the body. (Pain and temperature sensation coming from the surface of the body is called exteroceptive, while sensory information arising from tendons, muscles, or joint capsules is called proprioceptive.) General visceral afferent receptors are found in organs of the thorax, abdomen, and pelvis; their fibres convey, for example, pain information from the digestive tract. Both types of afferent fibre project centrally from cell bodies in dorsal-root ganglia.

General somatic efferent fibres originate from large ventral-horn cells and distribute to skeletal muscles in the body wall and in the extremities. General visceral efferent fibres also arise from cell bodies located within the spinal cord, but they exit only at thoracic and upper lumbar levels or at sacral levels (more specifically, at levels T_1-L_2 and S_2-S_4). Fibres from T_1-L_2 enter the sympathetic trunk, where they either form synaptic contacts within a ganglion, ascend or descend within the trunk, or exit the trunk and proceed to ganglia situated closer to their target organs. Fibres from S_2-S_4, on the other hand, leave the cord as the pelvic nerve and proceed to terminal ganglia located in the target organs. Postganglionic fibres arising from ganglia in the sympathetic trunk rejoin the spinal nerves and distribute to blood vessels, sweat glands, and the arrector pili muscles of the skin, while postganglionic fibres arising from prevertebral and terminal ganglia innervate viscera of the thorax, abdomen, and pelvis.

Cervical Plexus

Cervical levels C_1-C_4 are the main contributors to the group of nerves called the cervical plexus; in addition, small branches of the plexus link C_1 and C_2 with the vagus nerve, C_1 and C_2 with the hypoglossal nerve, and C_2-C_4 with the accessory nerve. Sensory branches of the cervical plexus are the lesser occipital nerve (to the scalp behind the ear), the great auricular nerve (to the ear and to the skin over the mastoid and parotid areas), transverse cervical cutaneous nerves (to the lateral and ventral neck surfaces), and supraclavicular nerves (along the clavicle, shoulder, and upper chest). Motor branches of the plexus serve muscles that stabilize and flex the neck, muscles that stabilize the hyoid bone (to assist in actions like swallowing), and muscles that elevate the upper ribs.

Originating from C_4, with small contributions from C_3 and C_5, are the phrenic nerves, which carry sensory information from parts of the pleura of the lungs and pericardium of the heart as well as motor impulses to muscles of the diaphragm.

Brachial Plexus

Cervical levels C_5–C_8 and thoracic level T_1 contribute to the formation of the brachial plexus; small nerve bundles also arrive from C_4 and T_2. Spinal nerves from these levels converge to form superior (C_5 and C_6), middle (C_7), and inferior (C_8 and T_1) trunks, which in turn split into anterior and posterior divisions. The divisions then form cords (posterior, lateral, and medial), which provide motor, sensory, and autonomic fibres to the shoulder and upper extremity.

Nerves to shoulder and pectoral muscles include the dorsal scapular (to the rhomboid muscles), suprascapular (to supraspinatus and infraspinatus), medial and lateral pectoral (to pectoralis minor and major), long thoracic (to serratus anterior), thoracodorsal (to latissimus dorsi), and subscapular (to teres major and subscapular). The axillary nerve carries motor fibres to the deltoid and teres minor muscles as well as sensory fibres to the lateral surface of the shoulder and upper arm. The biceps, brachialis, and coracobrachialis muscles, as well as the lateral surface of the forearm, are served by the musculocutaneous nerve.

The three major nerves of the arm, forearm, and hand are the radial, median, and ulnar. The radial nerve innervates the triceps, anconeus, and brachioradialis muscles, eight extensors of the wrist and digits, and one abductor

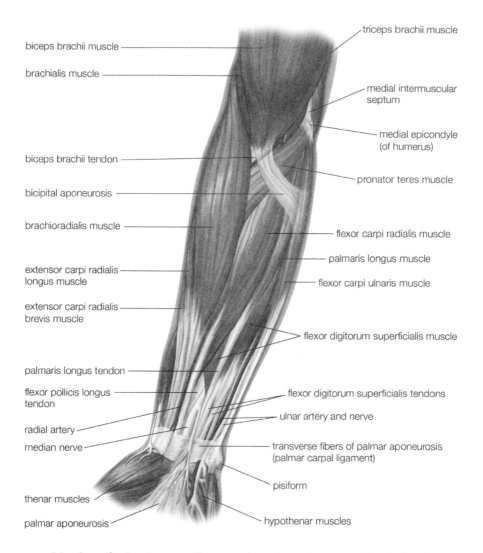

biceps brachii muscle

brachialis muscle

biceps brachii tendon

bicipital aponeurosis

brachioradialis muscle

extensor carpi radialis longus muscle

extensor carpi radialis brevis muscle

palmaris longus tendon

flexor pollicis longus tendon

radial artery

median nerve

thenar muscles

palmar aponeurosis

triceps brachii muscle

medial intermuscular septum

medial epicondyle (of humerus)

pronator teres muscle

flexor carpi radialis muscle

palmaris longus muscle

flexor carpi ulnaris muscle

flexor digitorum superficialis muscle

flexor digitorum superficialis tendons

ulnar artery and nerve

transverse fibers of palmar aponeurosis (palmar carpal ligament)

pisiform

hypothenar muscles

Muscles of the human forearm (anterior view, superficial layer). Encyclopædia Britannica, Inc.

of the hand; it is also sensory to part of the hand. The median nerve branches in the forearm to serve the palmaris longus, two pronator muscles, four flexor muscles, thenar muscles, and lumbrical muscles; most of these serve the wrist and hand. The ulnar nerve serves two flexor muscles and a variety of small muscles of the wrist and hand.

Cutaneous innervation of the upper extremity originates, via the brachial plexus, from spinal cord levels C_3-T_2. The shoulder is served by supraclavicular branches (C_3, C_4) of the cervical plexus, while the anterior and lateral aspects of the arm and forearm have sensory innervation via the axillary (C_5, C_6) nerve as well as the dorsal (C_5, C_6), lateral (C_5, C_6), and medial (C_8, T_1) antebrachial cutaneous nerves. These same nerves have branches that wrap around to serve portions of the posterior and medial surfaces of the extremity. The palm of the hand is served by the median (C_6-C_8) and ulnar (C_8, T_1) nerves. The ulnar nerve also wraps around to serve medial areas of the dorsum, or back, of the hand. An imaginary line drawn down the midline of the ring finger represents the junction of the ulnar-radial distribution on the back of the hand and the ulnar-median distribution on the palm. A small part of the thumb and the distal thirds of the index, middle, and lateral surface of the ring finger are served by the median nerve. The inner arm and the armpit is served by the intercostobrachial and the posterior and medial brachial cutaneous nerves (T_1-T_2).

Lumbar Plexus

Spinal nerves from lumbar levels L_1-L_4 contribute to the formation of the lumbar plexus, which, along with the sacral plexus, provides motor, sensory, and autonomic fibres to gluteal and inguinal regions and to the lower extremities. Lumbar roots are organized into dorsal and ventral divisions.

Minor cutaneous and muscular branches of the lumbar plexus include the iliohypogastric, genitofemoral, and ilioinguinal (projecting to the lower abdomen and to inguinal and genital regions) and the lateral femoral cutaneous nerve (to skin on the lateral thigh). Two major branches of the lumbar plexus are the obturator and femoral nerves. The obturator enters the thigh through the obturator foramen; motor branches proceed to the obturator internus and gracilis muscles as well as the adductor muscles, while sensory branches supply the articular capsule of the knee joint. An accessory obturator nerve supplies the pectineus muscle of the thigh and is sensory to the hip joint.

The sartorius muscle and medial and anterior surfaces of the thigh are served by branches of the anterior division of the femoral nerve. The posterior division of the femoral nerve provides sensory fibres to the inner surface of the leg (saphenous nerve), to the quadriceps muscles (muscular branches), to the hip and knee joints, and to the articularis genu muscle.

Sacral Plexus

The ventral rami of L_5 and S_1–S_3 form the sacral plexus, with contributions from L_4 and S_4. Branches from this plexus innervate gluteal muscles, muscles forming the internal surface of the pelvic basin (including those forming the levator ani), and muscles that run between the femur and pelvis to stabilize the hip joint (such as the obturator, piriformis, and quadratus femoris muscles). These muscles lend their names to the nerves that innervate them. Cutaneous branches from the plexus serve the buttocks, perineum, and posterior surface of the thigh.

The major nerve of the sacral plexus, and the largest nerve in the body, is the sciatic. Formed by the joining of ventral and dorsal divisions of the plexus, it passes through the greater sciatic foramen and descends in back of the thigh. There, sciatic branches innervate the biceps femoris, semitendinosus and semimembranosus muscles, and part of the adductor magnus muscle. In the popliteal fossa (just above the knee), the sciatic

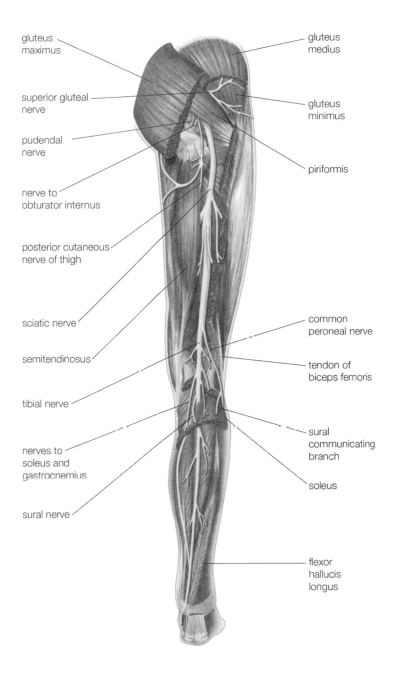

Posterior view of the right leg, showing the sciatic nerve and its branches.
Encyclopædia Britannica, Inc.

nerve divides into the tibial nerve and the common fibular (or peroneal) nerve. The tibial nerve (from the dorsal division) continues distally in the calf and innervates the gastrocnemius muscle, deep leg muscles such as the popliteus, soleus, and tibialis posterior, and the flexor muscles, lumbrical muscles, and other muscles of the ankle and plantar aspects of the foot. The peroneal nerve, from the ventral division, travels to the anterior surface of the leg and innervates the tibialis anterior, the fibularis muscles, and extensor muscles that elevate the foot and fan the toes. Cutaneous branches from the tibial and common fibular nerves serve the outer sides of the leg and the top and bottom of the foot and toes.

Coccygeal Plexus

The ventral rami of S_4, S_5, and Coc_1 form the coccygeal plexus, from which small anococcygeal nerves arise to innervate the skin over the coccyx (tailbone) and around the anus.

CRANIAL NERVES

Cranial nerves can be thought of as modified spinal nerves, since the general functional fibre types found in spinal nerves are also found in cranial nerves but are supplemented by special afferent or efferent fibres. The 12 pairs of cranial nerves are identified either by name or by Roman or Arabic numeral.

Fibres conveying information concerning olfaction, or smell (in cranial nerve I) and taste (in cranial nerves VII, IX, and X), are classified as special visceral afferent, while the designation of special somatic afferent is applied to fibres conveying vision (cranial nerve II) and equilibrium and hearing (cranial nerve VIII). Skeletal muscles that arise from the branchial arches are innervated by

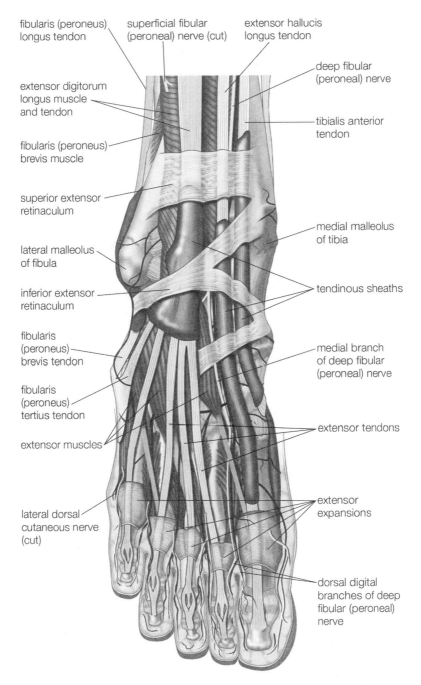

Dorsal view of the right foot, showing major muscles, tendons, and nerves.
Encyclopædia Britannica, Inc.

fibres of cranial nerves V, VII, IX, and X; these are classified as special visceral efferent fibres.

Olfactory Nerve (CN I or 1)

Bipolar cells in the nasal mucosa give rise to axons that enter the cranial cavity through foramina in the cribriform plate of the ethmoid bone. These cells and their axons, totaling about 20 to 24 in number, make up the olfactory nerve. Once in the cranial cavity, the fibres terminate in a small oval structure resting on the cribriform plate called the olfactory bulb. The functional component of olfactory fibres is special visceral afferent. Injury or disease of the olfactory nerve may result in anosmia, an inability to detect odours; it may also dull the sense of taste.

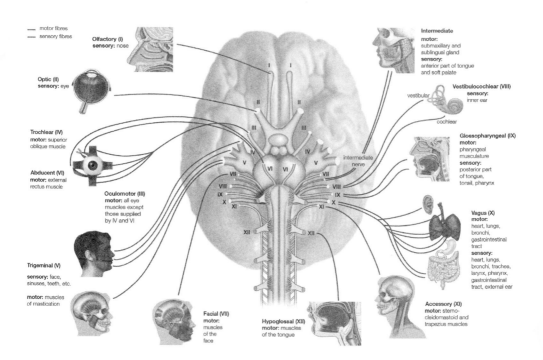

The cranial nerves (I–XII) *and their areas of innervation.* Encyclopædia Britannica, Inc.

Optic Nerve (CN II or 2)

Rods and cones in the retina of the eye receive information from the visual fields and, through intermediary cells, convey this input to retinal ganglion cells. Ganglion cell axons converge at the optic disc, pass through the sclera, and form the optic nerve. A branch from each eye enters the skull via the optic foramen, and they join to form the optic chiasm. At the chiasm, fibres from the nasal halves of each retina cross, while those from the temporal halves remain uncrossed. In this way the optic tracts, which extend from the chiasm to the thalamus, contain fibres conveying information from both eyes. Injury to one optic nerve therefore results in total blindness of that eye, while damage to the optic tract on one side results in partial blindness in both eyes.

Optic fibres also participate in accommodation of the lens and in the pupillary light reflex. Since the subarachnoid space around the brain is continuous with that around the optic nerve, increases in intracranial pressure can result in papilledema, or damage to the optic nerve, as it exits the bulb of the eye.

Oculomotor Nerve (CN III or 3)

The oculomotor nerve arises from two nuclei in the rostral midbrain. These are (1) the oculomotor nucleus, the source of general somatic efferent fibres to superior, medial, and inferior recti muscles, to the inferior oblique muscle, and to the levator palpebrae superious muscle, and (2) the Edinger-Westphal nucleus, which projects general visceral efferent preganglionic fibres to the ciliary ganglion.

The oculomotor nerve exits the ventral midbrain, pierces the dura mater, courses through the lateral wall of the cavernous sinus, and exits the cranial cavity via the superior orbital fissure. Within the orbit it branches into a superior ramus (to the superior rectus and levator muscles) and an inferior ramus (to the medial and inferior rectus muscles, the inferior oblique muscles, and the ciliary ganglion). Postganglionic fibres from the ciliary ganglion innervate the sphincter pupillae muscle of the iris as well as the ciliary muscle.

Oculomotor neurons project primarily to orbital muscles on the same side of the head. A lesion of the oculomotor nerve will result in paralysis of the three rectus muscles and the inferior oblique muscle (causing the eye to rotate downward and slightly outward), paralysis of the levator palpebrae superious muscle (drooping of the eyelids), and paralysis of the sphincter pupillae and ciliary muscles (so that the iris will remain dilated and the lens will not accommodate).

Trochlear Nerve (CN IV or 4)

The fourth cranial nerve is unique for three reasons. First, it is the only cranial nerve to exit the dorsal side of the brainstem. Second, fibres from the trochlear nucleus cross in the midbrain before they exit, so that trochlear neurons innervate the contralateral (opposite side) superior oblique muscle of the eye. Third, trochlear fibres have a long intracranial course before piercing the dura mater.

The trochlear nucleus is located in the caudal midbrain; the functional component of these cells is general somatic efferent. After exiting at the dorsal side of the midbrain, the trochlear nerve loops around the midbrain, pierces the dura mater, and passes through the lateral wall of the cavernous sinus. It then enters the orbit through the superior orbital fissure and innervates only the superior oblique muscle, which rotates the eye downward and slightly outward. Damage to the trochlear nerve will result in a loss of this eye movement and may produce double vision (diplopia).

Trigeminal Nerve (CN V or 5)

The trigeminal nerve is the largest of the cranial nerves. It has both motor and sensory components, the sensory fibres being general somatic afferent and the motor fibres being special visceral efferent. Most of the cell bodies of sensory fibres are located in the trigeminal ganglion, which is attached to the pons by the trigeminal root. These fibres convey pain and thermal sensations from the face, oral and nasal cavities, and parts of the dura mater and nasal sinuses, sensations of deep pressure, and information from sensory endings in muscles. Trigeminal motor fibres, projecting from nuclei in the pons, serve the muscles of mastication (chewing).

Lesions of the trigeminal nerve result in sensory losses over the face or in the oral cavity. Damage to the motor fibres results in paralysis of the masticatory muscles; as a result, the jaw may hang open or deviate toward the injured side when opened. Trigeminal neuralgia, or tic douloureux, is an intense pain originating mainly from areas supplied by sensory fibres of the maxillary and mandibular branches of this nerve.

The trigeminal ganglion gives rise to three large nerves: the ophthalmic, maxillary, and mandibular.

Ophthalmic Nerve

The ophthalmic nerve passes through the wall of the cavernous sinus and enters the orbit via the superior orbital fissure. Branches in the orbit are (1) the lacrimal nerve, serving the lacrimal gland, part of the upper eyelid, and the conjunctiva, (2) the nasociliary nerve, serving the mucosal lining of part of the nasal cavity, the tentorium cerebelli and some of the dura mater of the anterior cranial fossa, and skin on the dorsum and tip of the nose, and (3) the frontal nerve, serving the skin on the upper eyelid, the forehead, and the scalp above the eyes up to the vertex of the head.

Maxillary Nerve

The maxillary nerve courses through the cavernous sinus below the ophthalmic nerve and passes through the foramen rotundum into the orbital cavity. Branches of the maxillary nerve are (1) the meningeal branches, which serve the dura mater of the middle cranial fossa, (2) the alveolar nerves, serving the upper teeth and gingiva and the lining of the maxillary sinus, (3) the nasal and palatine nerves, which serve portions of the nasal cavity and the mucosa of the hard and soft palate, and (4) the infraorbital, zygomaticotemporal, and zygomaticofacial nerves, serving the upper lip, the lateral surfaces of the nose, the lower eyelid and conjunctiva, and the skin on the cheek and the side of the head behind the eye.

Mandibular Nerve

The mandibular nerve exits the cranial cavity via the foramen ovale and serves (1) the meninges and parts of the anterior cranial fossae (meningeal branches), (2) the temporomandibular joint, skin over part of the ear, and skin over the sides of the head above the ears (auriculotemporal nerve), (3) oral mucosa, the anterior two-thirds of the tongue, gingiva adjacent to the tongue, and the floor of the mouth (lingual nerve), and (4) the mandibular teeth (inferior alveolar nerve). Skin over the lateral and anterior surfaces of the mandible and the lower lip is served by cutaneous branches of the mandibular nerve.

Trigeminal motor fibres exit the cranial cavity via the foramen ovale along with the mandibular nerve. They serve the muscles of mastication (temporalis, masseter, medial and lateral pterygoid), three muscles involved in swallowing (anterior portions of the digastric muscle, the mylohyoid muscle, and the tensor veli palatini), and the tensor tympani, a muscle that has a damping effect on loud noises by stabilizing the tympanic membrane.

Abducens Nerve (CN VI or 6)

From its nucleus in the caudal pons, the abducens nerve exits the brainstem at the pons-medulla junction, pierces the dura mater, passes through the cavernous sinus close to the internal carotid artery, and exits the cranial vault via the superior orbital fissure. In the orbit the abducens nerve innervates the lateral rectus muscle, which turns the eye outward. Damage to the abducens nerve results in a tendency for the eye to deviate medially, or cross. Double vision may result on attempted lateral gaze. The nerve often is affected by increased intracranial pressure.

Facial Nerve (CN VII or 7)

The facial nerve is composed of a large root that innervates facial muscles and a small root (known as the intermediate nerve) that contains sensory and autonomic fibres. From the facial nucleus in the pons, facial motor fibres enter the internal auditory meatus, pass through the temporal bone, exit the skull via the stylomastoid foramen, and fan out over each side of the face in front of the ear. Fibres of the facial nerve are special visceral efferent; they innervate the small muscles of the external ear, the superficial muscles of the face, neck, and scalp, and the muscles of facial expression.

The intermediate nerve contains autonomic (parasympathetic) as well as general and special sensory fibres. Preganglionic autonomic fibres, classified as general visceral efferent, project from the superior salivatory nucleus in the pons. Exiting with the facial nerve, they pass to the pterygopalatine ganglion via the greater petrosal nerve (a branch of the facial nerve) and to the submandibular ganglion by way of the chorda tympani nerve (another branch of the facial nerve, which joins the lingual branch of the mandibular nerve). Postganglionic fibres from the pterygopalatine ganglion innervate the nasal and palatine glands and the lacrimal gland, while those from the sub-mandibular ganglion serve the submandibular and sublingual salivary glands. Among the sensory compo-nents of the intermediate nerve, general somatic afferent fibres relay sensation from the caudal surface of the ear, while special visceral afferent fibres originate from taste buds in the anterior two-thirds of the tongue, course in the lingual branch of the mandibular nerve, and then join the facial nerve via the chorda tympani branch. Both somatic and visceral afferent fibres have cell bodies in the geniculate ganglion, which is located on the facial nerve as it passes through the facial canal in the temporal bone.

Injury to the facial nerve at the brainstem produces a paralysis of facial muscles known as Bell palsy as well as a loss of taste sensation from the anterior two-thirds of the tongue. If damage occurs at the stylomastoid foramen, facial muscles will be paralyzed but taste will be intact.

Vestibulocochlear Nerve (CN VIII or 8)

This cranial nerve has a vestibular part, which functions in balance, equilibrium, and orientation in three-dimen-sional space, and a cochlear part, which functions in hearing. The functional component of these fibres is spe-cial somatic afferent; they originate from receptors located in the temporal bone.

Vestibular receptors are located in the semicircular canals of the ear, which provide input on rotatory move-ments (angular acceleration), and in the utricle and saccule, which generate information on linear acceleration and the influence of gravitational pull. This information is relayed by the vestibular fibres, whose bipolar cell bodies are located in the vestibular (Scarpa) ganglion. The central processes of these neurons exit the temporal bone via the internal acoustic meatus and enter the brainstem along-side the facial nerve.

Auditory receptors of the cochlear division are located in the organ of Corti and follow the spiral shape (about 2.5 turns) of the cochlea. Air movement against the eardrum initiates action of the ossicles of the ear, which, in turn, causes movement of fluid in the spiral cochlea. This fluid movement is converted by the organ of Corti into nerve impulses that are interpreted as auditory information. The bipolar cells of the spiral, or Corti, ganglion branch into central processes that course with the vestibular nerve. At the brainstem, cochlear fibres separate from vestibular fibres to end in the dorsal and ventral cochlear nuclei.

Lesions of the vestibular root result in eye movement disorders (e.g., nystagmus), unsteady gait with a tendency to fall toward the side of the lesion, nausea, and vertigo. Damage to the cochlea or cochlear nerve results in complete deafness, ringing in the ear (tinnitus), or both.

Glossopharyngeal Nerve (CN IX or 9)

The ninth cranial nerve, which exits the skull through the jugular foramen, has both motor and sensory components. Cell bodies of motor neurons, located in the nucleus ambiguus in the medulla oblongata, project as special visceral efferent fibres to the stylopharyngeal muscle. The action of the stylopharyngeus is to elevate the pharynx, as in gagging or swallowing. In addition, the inferior salivatory nucleus of the medulla sends general visceral efferent fibres to the otic ganglion via the lesser petrosal branch of the ninth nerve; postganglionic otic fibres innervate the parotid salivary gland.

Among the sensory components of the glossopharyngeal nerve, special visceral afferent fibres convey taste sensation from the back third of the tongue via lingual branches of the nerve. General visceral afferent fibres from the pharynx, the back of the tongue, parts of the soft palate and eustachian tube, and the carotid body and carotid sinus have their cell bodies in the superior and inferior ganglia, which are situated, respectively, within the jugular foramen and just outside the cranium. Sensory fibres in the carotid branch detect increased blood pressure in the carotid sinus and send impulses into the medulla that ultimately reduce heart rate and arterial pressure; this is known as the carotid sinus reflex.

Vagus Nerve (CN X or 10)

The vagus nerve has the most extensive distribution in the body of all the cranial nerves, innervating structures as diverse as the external surface of the eardrum and internal abdominal organs. The root of the nerve exits the cranial cavity via the jugular foramen. Within the foramen is the superior ganglion, containing cell bodies of general somatic afferent fibres, and just external to the foramen is the inferior ganglion, containing visceral afferent cells.

Pain and temperature sensations from the eardrum and external auditory canal and pain fibres from the dura mater of the posterior cranial fossa are conveyed on general somatic afferent fibres in the auricular and meningeal branches of the nerve. Taste buds on the root of the tongue and on the epiglottis contribute special visceral afferent fibres to the superior laryngeal branch. General visceral afferent fibres conveying sensation from the lower pharynx, larynx, trachea, esophagus, and organs of the thorax and abdomen to the left (splenic) flexure of the colon converge to form the posterior (right) and anterior (left) vagal nerves. Right and left vagal nerves are joined in the thorax by cardiac, pulmonary, and esophageal branches. In addition, general visceral afferent fibres from the larynx below the vocal folds join the vagus via the recurrent laryngeal nerves, while comparable input from the upper larynx and pharynx is relayed by the superior laryngeal nerves and by pharyngeal branches of the vagus. A vagal branch to the carotid body usually arises from the inferior ganglion.

Motor fibres of the vagus nerve include special visceral efferent fibres arising from the nucleus ambiguus of the medulla oblongata and innervating pharyngeal constrictor muscles and palatine muscles via pharyngeal branches of the vagus as well as the superior laryngeal nerve. All laryngeal musculature (excluding the cricothyroid but including the muscles of the vocal folds) are innervated by fibres arising in the nucleus ambiguus. Cells of the dorsal motor nucleus in the medulla distribute general visceral efferent fibres to plexuses or ganglia serving the pharynx, larynx, esophagus, and lungs. In addition, cardiac branches arise from plexuses in the lower neck and upper thorax, and, once in the abdomen, the vagus gives rise to gastric, celiac, hepatic, renal, intestinal, and splenic branches or plexuses.

Damage to one vagus nerve results in hoarseness and difficulty in swallowing or speaking. Injury to both nerves results in increased heart rate, paralysis of pharyngeal and laryngeal musculature, atonia of the esophagus and intestinal musculature, vomiting, and loss of visceral reflexes. Such a lesion is usually life-threatening, as paralysis of laryngeal muscles may result in asphyxiation.

Accessory Nerve (CN XI or 11)

The accessory nerve is formed by fibres from the medulla oblongata (known as the cranial root) and by fibres from cervical levels C_1–C_4 (known as the spinal root). The cranial root originates from the nucleus ambiguus and exits the medulla below the vagus nerve. Its fibres join the vagus and distribute to some muscles of the pharynx and larynx via pharyngeal and recurrent laryngeal branches of that nerve. For this reason, the cranial part of the accessory nerve is, for all practical purposes, part of the vagus nerve.

Fibres that arise from spinal levels exit the cord, coalesce and ascend as the spinal root of the accessory nerve, enter the cranial cavity through the foramen magnum, and then immediately leave through the jugular foramen. The accessory nerve then branches into the sternocleidomastoid muscle, which tilts the head toward one shoulder with an upward rotation of the face to the opposite side, and the trapezius muscle, which stabilizes and shrugs the shoulder.

Hypoglossal Nerve (CN XII or 12)

The hypoglossal nerve innervates certain muscles that control movement of the tongue. From the hypoglossal nucleus in the medulla oblongata, general somatic efferent fibres exit the cranial cavity through the hypoglossal canal and enter the neck in close proximity to the accessory and vagus nerves and the internal carotid artery. The nerve then loops down and forward into the floor of the mouth and branches into the tongue musculature from underneath. Hypoglossal fibres end in intrinsic tongue muscles, which modify the shape of the tongue (as in rolling the edges), as well as in extrinsic muscles that are responsible for changing its position in the mouth.

A lesion of the hypoglossal nerve on the same side of the head results in paralysis of the intrinsic and extrinsic musculature on the same side. The tongue atrophies and, on attempted protrusion, deviates toward the side of the lesion.

THE AUTONOMIC NERVOUS SYSTEM

The autonomic nervous system is the part of the peripheral nervous system that regulates the basic visceral processes needed for the maintenance of normal bodily functions. It operates independently of voluntary control, although certain events, such as stress, fear, sexual excitement, and alterations in the sleep-wake cycle, change the level of autonomic activity.

The autonomic system usually is defined as a motor system that innervates three major types of tissue: cardiac muscle, smooth muscle, and glands. However, it also relays visceral sensory information to the central nervous system and processes it so that alterations can be made in the activity of specific autonomic motor outflows, such as those that control the heart, blood vessels, and other visceral organs. It also stimulates the release of certain hormones involved in energy metabolism (e.g., insulin, glucagon, and epinephrine [also called adrenaline]) or cardiovascular functions (e.g., renin and vasopressin). These integrated responses maintain the normal internal environment of the body in an equilibrium state called homeostasis.

The autonomic system consists of two major divisions: the sympathetic nervous system and the parasympathetic nervous system. These often function in antagonistic ways. The motor outflow of both systems is formed by two serially connected sets of neurons. The first set, called preganglionic neurons, originates in the brainstem or the spinal cord, and the second set, called ganglion cells or postganglionic neurons, lies outside the central nervous system in collections of nerve cells called autonomic ganglia. Parasympathetic ganglia tend to lie close to or within the organs or tissues that their neurons innervate, whereas sympathetic ganglia are located at more distant sites from their target organs. Both systems have associated sensory fibres that send feedback into the central nervous system regarding the functional condition of target tissues.

A third division of the autonomic system, the enteric nervous system, consists of a collection of neurons embedded within the wall of the gastrointestinal tract and its derivatives. This system controls gastrointestinal motility and secretion.

SYMPATHETIC NERVOUS SYSTEM

The sympathetic nervous system normally functions to produce localized adjustments (such as sweating as a response to an increase in temperature) and reflex adjustments of the cardiovascular system. Under conditions of stress, however, the entire sympathetic nervous system is activated, producing an immediate, widespread response called the fight-or-flight response. This response is characterized by the release of large quantities of epinephrine from the adrenal gland, an increase in heart rate, an increase in cardiac output, skeletal muscle vasodilation, cutaneous and gastrointestinal vasoconstriction, pupillary dilation, bronchial dilation, and piloerection. The overall effect is to prepare the individual for imminent danger.

Sympathetic preganglionic neurons originate in the lateral horns of the 12 thoracic and the first 2 or 3 lumbar segments of the spinal cord. The axons of these neurons exit the spinal cord in the ventral roots and then synapse on either sympathetic ganglion cells or specialized cells in the adrenal gland called chromaffin cells.

Sympathetic Ganglia

Sympathetic ganglia can be divided into two major groups, paravertebral and prevertebral (or preaortic), on the basis of their location within the body. Paravertebral ganglia generally are located on each side of the vertebrae and are connected to form the sympathetic chain, or trunk. There are usually 21 or 22 pairs of these ganglia—3 in the cervical region, 10 or 11 in the thoracic region, 4 in the lumbar region, and 4 in the sacral region—and a single unpaired ganglion lying in front of the coccyx, called the ganglion impar.

The three cervical sympathetic ganglia are the superior cervical ganglion, the middle cervical ganglion, and the cervicothoracic ganglion (also called the stellate ganglion). The superior ganglion innervates viscera of the head, and the middle and stellate ganglia innervate viscera of the neck, thorax (i.e., the bronchi and heart), and upper limbs. The thoracic sympathetic ganglia innervate the trunk region, and the lumbar and sacral sympathetic ganglia innervate the pelvic floor and lower limbs. All the paravertebral ganglia provide sympathetic innervation to blood vessels in muscle and skin, arrector pili muscles attached to hairs, and sweat glands.

The three preaortic ganglia are the celiac, superior mesenteric, and inferior mesenteric. Lying on the anterior surface of the aorta, preaortic ganglia provide axons that are distributed with the three major gastrointestinal arteries arising from the aorta. Thus, the celiac ganglion innervates the stomach, liver, pancreas, and the duodenum, the first part of the small intestine; the superior mesenteric ganglion innervates the small intestine; and the inferior mesenteric ganglion innervates the descending colon, sigmoid colon, rectum, urinary bladder, and sexual organs.

Neurotransmitters and Receptors

Upon reaching their target organs by traveling with the blood vessels that supply them, sympathetic fibres terminate as a series of swellings close to the end organ. Because of this anatomical arrangement, autonomic transmission takes place across a junction rather than a synapse. "Presynaptic" sites can be identified because they contain aggregations of synaptic vesicles and membrane thickenings; postjunctional membranes, on the other hand, rarely possess morphological specializations, but they do contain specific receptors for various neurotransmitters.

The distance between pre- and postsynaptic elements can be quite large compared with typical synapses. For instance, the gap between cell membranes of a typical chemical synapse is 30–50 nanometres, while in blood vessels the distance is often greater than 100 nanometres or, in some cases, 1–2 micrometres (1,000–2,000 nanometres). Owing to these relatively large gaps between autonomic nerve terminals and their effector cells, neurotransmitters tend to act slowly; they become inactivated rather slowly as well. To compensate for this inefficiency, many effector cells, such as those in smooth and cardiac muscle, are connected by low-resistance pathways that allow for electrotonic coupling of the cells. In this way, if only one cell is activated, multiple cells will respond and work as a group.

At a first approximation, chemical transmission in the sympathetic system appears simple: preganglionic neurons use acetylcholine as a neurotransmitter, whereas most postganglionic neurons utilize norepinephrine (noradrenaline)—with the major exception that postganglionic neurons innervating sweat glands use acetylcholine. On closer inspection, however, neurotransmission is seen to be more complex, because multiple chemicals are released, and each functions as a specific chemical code affecting different receptors on the target cell. In addition, these chemical codes are self-regulatory, in that they act on presynaptic receptors located on their own axon terminals.

The chemical codes are specific to certain tissues. For example, most sympathetic neurons that innervate blood vessels secrete both norepinephrine and neuropeptide Y; sympathetic neurons that innervate the submucosal neural plexus of the gut contain both norepinephrine and somatostatin; and sympathetic neurons that innervate sweat glands contain calcitonin gene-related peptide, vasoactive intestinal polypeptide, and acetylcholine. In addition, other chemicals are released from autonomic neurons along with the so-called classical neurotransmitters, norepinephrine and acetylcholine. For instance, some neurons synthesize a gas, nitric oxide, that functions as a neuronal messenger molecule. Thus, neural transmission in the autonomic nervous system involves the release of combinations of different neuroactive agents that affect both pre- and postsynaptic receptors.

Neurotransmitters released from nerve terminals bind to specific receptors, which are specialized macromolecules embedded in the cell membrane. The binding action initiates a series of specific biochemical reactions in the target cell that produce a physiological response. In the sympathetic nervous system, for example, there are five types of adrenergic receptors (receptors binding epinephrine): α_1, α_2, β_1, β_2, and β_3. These adrenoceptors are found in different combinations in various cells throughout the body. Activation of α_1- adrenoceptors in arterioles causes blood-vessel constriction, whereas stimulation of α_2 autoreceptors (receptors located in sympathetic presynaptic nerve endings) functions to inhibit the release of norepinephrine. Other types of tissue have unique adrenoceptors. Heart rate and myocardial contractility, for example, are controlled by β_1-adrenoceptors; bronchial smooth muscle relaxation is mediated by β_2-adrenoceptors; and the breakdown of fat (lipolysis) is controlled by β_3-adrenoceptors.

Cholinergic receptors (receptors binding acetylcholine) also are found in the sympathetic system (as well as the parasympathetic system). Nicotinic cholinergic receptors stimulate sympathetic postganglionic neurons, adrenal chromaffin cells, and parasympathetic postganglionic neurons to release their chemicals. Muscarinic receptors are associated mainly with parasympathetic functions and are located in peripheral tissues (e.g., glands and smooth muscle). Peptidergic receptors exist in target cells as well.

The length of time that each type of chemical acts on its target cell is variable. As a rule, peptides cause slowly developing, long-lasting effects (one or more minutes), whereas the classical transmitters produce short-term effects (about 25 milliseconds).

PARASYMPATHETIC NERVOUS SYSTEM

The parasympathetic nervous system primarily modulates visceral organs such as glands. Responses are never activated en masse as in the fight-or-flight sympathetic response. While providing important control of many tissues, the parasympathetic system, unlike the sympathetic system, is not crucial for the maintenance of life.

The parasympathetic nervous system is organized in a manner similar to the sympathetic nervous system. Its motor component consists of preganglionic and postganglionic neurons. The preganglionic neurons are located in specific cell groups (also called nuclei) in the brainstem or in the lateral horns of the spinal cord at sacral levels (segments S_2–S_4). (Because parasympathetic fibres exit from these two sites, the system is sometimes referred to as the craniosacral outflow.) Preganglionic axons emerging from the brainstem project to parasympathetic ganglia that are located in the head (ciliary, pterygopalatine [also called sphenopalatine], and otic ganglia) or near the heart (cardiac ganglia), embedded in the end organ itself (e.g., the trachea, bronchi, and gastrointestinal tract), or situated a short distance from the urinary bladder (pelvic ganglion). Both pre- and postganglionic neurons secrete acetylcholine as a neurotransmitter, but, like sympathetic ganglion cells, they also contain other neuroactive chemical agents that function as cotransmitters.

The third cranial nerve (oculomotor nerve) contains parasympathetic nerve fibres that regulate the iris and lens of the eye. From their origin in the Edinger-Westphal nucleus of the midbrain, preganglionic axons travel to the orbit and synapse on the ciliary ganglion. The ciliary ganglion contains two types of postganglionic neurons: one innervates smooth muscle of the iris and is responsible for pupillary constriction, and the other innervates ciliary muscle and controls the curvature of the lens.

Various secretory glands located in the head are under parasympathetic control. These include the lacrimal gland, which supplies tears to the cornea of the eye; salivary glands (sublingual, submandibular, and parotid glands), which produce saliva; and nasal mucous glands, which secrete mucus throughout the nasal air passages. The parasympathetic preganglionic neurons that regulate these functions originate in the reticular formation of the medulla oblongata. One group of parasympathetic preganglionic neurons belongs to the superior salivatory nucleus and lies in the rostral part of the medullary reticular formation. These neurons send axons out of the medulla in a separate branch of the seventh cranial nerve (facial nerve) called the intermediate nerve. Some of the axons innervate the pterygopalatine ganglion, and others project to the submandibular ganglion. Pterygopalatine ganglion cells innervate the vasculature of the brain and eye as well as the lacrimal gland, nasal glands, and palatine glands, while neurons of the submandibular ganglion innervate the submandibular and sublingual salivary glands.

A second group of parasympathetic preganglionic neurons belongs to the inferior salivatory nucleus, located in the caudal part of the medullary reticular formation.

Neurons of this group send axons out of the medulla in the ninth cranial (glossopharyngeal) nerve and to the otic ganglion. From this site, postganglionic fibres travel to and innervate the parotid salivary gland.

Preganglionic parasympathetic fibres of the 10th cranial (vagus) nerve arise from two different sites in the medulla oblongata. Neurons that slow heart rate arise from a part of the ventral medulla called the nucleus ambiguus, while those that control functions of the gastrointestinal tract arise from the dorsal vagal nucleus. After exiting the medulla in the vagus nerve and traveling to their respective organs, the fibres synapse on ganglion cells embedded in the organs themselves. The vagus nerve also contains visceral afferent fibres that carry sensory information from organs of the neck (larynx, pharynx, and trachea), chest (heart and lungs), and gastrointestinal tract into a visceral sensory nucleus located in the medulla called the solitary tract nucleus.

Enteric Nervous System

The enteric nervous system is composed of two plexuses, or networks of neurons, embedded in the wall of the gastrointestinal tract. The outermost plexus, located between the inner circular and outer longitudinal smooth-muscle layers of the gut, is called the Auerbach, or myenteric, plexus. Neurons of this plexus regulate peristaltic waves that move digestive products from the oral to the anal opening. In addition, myenteric neurons control local muscular contractions that are responsible for stationary mixing and churning. The innermost group of neurons is called the Meissner, or submucosal, plexus. This plexus regulates the configuration of the luminal surface, controls glandular secretions, alters electrolyte and water transport, and regulates local blood flow.

Three functional classes of intrinsic enteric neurons are recognized: sensory neurons, interneurons, and motor neurons. Sensory neurons, activated by either mechanical or chemical stimulation of the innermost surface of the gut, transmit information to interneurons located within the Auerbach and the Meissner plexi, and the interneurons relay the information to motor neurons. Motor neurons in turn modulate the activity of a variety of target cells, including mucous glands, smooth muscle cells, endocrine cells, epithelial cells, and blood vessels.

Extrinsic neural pathways also are involved in the control of gastrointestinal functions. Three types exist: intestinofugal, sensory, and motor. Intestinofugal neurons reside in the gut wall; their axons travel to the preaortic sympathetic ganglia and control reflex arcs that involve large portions of the gastrointestinal tract. Sensory neurons relay information regarding distention and acidity to the central nervous system. There are two types of sensory neurons: sympathetic neurons, which originate from dorsal-root ganglia found at the thoracic and lumbar levels; and parasympathetic neurons, which originate in the nodose ganglion of the vagus nerve or in dorsal-root ganglia at sacral levels S_2–S_4. The former innervate the gastrointestinal tract from the pharynx to the left colic flexure, and the latter innervate the distal colon and rectum. Each portion of the gastrointestinal tract receives a dual sensory innervation: pain sensations travel via sympathetic afferent fibres, and sensations that signal information regarding the chemical environment of the gut travel by way of parasympathetic fibres and are not consciously perceived.

The third extrinsic pathway, exercising motor control over the gut, arises from parasympathetic preganglionic neurons found in the dorsal vagal nucleus of the medulla oblongata and from sympathetic preganglionic neurons in the lateral horns of the spinal cord. These pathways provide modulatory commands to the intrinsic enteric motor system and are nonessential in that basic functions can be maintained in their absence.

Through the pathways described above, the parasympathetic system activates digestive processes while the sympathetic system inhibits them. The sympathetic system inhibits digestive processes by two mechanisms: (1) contraction of circular smooth muscle sphincters located in the distal portion of the stomach (pyloric sphincter), small intestine (ileo-cecal sphincter), and rectum (internal anal sphincter), which act as valves to prevent the oral-to-anal passage (as well as reverse passage) of digestive products; and (2) inhibition of motor neurons throughout the length of the gut. In contrast, the parasympathetic system provides messages only to myenteric motor neurons.

CHAPTER 3

FUNCTIONS OF THE HUMAN NERVOUS SYSTEM

The human nervous system differs from that of other mammals chiefly in the great enlargement and elaboration of the cerebral hemispheres. Much of what is known of the functions of the human brain is derived from observations of the effects of disease, from the results of experimentation on animals, particularly monkeys, and from neuroimaging studies of animals and of healthy human subjects. Such sources of information have helped elucidate aspects of nervous activity underlying certain properties of the human brain, including processes related to vision, memory, speech, and emotion.

Although scientists' knowledge of the functions of this uniquely complex system is rapidly expanding, it is far from complete. Thus, there remain many important, unanswered questions about the human brain and nervous system.

IDENTIFYING NEURAL PATHWAYS

In order to understand how the human nervous system functions, scientists first had to identify the connecting elements, or pathways, that run between its various parts. Their research led them to the discovery of neural tracts and to the identification of less-well-defined connections between different regions of the brain and spinal cord. The identification of these pathways was not a simple matter, and indeed, in humans, many remain incompletely known or are simply conjectural.

A great deal of information about the human nervous system has been obtained by observing the effects of axonal destruction. If a nerve fibre is severed, the length of axon farthest from the cell body, or soma, will be deprived of the axonal flow of metabolites and will begin to deteriorate. The myelin sheath will also degenerate, so that, for some months after the injury, breakdown products of myelin will be seen under the microscope with special stains. This method is obviously of limited application in humans, as it requires precise lesions and subsequent examination before the myelin has been completely removed.

The staining of degenerated axons and of the terminals that form synapses with other neurons is also possible through the use of silver impregnation, but the techniques are laborious and results sometimes difficult to interpret. That a damaged neuron should show degenerative changes, however difficult to detect, is not unexpected, but the interdependence of neurons is sometimes shown by transneuronal degeneration. Neurons deprived of major input from axons that have been destroyed may themselves atrophy. This phenomenon is called antero-grade degeneration. In retrograde degeneration, similar changes may occur in neurons that have lost the main recipient of their outflow.

These anatomical methods are occasionally applicable to human disease. They can also be used postmortem when lesions of the central nervous system have been deliberately made—for example, in the surgical treatment of intractable pain. Other techniques can be used only in experiments on animals, but these are not always relevant to humans. For example, normal biochemical constituents labeled with a radioactive isotope can be injected into neurons and then transported the length of the axon, where they can be detected by picking up the radioactivity on an X-ray plate.

An observation technique dependent on retrograde axonal flow has been used extensively to demonstrate the origin of fibre tracts. In this technique, the enzyme peroxidase is taken up by axon terminals and is transported up the axon to the soma, where it can be shown by appropriate staining. The staining of neurotransmitter substances is possible in postmortem human material as well as in animals. Success, however, is dependent on examining relatively fresh or frozen material, and results may be greatly affected by previous treatment with neurologically active medications.

Electrical stimulation of a region of the nervous system generates nerve impulses in centres receiving input from the site of stimulation. This method, using microelectrodes, has been widely used in animal studies; however, the precise path followed by the artificially generated impulse may be difficult to establish.

Several highly specialized imaging techniques, such as computerized axial tomography (CAT), magnetic resonance imaging (MRI), and positron emission tomography (PET), have given scientists the ability to visualize and study the anatomy and function of the nervous system in living, healthy persons. A technique known as functional magnetic resonance imaging (fMRI) enables the detection of increases in blood flow in parallel with increases in brain activity. Functional MRI allows scientists to generate detailed maps of brain areas that underlie human mental activities in health and disease. This technique has been applied to the study of various functions of the brain, ranging from primary sensory responses to cognitive activities.

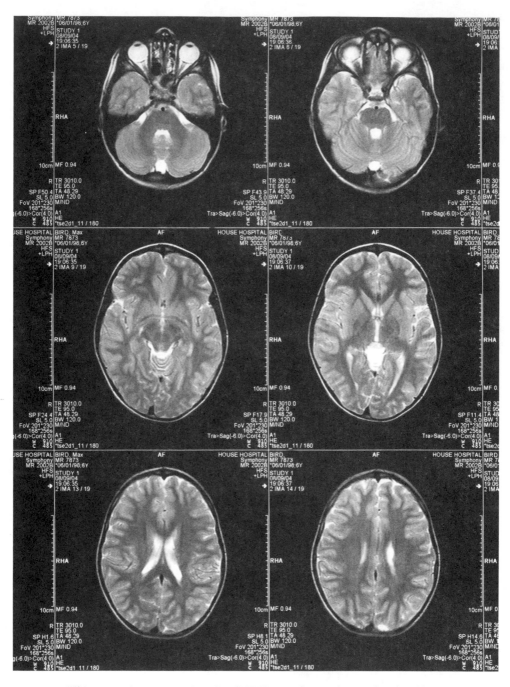

This magnetic resonance imaging (MRI) scan shows a human head and brain.
© www.istockphoto.com / Hayden Bird

RECEPTORS

Receptors are biological transducers that convert energy from both external and internal environments into electrical impulses. They may be massed together to form a sense organ, such as the eye or ear, or they may be scattered, as are those of the skin and viscera. Receptors are connected to the central nervous system by afferent nerve fibres. The region or area in the periphery from which a neuron within the central nervous system receives input is called its receptive field. Receptive fields are changing and not fixed entities.

Receptors are of many kinds and are classified in many ways. Steady-state receptors, for example, generate impulses as long as a particular state such as temperature remains constant. Changing-state receptors, on the other hand, respond to variation in the intensity or position of a stimulus. Receptors are also classified as exteroceptive (reporting the external environment), interoceptive (sampling the environment of the body itself), and proprioceptive (sensing the posture and movements of the body). Exteroceptors report the senses of sight, hearing, smell, taste, and touch. Interoceptors report the state of the bladder, the alimentary canal, the blood pressure, and the osmotic pressure of the blood plasma. Proprioceptors report the position and movements of parts of the body and the position of the body in space.

Receptors are also classified according to the kinds of stimulus to which they are sensitive. Chemical receptors, or chemoreceptors, are sensitive to substances taken into the mouth (taste or gustatory receptors), inhaled through the nose (smell or olfactory receptors), or found in the body itself (detectors of glucose or of acid-base balance in the blood). Receptors of the skin are classified as thermoreceptors, mechanoreceptors, and nociceptors—

the last being sensitive to stimulation that is noxious, or likely to damage the tissues of the body.

Thermoreceptors are of two types, warmth and cold. Warmth fibres are excited by rising temperature and inhibited by falling temperature, and cold fibres respond in the opposite manner.

Mechanoreceptors are also of several different types. Sensory nerve terminals around the base of hairs are activated by very slight movement of the hair, but they rapidly adapt to continued stimulation and stop firing. In hairless skin both rapidly and slowly adapting receptors provide information about the force of mechanical stimulation. The Pacinian corpuscles, elaborate structures found in the skin of the fingers and in other organs, are layers of fluid-filled membranes forming structures just visible to the naked eye at the terminals of axons. Local pressure exerted at the surface or within the body causes deformation of parts of the corpuscle, a shift of chemical ions (e.g., sodium, potassium), and the appearance of a receptor potential at the nerve ending. This receptor potential, on reaching sufficient (threshold) strength, acts to generate a nerve impulse within the corpuscle. These receptors are also activated by rapidly changing or alternating stimuli such as vibration.

All receptors report two features of stimulation: its intensity and its location. Intensity is signaled by the frequency of nerve impulse discharge of a neuron and also by the number of afferent nerves reporting the stimulation. As the strength of a stimulus increases, the rate of change in electrical potential of the receptor increases, and the frequency of nerve impulse generation likewise increases.

The location of a stimulus, whether in the external or internal environment, is readily determined by the nervous system. Localization of stimuli in the environment depends to a great extent on pairs of receptors, one on each side of the body. For example, children learn very early in life that a loud sound is probably coming from a nearer source than a weak sound. They localize the sound by noticing the difference in intensity and the minimal difference in time of arrival at the ears, increasing these differences by turning the head.

Localization of a stimulus on the skin depends upon the arrangement of nerve fibres in the skin and in the deep tissues beneath the skin, as well as upon the overlap of receptive fields. Most mechanical stimuli indent the skin, stimulating nerve fibres in the connective tissue below the skin. Any point on the skin is supplied by at least 3, and sometimes up to 40, nerve fibres, and no two points are supplied by precisely the same pattern of fibres.

Finer localization is achieved by what is called surround inhibition. In the retina, for example, there is an inhibitory area around the excited area. This mechanism accentuates the excited area. Surround excitation, on the other hand, is characterized by an excitatory area around an inhibitory area. In both cases contrast is enhanced and discrimination sharpened.

In seeking information about the environment, the nervous system presents the most-sensitive receptors to a stimulating object. At its simplest, this action is reflex. In the retina a small region about the size of a pinhead, called the fovea, is particularly sensitive to colour. When a part of the periphery of the visual field is excited, a reflex movement of the head and eyes focuses the light rays upon that part of the fovea. A similar reflex turns the head and eyes in the direction of a noise. As the English physiologist Charles Sherrington said in 1900, "In the limbs and mobile parts, when a spot of less discriminative sensitivity is touched, instinct moves the member, so that it brings to the object the part where its own sensitivity is delicate."

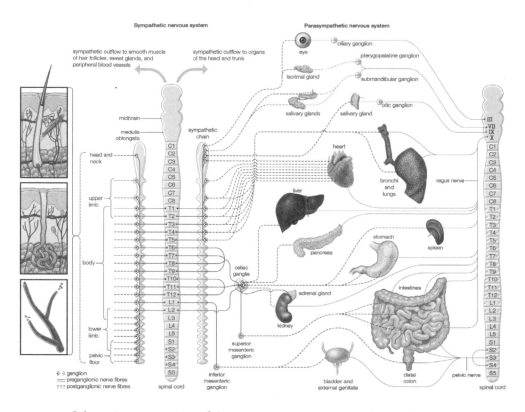

Schematic representation of the autonomic nervous system, showing distribution of sympathetic and parasympathetic nerves to the head, trunk, and limbs. Encyclopædia Britannica, Inc.

AUTONOMIC CONTROL OF ORGANS

The autonomic nervous system is regulated by cell groups in the brain that process visceral information arriving in specific neural networks, integrate that information, and then issue specific regulatory instructions through the appropriate autonomic outflows. Each end organ is processed in a unique way by functionally specific sets of neurons in which there is often coordination of both the sympathetic and parasympathetic nervous systems.

THE EYE

In order for the eye to function properly, specific auto-nomic functions must maintain adjustment of four types of smooth muscle: (1) smooth muscle of the iris, which controls the amount of light that passes through the pupil to the retina, (2) ciliary muscle on the inner aspect of the eye, which controls the ability to focus on nearby objects, (3) smooth muscle of arteries providing oxygen to the eye, and (4) smooth muscle of veins that drain blood from the eye and affect intraocular pressure. In addition, the cornea must be kept moist by secretion from the lacrimal gland.

When bright light is shined into an eye, the pupils of both eyes constrict. This response, called the light reflex, is regulated by three structures: the retina, the pretectum, and the midbrain. In the retina is a three-neuron circuit consisting of light-sensitive photoreceptors (rods), bipolar cells, and retinal ganglion cells. The latter transmit luminosity information to the pretectum, where particular types of neurons relay the information to parasympathetic preganglionic neurons located in the Edinger-Westphal nucleus of the midbrain. The axons of these neurons exit the ventral surface of the midbrain and synapse in the ciliary ganglion. From there, parasympathetic postganglionic neurons innervate the pupillary sphincter muscle, causing constriction.

In order to bring a nearby object into focus, several changes must occur in both the external and internal muscles of the eyes. The initial stimulus for accommodation is a blurred visual image that first reaches the visual cortex. Through a series of cortical connections, the blurred image reaches two specialized motor centres. One of these, located in the frontal cortex, sends motor commands to neurons in the oculomotor nucleus controlling the medial rectus muscles; this causes the eyes to converge. The other motor centre, located in the temporal lobe, functions as the accommodation area. Via multineuronal pathways, it activates specific parasympathetic pathways arising from the ciliary ganglion. This pathway causes the ciliary muscle to contract, thereby reducing tension on the lens and allowing it to become more rounded so the image of the near object can be focused on the central part of the retina. At the same time, the iris, also under control of the oculomotor parasympathetic system, constricts to further enhance the resolution of the lens.

THE ENDOCRINE SYSTEM

The adrenal glands, which lie above the kidney, are composed of the cortex and the medulla. The adrenal cortex synthesizes and secretes steroid hormones that are essential for life, but it is not under autonomic control. The adrenal medulla, on the other hand, is innervated by sympathetic preganglionic neurons. Within the adrenal medulla are chromaffin cells, which are homologous to sympathetic neurons and, like sympathetic neurons, are developed from embryonic neural crest cells. Chromaffin cells produce epinephrine (adrenaline) and, to a much lesser extent, norepinephrine as well as other chemicals such as chromogranins, enkephalins, and neuropeptide Y—all of which are released into the bloodstream and act as hormones. Epinephrine in particular affects many different types of tissues throughout the body and has a particularly potent effect on cells that possess β-adrenoceptors.

The release of epinephrine prevents hypoglycemia (low blood sugar) through the following mechanism. By binding to α_2-adrenoceptors embedded in the hormone-releasing cells of the pancreas, epinephrine inhibits the release of insulin. Since insulin promotes the absorption of glucose from the bloodstream into liver, skeletal muscle, and fat cells, inhibition of its release results in a greater amount of glucose that is available for entry into the brain. In addition, by binding to certain β-adrenoceptors, epinephrine stimulates the release of glucagon, a pancreatic peptide hormone that acts in the liver to convert glycogen to glucose. Under emergency conditions, epinephrine causes even more widespread effects on glucose metabolism. Glycogen in the liver and skeletal muscle is broken down to glucose; fat held in adipose cells is converted to fatty acids and glycerol; and production of glucose and ketone bodies (e.g., β-hydroxybutyric acid and acetoacetic acid) is increased in the liver. All of these substances can be used as energy sources for the body.

THE REPRODUCTIVE SYSTEM

The sexual response in both males and females can be defined by three physiological events. The first stage begins with psychogenic impulses in higher neural centres, which travel through multineuronal pathways and cause excitation of sacral parasympathetic outflow innervating vascular tissues of the penis or clitoris. This results in dilation of these arteries and erection of the penis or clitoris.

The second stage involves secretion of glandular fluids, which is mediated by sympathetic neurons arising in the T_{12}–L_2 levels of the lateral horns. In the male, this stage involves contraction of the epididymis, vas deferens, seminal vesicles, and prostate gland, with the overall effect of moving fluids into the urethra; at the same time, sympathetic activation causes a closure of the internal urinary sphincter to prevent retrograde ejaculation of semen into the bladder. In the female, the response involves mucous secretions of the greater vestibular glands, resulting in lubrication of the vaginal orifice.

The third phase involves a muscular response in which somatic efferent fibres in the pudendal nerve produce rhythmic contractions of the bulbocavernous and ischio-cavernosus muscles in the male, causing ejaculation. In the female, homologous muscles of the pelvic floor undergo rhythmic contractions controlled by somatic efferent neurons from the S_2–S_4 ventral horns.

THE CARDIOVASCULAR SYSTEM

The function of the cardiovascular system is to maintain an adequate supply of oxygen to all tissues of the body. In order to maintain this function, the autonomic system must process visceral information and coordinate neural elements that innervate the heart, blood vessels, and respiration. In addition, certain hormones such as angiotensin II and vasopressin are released and act in concert with the autonomic nervous system.

The cardiovascular system is regulated by sets of neurons that form two major types of reflex circuit. One type is triggered by mechanoreceptors found in the major arteries near the heart and in the heart itself. Receptors sensitive to high pressure are located in the wall of the aortic arch and the carotid sinuses. These receptors are innervated by the aortic branch of the vagus nerve and by a branch of the glossopharyngeal nerve. Both branches send information regarding increases in arterial blood pressure into the medulla oblongata and synapse in the nucleus of the solitary tract. Another group of mechano-receptors provides information about venous pressure and volume; these are low-pressure receptors located in the walls of the major veins as they enter the heart and within the walls of the atria. Low-pressure afferents also relay sensory information to the solitary tract.

Mechanoreceptors trigger what is called the baroreceptor reflex, which causes a decrease in the discharge of sympathetic vasomotor and cardiac outflows whenever an increase in blood pressure occurs. In addition, the baroreceptor reflex causes stimulation of vagal cardioinhibitory neurons, which produces a decrease in heart rate, a decrease in cardiac contractility, and dilation of peripheral blood vessels. Overall, the net effect is to lower blood pressure.

The second major class of afferents that trigger reflex responses are chemoreceptors found in the major arteries near the heart in groups close to the high-pressure mechanoreceptors. Functioning as oxygen sensors, these receptors are innervated by separate sets of fibres that travel parallel with the baroreceptor nerves, and they also project to the nucleus of the solitary tract. Overall, the chemoreceptor reflex regulates respiration, cardiac output, and regional blood flow, ensuring that proper amounts of oxygen are delivered to the brain and heart.

Vasopressin is a peptide hormone that is synthesized in magnocellular neurons of the supraoptic and paraventricular nuclei of the hypothalamus. These neurons send their axons into the posterior lobe of the pituitary gland, from which vasopressin is released into nearby capillaries and distributed throughout the body.

Vasopressin has two main functions: volume regulation and vasomotor tone. It acts to increase water retention by increasing the permeability of kidney tubules to water as the kidney filters blood plasma. As more water is reabsorbed, extracellular fluid volume is increased, and this in turn increases venous volume and, ultimately, blood pressure. Under emergency conditions, vasopressin also selectively constricts certain vascular beds that are nonessential for life (e.g., gastrointestinal, muscle); this shunts blood to critical tissues such as the heart and brain.

Two major stimuli trigger the release of vasopressin: increases in extracellular fluid osmolality and decreases in blood volume (as in hemorrhage). Osmotic stimuli cause vasopressin to be released by acting on specialized brain centres called circumventricular organs surrounding the third and fourth ventricles of the brain. These "osmosensitive" areas contain neurons with central projections that alter autonomic and neuroendocrine functions and possess a unique vascular system that permits diffusion of large molecules such as peptides and ions to cross readily from the plasma to the brain. Normally, such chemical agents do not have free passage, because the capillaries form a blood-brain barrier, but at these special sites they have direct access to central neurons. One of the areas, called the organum vasculosum of the lamina terminalis, lies in the third ventricle and is involved in osmo- and sodium regulation. Another circumventricular organ, called the subfornical organ, lies in the dorsal part of the third ventricle; it is particularly sensitive to hormones such as angiotensin II and signals that changes are needed for the regulation of salt and water balance. Both regions project directly to vasopressin-producing hypothalamic neurons. The area postrema, which lies on the floor of the fourth ventricle in the medulla oblongata, is also involved as a special chemical sensor of the plasma.

When blood is lost through hemorrhage, atrial receptors and baroreceptors relay volume and pressure information, via the vagus nerve, into the nucleus of the solitary tract. Neurons in this nucleus send commands to other relay neurons that project directly to the magnocellular hypothalamic neurons and cause the release of vasopressin.

THE URINARY SYSTEM

Functions of the urinary bladder depend entirely on the autonomic nervous system. For example, urine is retained by activation of sympathetic pathways originating from lateral horns in spinal segments T_{11}–L_2; these cause contraction of smooth muscle that forms the internal urinary sphincter. The external urinary sphincter, which works in concert with the internal sphincter, is made up of skeletal muscle controlled by motor fibres of the pudendal nerve. These fibres, arising from ventral horns of segments S_2–S_4, provide tonic excitation of the external sphincter. Because they are under voluntary control, micturition is initiated by higher brain centres. Voluntary inhibition of the sacral motor outflow results in relaxation of the external urinary sphincter. Simultaneously, an increase in abdominal pressure, caused by contraction of muscles of the abdominal wall, initiates the flow of urine. This is followed by a reflex inhibition of sympathetic outflow, resulting in relaxation of the internal urinary sphincter, and by activation of parasympathetic outflow to smooth muscle that causes the bladder to contract and expel the urine.

While the autonomic nervous system is not crucial to functions of the kidney, the fine-tuning of certain processes, such as water maintenance, electrolyte balance, and the production of the vasoactive hormones renin and erythropoietin, is regulated by sympathetic fibres.

HIGHER CEREBRAL FUNCTIONS

The neurons of the cerebral cortex constitute the highest level of control in the hierarchy of the nervous system. Consequently, the terms *higher cerebral functions* and *higher cortical functions* are used by neurologists and neuroscientists to refer to all conscious mental activity, such as thinking, remembering, and reasoning, and to complex volitional behaviour such as speaking and carrying out purposive movement. The terms also refer to the processing of information in the cerebral cortex, most of which takes place unconsciously.

ANALYTICAL APPROACHES

Neuroscientists investigate the structure and functions of the cerebral cortex, but the processes involved in thinking are also studied by cognitive psychologists, who group the mental activities known to the neuroscientist as higher cortical functions under the headings cognitive function or human information processing. From this perspective, complex information processing is the hallmark of cognitive function. Cognitive science attempts to identify and define the processes involved in thinking without regard to their physiological basis. The resulting models of cognitive function resemble flowcharts for a computer program more than neural networks—and, indeed, they frequently make use of computer terminology and analogies.

The discipline of neuropsychology, by studying the relationship between behaviour and brain function, bridges the gap between neural and cognitive science. Examples of this bridging role include studies in which cognitive models are used as conceptual frameworks to help explain the behaviour of patients who have suffered damage to different parts of the brain. Thus, damage to the frontal lobes can be conceptualized as a failure of the "central executive" component of working memory, and a failure of the "generate" function in another model of mental imagery would fit with some of the consequences of left parietal lobe damage.

The analysis of changes in behaviour and ability following damage to the brain is by far the oldest and probably the most-informative method adopted for studying higher cortical functions. Usually these changes take the form of what is known as a deficit—that is, an impairment of the ability to act or think in some way. With certain stipulations, one can assume that the damaged part of the brain is involved in the function that has been lost. However, people vary considerably in their abilities, and most brain lesions occur in subjects whose behaviour was not formally studied before they became ill. Lesions are rarely precisely congruent with the brain area responsible for a given function, and their exact location and extent can be difficult to determine even with modern imaging techniques. Abnormal behaviour after brain injury, therefore, is often difficult to attribute to precisely defined damage or dysfunction.

It would also be naive to suppose that a function is represented in a particular brain area just because it is disrupted after damage to that area. For example, a tennis champion does not play well with a broken ankle, but this would not lead one to conclude that the ankle is the centre in which athletic skill resides. Reasonably certain conclusions about brain-behaviour relationships, therefore, can be drawn only if similar well-defined changes occur reliably in a substantial number of patients suffering from similar lesions or disease states.

The most prominent series of observations clearly belonging to modern neuropsychology were made by Paul Broca in the 1860s. He reported the cases of several patients whose speech had been affected following damage to the left frontal lobe and provided autopsy evidence of the location of the lesion. Broca explicitly recognized the left hemisphere's control of language, one of the fundamental phenomena of higher cortical function.

In 1874 the German neurologist Carl Wernicke described a case in which a lesion in a different part of the left hemisphere, the posterior temporal region, affected language in a different way. In contrast to Broca's cases, language comprehension was more affected than language output. This meant that two different aspects of higher cortical function had been found to be localized in different parts of the brain. In the next few decades there was a rapid expansion in the number of cognitive processes studied and tentatively localized.

Wernicke was one of the first to recognize the importance of the interaction between connected brain areas and to view higher cortical function as the buildup of complex mental processes through the coordinated activities of local regions dealing with relatively simple, predominantly sensory-motor functions. In doing so, he opposed the view of the brain as an equipotential organ acting en masse.

Since Wernicke's time, scientific views have swung between the localization and mass-action theories. Major advances in the 20th century included vast increases in knowledge, the discovery of new ways of studying the anatomy and physiology of the brain, and the introduction of better quantitative methods in the study of behaviour.

HEMISPHERIC ASYMMETRY, HANDEDNESS, AND CEREBRAL DOMINANCE

Broca's declaration that the left hemisphere is predominantly responsible for language-related behaviour is the clearest and most dramatic example of an asymmetry of function in the human brain. This functional asymmetry is related to hand preference and probably to anatomical differences, although neither relationship is simple.

Evidence from a number of converging sources, notably the high incidence of the language disturbance aphasia after left- but not right-hemisphere damage, indicates that the left hemisphere is dominant for the comprehension and expression of language in close to 99 percent of right-handed people. At least 60 percent of left-handed and ambidextrous people also have left-hemisphere language, but up to 30 percent have predominantly right-hemisphere language. The remainder have language represented to some degree in both hemispheres.

The posterior temporal region of the brain, which is one of the regions responsible for language in the dominant hemisphere, is physically asymmetrical; specifically, the area known as the planum temporale is larger in the left hemisphere in most people. This asymmetry is more common in right-handers, while left-handed individuals are likely to have more nearly symmetrical brains. Reduced anatomical asymmetry has also been found in people with right-hemisphere dominance for speech and in some people with the reading disorder dyslexia. These results point to some relationship between handedness, cerebral dominance for language, anatomical asymmetry in the temporal lobe, and some aspects of language competence. Certainly there is a tendency for right-handedness, left-hemisphere dominance for language, and a larger left planum temporale to occur together. However, there are exceptions; for example, a few right-handers are right-hemisphere dominant for speech, and some right-handers who have left-hemisphere speech do not have a larger left planum temporale. In people who are atypical in one of these respects—for example, by being left-handed—the relationship between handedness, cerebral dominance, and anatomical asymmetry is much less consistent. Therefore, language is not invariably located in the hemisphere opposite the dominant hand or in the hemisphere with the larger planum temporale.

Studies of individuals being treated for epilepsy in whom the corpus callosum (the bundle of nerve fibres connecting the two halves of the brain) has been severed, allowing the two hemispheres to function largely independently, have revealed that the right hemisphere has more language competence than was thought. These individuals show evidence of comprehension of words presented to the isolated right hemisphere, although that hemisphere is not able to initiate speech. The speech of individuals with a lesion of the right hemisphere may lack normal melodic quality, and they may have difficulty expressing and understanding such things as emotional overtones. They may also have difficulty appreciating some of the more subtle, connotative aspects of language, such as puns, figures of speech, and jokes. Nevertheless, the dominance of the left hemisphere for language, particularly the syntactic aspects of language and language output, is the clearest example yet discovered of the lateralization of higher cortical function.

The left hemisphere also appears to be more involved than the right in the programming of complex sequences of movement and in some aspects of awareness of one's own body. Thus, apraxia is more common after damage to the left hemisphere. In apraxia, the individual has difficulty performing actions involving several movements or the manipulation of objects in an appropriate and skillful way. The difficulty appears to be in programming the motor system to control the sequence of movements required to perform a complex action in the appropriate order and with the appropriate timing.

Confusion of right and left is also found after left-hemisphere damage, making it appear that the left hemisphere is largely responsible for collating somatosensory information into a special awareness of the body called the body image. Finger agnosia is a condition in which the individual does not appear to "know" which finger is which and is unable to indicate which one the examiner touches without the aid of vision. The phenomenon of the phantom limb, whereby patients "feel" sensations in amputated limbs, indicates that the brain's internal representation of the body may persist intact for some time after the loss of a body part. This internal representation appears to be maintained chiefly by the left hemisphere.

The special functions of the right hemisphere were recognized later than those of the left hemisphere, although a case of "imperception" reported by the English neurologist John Hughlings Jackson in 1876 foreshadowed later findings. Jackson's patient, who had a lesion in the posterior part of the right hemisphere, lost her way in familiar surroundings, failed to recognize familiar places and people, and had difficulty in dressing herself—all of which became well-recognized consequences of right-hemisphere damage. The right hemisphere appears to be specialized for some aspects of higher-level visual perception, spatial orientation, and sense of direction, and it probably plays a dominant role in the recognition of objects and faces. The specialization of the right hemisphere, however, is less absolute than that of the left hemisphere in that these skills are less lateralized than language.

There has been considerable speculation as to why the human brain is functionally asymmetrical. Initially, both functional and anatomical asymmetry were thought, like language, to be a uniquely human trait, but less-pronounced asymmetries have been found in lower animals. One theory is that it is necessary to have language represented in a single hemisphere to avoid competition between the hemispheres for control of the muscles involved in speech. Another theory is that it is efficient to have the language system represented in a restricted area on one side of the brain because information needs to be transferred over short distances and fewer connections. A third theory is that the dominance of the left hemisphere over the right hand and skilled movement preceded its dominance over language. According to this view, language subsequently developed in the same hemisphere because language implies speech, which requires precise programming of sequences of movement in the articulatory musculature. None of these theories has been conclusively proved correct or has been generally accepted. Also, there remain some facts that are difficult to explain by any theory. For example, all of the above theories would predict that bilateral and, in some cases, right-hemisphere language representation would be disadvantageous, but this does not seem to be generally true.

LANGUAGE

The language area of the brain surrounds the Sylvian fissure in the dominant hemisphere and is divided into two major components named after Paul Broca and Carl Wernicke. The Broca area lies in the third frontal convolution, just anterior to the face area of the motor cortex and just above the Sylvian fissure. This is often described as the motor, or expressive, speech area; damage to it results in Broca aphasia, a language disorder characterized by deliberate, telegraphic speech with very simple grammatical structure, though the speaker may be quite clear as to what he or she wishes to say and may communicate successfully. The Wernicke area is in the superior part of the posterior temporal lobe; it is close to the auditory cortex and is considered to be the receptive language, or language-comprehension, centre. An individual with Wernicke aphasia has difficulty understanding language; speech is typically

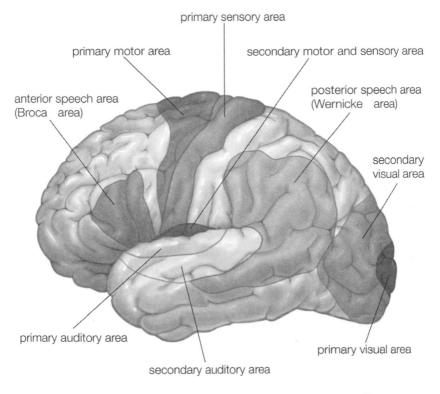

primary sensory area

primary motor area

secondary motor and sensory area

anterior speech area
(Broca area)

posterior speech area
(Wernicke area)

secondary
visual area

primary auditory area

primary visual area

secondary auditory area

Functional areas of the human brain. Encyclopædia Britannica, Inc.

fluent but is empty of content and characterized by circumlocutions, a high incidence of vague words like "thing," and sometimes neologisms and senseless "word salad." The entire posterior language area extends into the parietal lobe and is connected to the Broca area by a fibre tract called the arcuate fasciculus. Damage to this tract may result in conduction aphasia, a disorder in which the individual can understand and speak but has difficulty in repeating what is said to him or her. The suggestion is that, in this condition, language can be comprehended by the posterior zone and spoken by the anterior zone, but is not easily shuttled from one to the other.

Aphasia is a disorder of language and not of speech (although an apraxia of speech, in which the programming of motor speech output is affected, may accompany aphasia). The writing and reading of aphasic individuals, therefore, usually commits the same type of error as their speech, while the reverse is not the case. Isolated disorders of writing (dysgraphia) or, more commonly, reading (dyslexia) may occur as well, but these reflect a disruption of additional processing required for these activities over and above that required for language.

One particular form of dyslexia, dyslexia without dysgraphia, is an example of a disconnection syndrome—a disorder resulting from the disconnection of two areas of the brain rather than from damage to a centre. This type of dyslexia, also called letter-by-letter reading, is not associated with a writing disturbance; individuals tend to attempt to read by spelling words out loud, letter by letter. It usually results from a lesion in the posterior part of the left hemisphere that disconnects the visual areas of the brain from the language areas. This renders the language areas effectively blind, so that they cannot interpret visible language such as the written word. Writing is unaffected because the right hand is still connected to the left hemisphere, and, if letters can be spoken out loud correctly (which is not always the case), the individual will be able to hear himself or herself say them and reintegrate them into words. Disconnection syndromes are an important concept in understanding behavioral disorders associated with brain damage. The possibility that deficits are caused by disconnection must always be borne in mind.

MEMORY

Memory refers to the storage of information that is necessary for the performance of many cognitive tasks. Working, or short-term, memory is the memory one uses, for example, to remember a telephone number after looking it up in a directory and while dialing. In order to understand this sentence, for example, a reader must maintain the first half of the sentence in working memory while reading the second half. The capacity of working memory is limited, and it decreases if not exercised. Long-term memory, also called secondary or reference memory, stores information for longer periods. The capacity of long-term memory is unlimited, and it can endure indefinitely. In addition, psychologists distinguish episodic memory, a memory of specific events or episodes normally described by the verb *remember*, from semantic memory, a knowledge of facts normally said to be known rather than remembered.

Memory is probably stored over wide areas of the brain rather than in any single location. However, amnesia, a memory disorder, can occur because of localized bilateral lesions in the limbic system—notably the hippocampus on the medial side of the temporal lobe, some parts of the thalamus, and their connections. This probably implies that these structures, rather than actually constituting a memory store, are important in the development of memories and in their recall. Memory impairment resulting from damage in these areas is a disorder of long-term episodic memory and is predominantly an anterograde amnesia—it typically affects the memory of events occurring after the illness or accident causing the amnesia more than it does memories of the past. Substantial retrograde amnesia (loss of the memory of events occurring before the onset of the injury) rarely, if ever, occurs without significant anterograde amnesia as a result of brain damage, although it may occur alone in psychiatric disorders.

Although amnesia is a disorder of long-term episodic memory and leaves short-term and semantic memory intact, both of the latter can be affected by brain damage. Some parietal lobe lesions may affect short-term memory without affecting long-term memory. Short-term memory impairment—at least for verbal material—may be further subdivided into auditory and visual domains; however, these disorders result in difficulty in understanding spoken and written language rather than in memory impairment (i.e., they appear more like aphasia and dyslexia). Impairment of semantic memory also results in an impairment that resembles a loss of concepts or a language deficit more than it resembles a memory impairment. Some forms of visual agnosia have been interpreted as semantic memory impairment, since patients are unable to recognize objects such as chairs because they no longer "know" what chairs are or what they look like (or can no longer access that knowledge).

EXECUTIVE FUNCTIONS OF THE FRONTAL LOBES

The frontal lobes are the part of the brain most remote from sensory input and whose functions are the most difficult to capture. They can be thought of as the executive that controls and directs the operation of brain systems dealing with cognitive function. The deficits seen after frontal lobe damage are described as a "dysexecutive syndrome."

Frontal lobe damage can affect people in any of several ways. On the one hand, they may have difficulty initiating a task or a behaviour, in extreme cases being virtually unable to move or speak, but more often they will simply have difficulty in initiating a task. On the other hand, individuals with frontal lobe damage may perseverate (continue to repeat a behaviour), being apparently unable to stop a behaviour once it is started. Rather than appearing apathetic and hypoactive, patients may be uninhibited and may appear rude. Such people may also have difficulty in planning and problem solving and may be incapable of creative thinking. Mild cases of this deficit may be determined by a difficulty in solving mental arithmetic problems that are filled with words, even though the patient is capable of remembering the question and performing the required calculation. In such cases it appears that the patient simply cannot select the appropriate cognitive strategy to solve the problem.

A unifying theme in these disorders is the notion of inadequate control of organization of pieces of behaviour that may in themselves be well formed. Patients with frontal lobe damage are easily distracted. Although their deficits may be superficially less dramatic than those associated with posterior lesions, they can have a drastic effect on everyday function. Irritability and personality change are also frequently seen after frontal lobe damage.

CHAPTER 4

THE NERVOUS SYSTEM IN MOTION

Movements of the body are brought about by the harmonious contraction and relaxation of selected muscles. Contraction occurs when nerve impulses are transmitted across neuromuscular junctions to the membrane covering each muscle fibre. Most muscles are not continuously contracting but are kept in a state ready to contract. The slightest movement or even the intention to move results in widespread activity of the muscles of the trunk and limbs.

Movements may be intrinsic to the body itself and carried out by muscles of the trunk and body cavity. Examples are those involved in breathing, swallowing, laughing, sneezing, urinating, and defecating. Such movements are largely carried out by smooth muscles of the viscera (alimentary canal and bladder, for example); they are innervated by efferent sympathetic and parasympathetic nerves. Other movements relate the body to the environment, either for moving or for signaling to other individuals. These are carried out by the skeletal muscles of the trunk and limbs. Skeletal muscles are attached to bones and produce movement at the joints. They are innervated by efferent motor nerves and sometimes by efferent sympathetic and parasympathetic nerves.

Every movement of the body has to be correct for force, speed, and position. These aspects of movement are continuously reported to the central nervous system by receptors sensitive to position, posture, equilibrium, and

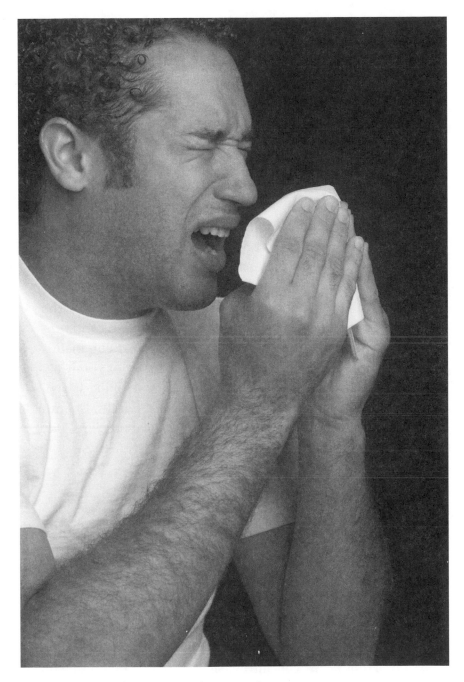

Sneezing is a reflexive action. Shutterstock.com

internal conditions of the body. These receptors are called proprioceptors, and those proprioceptors that keep a continuous report on the position of limbs are the muscle spindles and tendon organs.

Movements can be organized at several levels of the nervous system. At the lowest level are movements of the viscera, some of which do not involve the central nervous system, being controlled by neurons of the autonomic nervous system within the viscera themselves. Movements of the trunk and limbs occur at the next level of the spinal cord. If the spinal cord is severed so that no nerve impulses arrive from the brain, certain movements of the trunk and limbs below the level of the injury can still occur. At a higher level, respiratory movements are controlled by the lower brainstem. The upper brainstem controls muscles of the eye, the bladder, and basic movements of walking and running. At the next level is the hypothalamus. It commands certain totalities of movement, such as those of vomiting, urinating and defecating, and curling up and falling asleep. At the highest level is gray matter of the cerebral hemispheres, both the cortex and the subcortical basal ganglia. This is the level of conscious control of movements.

REFLEX ACTIONS

Of the many kinds of neural activity, there is one simple kind in which a stimulus leads to an immediate action. This is reflex activity. The word *reflex* (from Latin *reflexus*, "reflection") was introduced into biology by 19th-century English neurologist Marshall Hall, who fashioned the word because he thought of the muscles as reflecting a stimulus much as a wall reflects a ball thrown against it. By reflex, Hall meant the automatic response of a muscle or several muscles to a stimulus that excites an afferent nerve. The term is now used to describe an action that is an inborn central nervous system activity, not involving consciousness, in which a particular stimulus, by exciting an afferent nerve, produces a stereotyped, immediate response of muscle or gland.

The anatomical pathway of a reflex is called the reflex arc. It consists of an afferent (or sensory) nerve, usually one or more interneurons within the central nervous system, and an efferent (motor, secretory, or secreto-motor) nerve. Most reflexes have several synapses in the reflex arc. The stretch reflex is exceptional in that, with no interneuron in the arc, it has only one synapse between the afferent nerve fibre and the motor neuron. The flexor reflex, which removes a limb from a noxious stimulus, has a minimum of two interneurons and three synapses.

Probably the best-known reflex is the pupillary light reflex. If a light is flashed near one eye, the pupils of both eyes contract. Light is the stimulus; impulses reach the brain via the optic nerve; and the response is conveyed to the pupillary musculature by autonomic nerves that supply the eye. Another reflex involving the eye is known as the lacrimal reflex. When something irritates the conjunctiva or cornea of the eye, the lacrimal reflex causes nerve impulses to pass along the fifth cranial nerve (trigeminal) and reach the midbrain. The efferent limb of this reflex arc is autonomic and mainly parasympathetic. These nerve fibres stimulate the lacrimal glands of the orbit, causing the outpouring of tears. Other reflexes of the midbrain and medulla oblongata are the cough and sneeze reflexes. The cough reflex is caused by an irritant in the trachea and the sneeze reflex by one in the nose. In both, the reflex response involves many muscles; this includes a temporary lapse of respiration in order to expel the irritant.

The first reflexes develop in the womb. By seven and a half weeks after conception, the first reflex can be observed; stimulation around the mouth of the fetus causes the lips to be turned toward the stimulus. By birth, sucking and swallowing reflexes are ready for use. Touching the baby's lips induces sucking, and touching the back of its throat induces swallowing.

Although the word *stereotyped* is used to define a reflex, this does not mean that the reflex response is invariable and unchangeable. When a stimulus is repeated regularly, two changes occur in the reflex response—sensitization and habituation. Sensitization is an increase in response; in general, it occurs during the first 10 to 20 responses. Habituation is a decrease in response; it continues until, eventually, the response is extinguished. When the stimulus is irregularly repeated, habituation does not occur or is minimal.

There are also long-term changes in reflexes, which may be seen in experimental spinal cord transections performed on kittens. Repeated stimulation of the skin below the level of the lesion, such as rubbing the same area for 20 minutes every day, causes a change in latency (the interval between the stimulus and the onset of response) of certain reflexes, with diminution and finally extinction of the response. Although this procedure takes several weeks, it shows that, with daily stimulation, one reflex response can be changed into another. Repeated activation of synapses increases their efficiency, causing a lasting change. When this repeated stimulation ceases, synaptic functions regress, and reflex responses return to their original form.

Although a reflex response is said to be rapid and immediate, some reflexes, called recruiting reflexes, can hardly be evoked by a single stimulus. Instead, they require increasing stimulation to induce a response. The reflex contraction of the bladder, for example, requires an increasing amount of urine to stretch the muscle and to obtain muscular contraction.

Reflexes can be altered by impulses from higher levels of the central nervous system. For example, the cough reflex can be suppressed easily, and even the gag reflex (the movements of incipient vomiting resulting from mechanical stimulation of the wall of the pharynx) can be suppressed with training. The so-called conditioned reflexes are not reflexes at all but complicated acts of learned behaviour. Salivation is one such conditioned reflex; it occurs only when a person is conscious of the presence of food or when one imagines food.

SENSORY RECEPTORS OF MOVEMENT

Only a minority of the nerve fibres supplying a muscle are ordinary motor fibres that actually make it contract. The rest are either afferent sensory fibres telling the central nervous system what the muscle is doing or specialized motor fibres regulating the behaviour of the sensory nerve endings. If the constant feedback of proprioceptive information from the muscles, tendons, and joints is cut off, movements can still occur, but they cannot be adjusted to suit changing conditions; nor can new motor skills be developed.

The sensory receptors chiefly concerned with body movement are the muscle spindles and tendon organs. The muscle spindle is vastly more complicated than the tendon organ, so that, although it has been much more intensively studied, it is less well understood.

Tendon Organs

The tendon organ consists simply of an afferent nerve fibre that terminates in a number of branches upon slips of tendon where the tendons join onto muscle fibres. By lying in series with muscle, the tendon organ is well placed to signal muscular tension. In fact, the afferent fibre of the tendon organ is sufficiently sensitive to generate a useful signal on the contraction of a single muscle fibre. In this way tendon organs provide a continuous flow of information on the level of muscular contraction.

Muscle Spindles

The familiar knee-jerk reflex, tested routinely by physicians, is a spinal reflex in which a brief, rapid tap on the knee excites muscle spindle afferent neurons, which then excite the motor neurons of the stretched muscle via a single synapse in the spinal cord. In this simplest of reflexes, which is not transmitted through interneurons of the spinal cord, the delay (approximately 0.02 second) primarily occurs in the conduction of impulses to and from the spinal cord.

Information provided by muscle spindles is also utilized by the cerebellum and the cerebral cortex in ways that continue to elude detailed analysis. One example is kinesthesia, or the subjective sensory awareness of the position of limbs in space. It might be supposed (as it long was) that sensory receptors in joints, not the muscles, provide kinesthetic signals, since people are very aware of joint angle and less aware of the length of the various muscles involved. In fact, kinesthesia depends largely upon the integration within the cerebral cortex of signals from the muscle spindles.

Features of the structure and function of the muscle spindle continue to be discovered. Within it are several specialized muscle fibres, known as intrafusal muscle fibres (from Latin *fusus*, "spindle"). The muscle spindle is several millimetres long, and approximately five intrafusal muscle fibres run throughout its length. They are considerably thinner and shorter than ordinary skeletal muscle fibres, although they show similar contractions and have the same histological appearance.

The characteristic central swelling of the spindle (giving it a shape reminiscent of the spindle of a spinning wheel) is produced by fluid contained in a capsule surrounding the central millimetre of the intrafusal fibres.

Classically, the nerve terminals are considered to be of three kinds: primary sensory endings, secondary sensory endings, and plate motor endings. There are approximately equal numbers of primary and secondary sensory endings, so they may be considered equally important. However, the primary, or annulo-spiral, ending has traditionally attracted the most attention, largely through its prominent appearance and the simplicity of its chief reflex action, the tendon jerk. It consists of a large axon, which branches to wind spirals around the equatorial region of every intrafusal fibre. The secondary ending is supplied by a smaller axon. It has less-dramatic "flower spray" terminals lying primarily upon the smaller intrafusal fibres to one side of the primary endings. The reflex action of the secondary endings is incompletely understood. The plate motor endings lie toward the ends of the intrafusal fibres. They are fairly similar to the motor end plates of the skeletal, or extrafusal, muscle fibres.

The working of this elaborate piece of biological machinery is not yet fully understood. The muscle spindle lies parallel with the main muscle fibres and so sends a signal whenever the muscle changes its length. Both types of sensory endings increase their discharge of impulses when the muscle is stretched and reduce their firing when the muscle is slackened. The primary ending differs from the secondary ending in two important respects: first, it is much more sensitive to changing length of the muscle; second, it is much more sensitive to small stimuli than large ones. Together, these properties explain the exquisite sensitivity of the primary sensory ending to the stimulus of a tendon tap, which has little effect on the secondary ending or on the tendon organ. The essential principle is that the ability of the muscle spindle to signal a wide range of movement is increased by its having two separate output channels of different sensitivity.

Most of the intrafusal fibres of the muscle spindle receive specialized fusimotor nerve fibres. These are much smaller than the motor axons innervating extrafusal muscle fibres and are given the name gamma (γ) efferents. Because their only function is to regulate the behaviour of the muscle spindles, their stimulation produces no significant contraction of the muscle as a whole. The γ efferents are of two functionally distinct kinds with different effects on the afferent fibres — especially on the primary ending. One type, the dynamic fusimotor axon, increases the normal sensitivity of the primary ending to movement; the other type, the static fusimotor axon, decreases its sensitivity, causing it to behave much more like a secondary ending. Thus, the two types of efferent fibre provide a means whereby the sensitivity of the muscle spindle to external stimuli may be regulated over a very wide range. Stimulation of both types also increases the rate of firing of the afferent fibres when the length of the muscle is constant; this is called a biasing action. It is thought that they produce these different effects by supplying different types of intrafusal fibre.

In addition to receiving specialized fusimotor fibres, the muscle spindle may also receive, though on a less-regular basis, branches of ordinary extrafusal motor axons. Called alpha (α) efferents, these fibres have either a static or a dynamic effect. The physiologically important point is that most of the motor supply to the muscle spindles is largely independent of that of the ordinary muscle fibres, and only a small part is obligatorily coupled with them. The specific mechanisms by which the sensitivity of the spindle is regulated remain obscure; they may differ from muscle to muscle and for movements of different kinds.

BASIC ORGANIZATION OF MOVEMENT

The neural inputs that coordinate reflex movements involve the innervation of generally antagonistic muscles. These circuits of communication enable complex responses—such as the simultaneous stimulation of an extensor muscle and inhibition of the opposite flexor muscle or the simultaneous stimulation of both the flexor and the extensor muscles. The different ways in which reflex pathways can be organized are illustrated by stretch reflexes, reciprocal innervation, and postural reflexes.

Stretch Reflexes

Primary afferent fibres are responsible for the stretch reflex, in which pulling the tendon of a muscle causes the muscle to contract. The basis for this simple spinal reflex is a monosynaptic excitation of the motor neurons of the stretched muscle. At the same time, however, motor neurons of the antagonist muscle (the muscle that moves the limb in the opposite direction) are inhibited. This action is mediated by an inhibitory interneuron interposed between the afferent neuron and the motor neuron. These reflexes have a transitory, or phasic, action even though the afferent impulses continue unabated; this is probably because they become submerged in more-complex delayed reflex responses elicited by the same and other afferent inputs.

Traditionally, it was thought that the stretch reflex provided uniquely for the automatic reflex control of standing, so that if the body swayed, then the stretched muscle would automatically take up the load and the antagonist would be switched off. This is now recognized to be only a part of the process, since more-powerful, slightly delayed reflex responses occur not only in the stretched muscle but also in others that help restore balance but have not themselves been stretched. Some of these responses seem to be spinal reflexes, but in humans, with their large brains, there is evidence that others are transcortical reflexes, in which the afferent impulse is transmitted rapidly up to the motor areas of the cerebral cortex to influence the level of ongoing voluntary motor impulses.

Reciprocal Innervation

Any cold, hot, or noxious stimulus coming in contact with the skin of the foot contracts the flexor muscle of that limb, relaxes the extensor muscles of the same limb, and extends the opposite limb. The purpose of these movements is to remove one limb from harm while shifting weight to the opposite limb. These movements constitute the first and immediate response to a stimulus, but a slower and longer-lasting reflex response is also possible. For example, noxious stimulation of the deep tissues of the limb can cause a prolonged discharge of impulses conducted by nonmyelinated afferent fibres to the spinal cord. The result is prolonged flexion of the damaged limb or at least a pattern of posture and movement favouring flexion. These effects last far longer than the original discharges from the afferent neurons of the damaged region—often continuing not for minutes but for weeks or months.

The flexor and extensor reflexes are only two examples of the sequential ordering of muscular contraction and relaxation. Underlying this basic organization is the principle of reciprocal innervation—the contraction of one muscle or group of muscles with the relaxation of muscles that have the opposite function. In reciprocal innervation, afferent nerve fibres from the contracting muscle excite inhibitory interneurons in the spinal cord; the interneurons, by inhibiting certain motor neurons, cause an antagonist muscle to relax.

Reciprocal innervation is apparent in eye movements. On looking to the right, the right lateral rectus and left medial rectus muscles of the eye contract, while the antagonist left lateral rectus and right medial rectus muscles relax. One eye cannot be turned without turning the other eye in the same direction (except in the movement of convergence, when both eyes turn medially toward the nose in looking at a near object).

Reciprocal innervation does not underlie all movement. For example, in order to fix the knee joint, antagonist muscles must contract simultaneously. In the movement of walking, there is both reciprocal innervation and simultaneous contraction of different sets of muscles. Because this basic organization of movement takes place at lower levels of the nervous system, the training of skilled movements such as walking requires the suppression of some lower-level reflexes as well as a proper arrangement of the reciprocal inhibition and simultaneous contraction of antagonist muscles.

Posture

Posture is the position and carriage of the limbs and the body as a whole. Except when lying down, the first postural requirement is to counteract the pull of gravity, which pulls the body toward the ground. This force induces stretch reflexes to keep the lower limbs extended and the back upright. The muscles are not kept contracted all the time, however. As the posture changes and the centre of gravity shifts, different muscles are stretched and contracted. Another important reflex is the extensor thrust reflex of the lower limb. Pressure on the foot stretches the ligaments of the sole, which causes reflex contraction of both flexor and extensor muscles, making the leg into a rigid pillar. As soon as the sole of the foot leaves the ground, the reflex response ceases, and the limb is free to move again.

The body is balanced when the centre of gravity is above the base formed by the feet. When the centre of gravity moves outside this base, the body starts to fall and has to bring the centre back to the base. Striding forward in walking depends on leaning forward so that the centre of gravity moves in front of the feet. When a baby is learning to walk, he or she must either take a step forward or fall down. Both happen; eventually the former happens more frequently than the latter.

Ballerinas use constant postural adjustments to balance their centres of gravity as they dance. Shutterstock.com

In addition to continuous postural adjustment for the changing centre of gravity, all movements require that certain parts of the body be fixed so that other parts can be supported as they move. For instance, when manipulating objects with the fingers, the forearm and arm are fixed. This does not mean that they do not move; they move so as to support the fine movements of the fingers. This changing postural fixation is carried out automatically and unconsciously. Before any movement occurs, the essential posture is arranged, and it continues to be adjusted throughout the movement.

LOWER-LEVEL MECHANISMS OF MOVEMENT

In the mid-20th century, German physiologist Erich Walter von Holst showed that many series of movements of invertebrates and vertebrates are organized endogenously. This discovery opened up a new realm in the study of movement, one that extended far beyond reflexes. Von Holst's general hypothesis was that within the gray matter there are networks of local neurons that generate alternating or cyclical patterns of movement. He proposed that these are the mechanisms of rhythmically repeated movements such as those of locomotion, breathing, scratching, feeding, and chewing.

In fish, Von Holst demonstrated that the movements of the fins in swimming that need careful and correct timing and coordination continued even after the sensory dorsal roots of the spinal cord had been cut, so that there could be no sensory input to trigger reflexes. In these animals, command neurons in the lower medulla oblongata switch on the rhythmic movement built into the spinal cord, so that even when the brain has been cut out, the motor impulses and rhythmic movements continue.

Von Holst's theory differs from previous concepts in that it attributes little or no importance to the role of feedback from the parts of the body being moved. Instead, it proposes, as the essential mechanism of repetitive movements, certain central pacemakers or oscillators. The role of feedback, according to this theory, is merely to modulate the central oscillator. This is seen in the swimming movements in fish and even in purring rhythms in cats, which continue after dorsal roots have been cut.

In certain kinds of movement, the input of dorsal roots is essential, but the movement needs to be defined in every case. For example, stepping movements of certain vertebrates, of which the mechanisms are within the spinal cord, can occur only with intact dorsal roots.

Higher levels of the brain can set spinal centres in motion, stop them, and change the amplitude and frequency of repetitive movements. In the case of humans, when the spinal cord is cut off from the brain by disease or trauma, the movements that occur are uncontrolled. The movements of locomotion, seen in lower vertebrates, do not occur. This is because the cerebral hemispheres in humans have taken over the organization of movements that in lower species are organized at lower levels of the central nervous system, such as the reticular formation of the brainstem and the spinal cord.

Within the centre of the brainstem, the reticular formation consists of vast numbers of neurons and their interconnections. The majority of the neurons have motor functions, and many of their fibres branch. This branching allows a single fibre to affect several different levels of the spinal cord. For example, one nerve fibre may excite motor neurons of the neck and of various regions of the back. This is one way in which commands from the higher neural level are sent to several segments of the spinal cord.

The movements of breathing are instigated and regulated by chemoreceptors in blood vessel walls, which sense carbon dioxide tension in the blood plasma. The essential drive or central rhythm generator consists of pacemaker neurons in the reticular formation of the pons and throughout the medulla oblongata. These neurons show rhythmic changes in electrical potential, which are relayed by reticulospinal tracts to the spinal neurons concerned with respiration.

Other movements intrinsic to the body are those needed for urination and defecation. Cats and dogs from which the cerebral cortex has been removed urinate and defecate in a normal manner. This is because nuclei in the midbrain near those that organize the movements of locomotion control these movements, so that urination and defecation occur whenever there are enough waste products to be expelled. This is also the condition of the healthy human baby. But as the infant grows up, he learns to fit these events into the social circumstances of living, which requires higher-level control by the cerebral hemispheres.

HIGHER-LEVEL MECHANISMS OF MOVEMENT

Because of the many differences in the movements used in standing, coughing, laughing, or playing a scale on the piano, it is convenient to think of movements as lower and more automatic or as higher and less automatic. According to this concept, movements are not placed in totally different categories but are regarded as different in degree.

Cerebral Hemispheres

Basic organizations of movement, such as reciprocal innervation, are organized at levels of the central nervous system lower than the cerebral hemispheres—at both the spinal and the brainstem level. Examples of brainstem reflexes are turning of the eyes and head toward a light or sound. The same movements, of course, also can be organized consciously when one decides to turn the head and eyes to look. The cerebral hemispheres themselves can organize certain series of movements, called programmed movements, that need to be performed so rapidly that there is no time for correction of error by local feedback. For this reason the program is arranged before the movements begin. Examples of such movements are those of a pianist performing a trill or of an athlete hitting a ball.

Most of the movements organized by the cerebral cortex are carried out automatically. But when a new series of movements is being learned, or when a movement is difficult, the attributes usually associated with the higher levels of the brain—such as planning, internal speech, remembering, and learning—are used.

The primary motor area is the motor strip of the precentral gyrus. Immediately behind it is the postcentral gyrus, also called the primary sensory area. Each of these areas displays a maplike correspondence with various body parts, the legs represented near the top of the hemispheres and the arms and face lower on the cortical surface. Each of these areas is to some extent both motor and sensory. The motor region, for example, receives input from the skin, joints, and muscles via the postcentral gyrus behind and the thalamus below.

Experiments in monkeys have shown that the motor strip is able to arrange activity of muscles to produce the correct force for the loading conditions of the limbs. To do this, the motor strip continually receives information from the primary sensory area both before and during the movement. Cutaneous areas having the greatest tactile acuity have the largest representation in the primary sen-

Cutaneous nerves of head and neck

auriculotemporal nerve

zygomaticotemporal nerve

supraorbital nerve

palpebral branch of lacrimal nerve

supratrochlear nerve

infratrochlear nerve

external nasal branch of anterior ethmoidal nerve

greater occipital nerve

3rd occipital nerve

lesser occipital nerve

infraorbital nerve

zygomatico-facial nerve

buccal nerve

mental nerve

great auricular nerve

transverse cervical nerve

supraclavicular nerve

Cutaneous nerves of the head and neck. Encyclopædia Britannica, Inc.

sory area; these areas are connected to equally large areas in the primary motor area.

In front of the motor strip is an area known as the pre-motor cortex or area. When it is stimulated in a monkey, the animal turns its head and eyes as though it is looking in a particular direction. This cortical area, then, organizes the guiding of movements by vision and hearing.

The secondary motor area is at the lower end of the precentral gyrus. It is secondary not only because it was discovered after the primary motor area but also because it does not function in a discrete manner like the primary area. Stimulation of this small area produces movements of large parts of the body. It is also a sensory area, as sensations in the parts of the body being moved are felt during stimulation.

On the medial surface of the hemisphere, in front of the motor strip, is the supplementary motor area. Stimulation of this area can produce vocalization or interrupt speech. Large movements of both sides of the body—often symmetrical movements of the two limbs— also may occur. Stimulation also produces movements of the opposite side of the body, such as raising the upper limb and turning the head and eyes as if looking at something opposite. In experiments on monkeys, when the animal chooses to respond to one kind of sensation rather than to another, it is the supplementary area that is active rather than the precentral area. In these animals, the fibres descending from the supplementary motor area run to the spinal cord and terminate throughout its whole length. Fibres also are sent to the precentral gyri of both hemispheres, the reticular formation of the pons, the hypothalamus, the midbrain, and many other masses of cerebral gray matter such as the caudate nucleus and the globus pallidus. The supplementary motor area is upstream from the primary motor area; it initiates movements, whereas the motor strip of the precentral gyrus is part of the apparatus for carrying them out.

Other regions of the cerebral hemisphere from which movements are produced by electrical stimulation are the insula and the surface of the temporal lobe. The insula is a region below the frontal and temporal lobes that, when stimulated, causes movements of the face, larynx, and neck. Stimulation of the anterior end of one temporal lobe causes movements of the head and body toward the other side.

Fibres from the anterior part of the cingulate gyrus are involved in the control of urination and defecation. The organization of these functions also depends on regions anterior to the cingulate gyrus in the medial wall of the frontal lobe. These regions form a part of the limbic lobe, which is responsible, along with their autonomic components, for some emotional states.

Movements closely guided by vision have their own pathways. Occipital visual areas send fibres to the pons and from there to the cerebellum. Also just in front of the visual cortex in the parietal lobe are neurons organizing certain types of eye movement. In the monkey, these neurons are at rest during steady gaze, becoming active when the animal turns its eyes to look at something. The fact that the movements constitute a high level of motor behaviour is shown by the activation of these neurons only when the animal is attempting to satisfy an appetite by using its upper limbs and hands; using the limbs for other purposes does not activate them. The neurons are also active when the animal is carrying out the movements of grooming, which also satisfies an innate drive.

One of the main pathways for cortically directed movement of the limbs is the corticospinal tract. This tract developed among animals that used their forelimbs for exploring and affecting the environment as well as for locomotion. It is largest in humans. Fibres of the tract go to various regions of the brainstem and the spinal cord that organize movement. Excitation via the corticospinal tract is then brought to many muscles, all of them presumably working together in a coordinated manner. This is achieved by the anatomical arrangement of the motor neurons and by the termination of the corticospinal tract on interneurons, which convey a coordinated pattern of stimulation to the motor neurons.

The corticospinal tract is not merely a pathway to medullary and spinal motor neurons. Activity in this tract can suppress the input from cutaneous areas while facilitating proprioceptive input. This is probably an important mechanism in the organization of movement. The corticospinal neurons themselves receive constant input from the cerebellum needed for internal feedback. Much of this input originates in the muscles, joints, and skin of the body parts being moved.

Cerebellum

Although a cycle of simple repetitive movements can be organized without sensory feedback, more-sophisticated movements require feedback as well as what is called feed-forward control. This is provided by the cerebellum. Many parts of the brain have to be kept informed of movements in order to detect error and continually correct the movement. The cerebellum continuously receives input from the trunk, limbs, eyes, ears, and vestibular apparatus, maintaining in turn a continuous transfer of information to the motor parts of the thalamus and to the cerebral cortex.

As a movement is being prepared, a replica of the instructions is sent to the cerebellum, which sends back its own information to the cerebral cortex. The cortex, meanwhile, sends information about the movement to

various afferent neurons that are about to receive information from receptors in the body parts where the
movement is about to begin. This comparison between
instructions sent and movement performed is a fundamental requirement of all complicated movements. The
discharge of impulses from motor to sensory regions is
called the corollary discharge. The mechanisms involving
the cerebellum do not come to consciousness. There are
no sensory consequences of damage to the cerebellum, for
the cerebellum is a motor structure.

As series of movements are learned and improved with
practice, a replica of the movement is probably retained in
the cerebral hemispheres. (The mechanisms of this postu-
lated replica are as yet unknown.) Whenever the learned
movements are repeated, they are formed and guided by
the replica. This hypothesis of controlling movement
by previously practiced patterns was developed by von
Holst. He gave the name *efference* to the totality of motor
impulses necessary for a movement, and he proposed that,
whenever the efference is produced, it leaves an image of
itself somewhere in the central nervous system. He called
this image the efference copy. According to von Holst's
theory, as the movement is repeated, afferent impulses,
called the re-afference, return to the brain from receptors
activated by muscular activity. There is then a comparison
between the efference copy and the re-afference. When
they are identical, the movement is "correct" in relation to
its previous performance. When the re-afference differs
from the efference copy, corrections have to be made so as
to bring the present pattern of movement back to the
original image left in the brain.

If the cerebellum is damaged or degenerates, any error
between the movement being performed and the efference copy will no longer be corrected, and the postural
adjustments sent from the cerebral hemispheres will no

longer be implemented. The force and extent of movements also will be abnormal, the movement going too far or not far enough. The various muscles may not come into play at the right time, and there will be a disturbance in the relationship of antagonist muscles, so that the accurate arrival on target will be replaced by oscillation.

Basal Ganglia

Most of what is known about the contribution of the basal ganglia has been obtained from studying abnormal conditions that occur when these nuclei are affected by disease. In Parkinson disease there is a loss of the pigmented neurons of the substantia nigra, which release the neurotransmitter dopamine at synapses in the basal ganglia. Individuals with this disease have a certain type of muscle stiffness called rigidity, a typical tremor, flexed posture, and difficulty in maintaining equilibrium. They have difficulty in initiating movements, including walking, and they cannot put adequate force into fast movements. They have particular difficulty in changing from one movement to its opposite, in carrying out two movements simultaneously, and in stopping one movement while starting another.

The organization of posture, which is based on vestibular, proprioceptive, and visual input to the globus pallidus, is severely damaged when this region of the basal ganglia degenerates. Because a changing posture of the various parts of the body is a prerequisite of every movement, degeneration of this region upsets all movement. Visual reflexes contributing to motion also act through the globus pallidus. One patient may be unable to go forward if he or she has to pass through a narrow door, and another may not be able to do so if he or she has to go into a wide expanse such as a field.

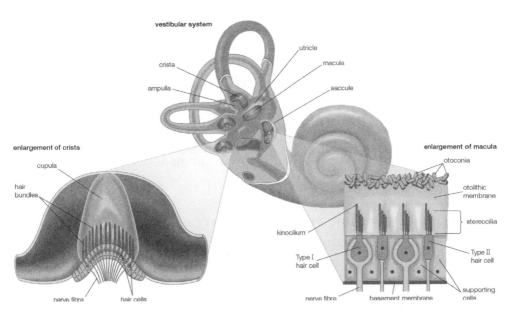

The membranous labyrinth of the vestibular system, which contains the organs of balance: (lower left) *the cristae of the semicircular ducts and* (lower right) *the maculae of the utricle and saccule.* Encyclopædia Britannica, Inc.

THE VESTIBULAR SYSTEM

Humans have evolved sophisticated sensory receptors to detect features of the environment in which they live. In addition to the special senses such as hearing and sight, there are unobtrusive sensory systems such as the vestibular system, which is sensitive to acceleration.

Acceleration can be considered as occurring in two forms—linear and angular. One familiar type of linear acceleration is gravity. Because this environmental feature, unlike any other encountered by an organism, is always present, highly sophisticated systems have developed to detect gravity and enable humans to maintain their position relative to Earth. A common form of angular acceleration is that induced by rotation, such as a turning of the head. Through the vestibular apparatus these forces are detected, and appropriate motor activities are organized to counter the postural perturbations that they induce.

The vestibular sensory organ is a paired structure located symmetrically on either side of the head within the inner ear. Inside each end organ are the hair cells, the detection units for both linear and angular acceleration. Extending from each hair cell are fine, hairlike cilia; displacement of the cilia alters the electrical potential of the cell. Bending the cilia in one direction causes the cell membrane to depolarize, while hyperpolarization is induced by movement in the opposite direction. Changes in membrane potential induce alteration in the firing of nerve impulses by the afferent neurons supplying each hair cell.

The two types of acceleration are detected by two types of vestibular end organ. Linear acceleration is sensed by a pair of organs—the saccule and utricle—while there are three receptor organs—called semicircular canals—in each vestibular apparatus for the detection of angular acceleration.

SACCULE AND UTRICLE

Each saccule and utricle has a single cluster, or macula, of hair cells located in the vertical and horizontal planes, respectively. Resting upon the hair cells is a gelatinous membrane in which are embedded calcareous granules called otoliths. Changes in linear acceleration alter the pressure on the otoliths, causing displacement of the cilia and providing an adequate stimulus for membrane depolarization. Within each macula the hair cells are arranged in two groups oriented in opposite directions, so that the receptor functions in a push-pull fashion within each organ. Since many of the nerve fibres traveling from the hair cells to the brain are constantly active, this arrangement makes the receptors a highly sensitive detection system for both vertical and horizontal linear acceleration.

SEMICIRCULAR CANALS

The angular acceleration detectors within the semicircular canals function in a different way. The three canals—which in fact are considerably more than a semicircle in circumference—are oriented at approximately right angles to one another. Two are vertically placed, and one is at about 30° to the horizontal. In this arrangement the anterior canal of one side of the head is in the plane of the posterior canal of the other side. A ridge, or crista, covered by sensory hair cells is located at the end of each canal within an expanded chamber called the ampulla. Rotation of the canals about an imaginary axis passing through the centre of each semicircle causes endolymphatic fluid to flow toward or away from the crista, generating a force that bends the cilia by displacement of a gelatinous plate resting upon the hairs. The cells of the vertical canals are oriented in such a way that centrifugal movement away from the cristae depolarizes the hair cell membranes of the vertical canals, while the opposite applies to the horizontal canal.

NERVE SUPPLY

As in the case of the utricle and saccule, some of the nerve fibres conveying information from the cells are constantly active. The hair cells receive nerve impulses from the brain (via efferent fibres) and send them to the central nervous system (via afferent fibres). Excitatory efferent fibres increase the sensitivity of the hair cells, while inhibitory fibres decrease sensitivity. This system gives the semicircular canals a plasticity that is essential to maintaining optimal activity under different environmental conditions—including such extraordinary states as space travel.

The vestibular apparatus is supplied by neurons that make up the vestibular portion of the vestibulocochlear, or eighth cranial, nerve. The somata, or cell bodies, of the afferent fibres lie in the vestibular ganglia near the end organ. Most of the nerve fibres pass from there to vestibular nuclei in the pons, while others pass directly to the cerebellum. The efferent fibres of the vestibular nerve arise from nuclei in the pons.

VESTIBULAR FUNCTIONS

For vision to be effective, the retinal image must be stationary. This can be achieved only by maintaining the position of the eyes relative to the Earth and using this as a stable platform for following a moving object. The vestibular system plays a critical part in this, mainly through complex and incompletely understood connections between the vestibular apparatus and the musculature of the eyes.

Rotation of the head in any direction is detected by the semicircular canals, and a velocity signal is then passed via the vestibular nuclei to the somatic and extraocular muscles. In the case of the eye muscles, the velocity signal reaching the brainstem is in some way integrated with impulses signaling the position of the eyes, thus ensuring that the eyes maintain their position relative to space and the observed object. This integration partly occurs in the vestibular nuclei, the source of secondary neurons destined for the extraocular muscle nuclei of both sides.

VESTIBULO-OCULAR REFLEX

When the head is oscillated, the eyes maintain their position in space but move in relation to the head. This so-called vestibulo-ocular reflex operates in both horizontal and vertical planes owing to the arrangement of the three semicircular canals, and it maintains such stability that the observed object does not oscillate until quite high velocities are attained. The other components of the vestibular system, the saccule and utricle, also contribute to the vestibulo-ocular reflex. Under normal circumstances the otolith receptors cause torsional movement of the eyes. For example, tilting the head toward one shoulder results in counterrolling of the eyes, thereby stabilizing the image upon the retina. The two components of the vestibulo-ocular reflex interact, enabling appropriate eye movements to be generated when both linear and angular accelerations are changing.

While the vestibulo-ocular reflex is the best understood of the vestibulo-motor connections, information from the vestibular receptors is also known to be passed via vestibular and other brainstem nuclei to the somatic musculature of the trunk and limbs. Through these pathways, body posture is adjusted to counter acceleration forces applied to the vestibule. These reflexes are so important in maintaining vertical posture that severe short-term consequences on posture are seen if the vestibulocochlear nerve is cut.

CONSCIOUS SENSATION

Besides maintaining input for the generation of motor reflexes, vestibular impulses reach consciousness and create a powerful sensation. A person being rotated knows when he or she is accelerating even in the absence of an object upon which the individual can fix his or her eyes. This occurs because acceleration is the adequate stimulus for the semicircular canals. Similarly, information detected by the otoliths is brought readily to consciousness; for example, a person is aware when a darkened elevator accelerates up or down. The pathways to the cerebral cortex, which mediate conscious sensation, are not fully known, but there is evidence that areas of the parietal and temporal lobes receive connections via the thalamus.

An important aspect of vestibular physiology is the interaction of vestibular impulses, which signal changes of position, and impulses from other sensory receptors that signal changes in bodily movement. For example, when the head turns to one side about a vertical axis, not only is the horizontal canal of that side stimulated and that of the other side inhibited, but receptors in the neck joints and muscles are also stimulated, and the retina indicates movement if fixation is not maintained perfectly. This information is fed to the brain via sensory pathways in the spinal cord and various visual sensory systems. Therefore, within the vestibular nuclei of the pons, neurons that respond to acceleration signals from the semicircular canals receive impulses from other sources as well.

Other information from visual and spinal sensory systems passes to the cerebellum, which also receives direct impulses from the vestibular apparatus that bypass the vestibular nuclei. In this way the cerebellum has the opportunity to compare signals and assess the degree of mismatch between them. (Motion sickness is often generated by a mismatch between the various inputs signaling orientation within space. People will frequently be seasick if they are below the deck of a boat and the visual system signals no movement while the vestibular system indicates motion.) The vestibulo-ocular reflex also may be underactive, so that for a given head movement the eyes do not deviate sufficiently within the orbit and the observed object does not remain stationary upon the retina. Thus, the image slips and cannot be seen clearly during movement. The cerebellum has the opportunity to detect this mismatch between the required position of the eyes with respect to the environment and the movement actually achieved. Through inhibitory connections to the vestibular nuclei, the cerebellum can then adjust the vestibulo-ocular reflex so that a more appropriate movement of the eyes is achieved with the next acceleration signal. In other words, there is a continual updating of the vestibulo-ocular reflex via the cerebellum or structures associated with it.

A similar situation also obtains for somatosensory input from the spinal cord. A dramatic demonstration of short-term adaptation via the visual system occurs when someone wears glasses with prism lenses that reverse the perception of the environment in the horizontal plane, making everything appear upside down. The person is at first unable to move about because any rotation of the head results in apparent movement of the environment in the wrong direction. However, over a few days normal mobility gradually returns. During this time, the vestibulo-ocular reflex is at first diminished in amplitude and then is reversed. Removal of the prisms results in a rapid return to the normal state. These experiments are a powerful demonstration of the plasticity of the vestibulo-ocular reflex, which can continue functioning throughout life in spite of the various insults that befall it.

CHAPTER 5

PERCEPTION, SENSATION, AND NEUROPLASTICITY

The brain is constantly working to interpret information that it receives from the surrounding environment. Likewise, humans are constantly altering their behaviours in response to these interpretations. Human behaviour is largely guided by sensation and perception, and thus changes in environment and in the brain's response to environmental inputs can in turn lead to alterations in behaviour.

The brain itself can also change—new neural connections are developed and reinforced in response to new behaviours, such as learning to play an instrument or learning to read. In addition, when preexisting neural connections are no longer reinforced through use, the affected connections recede, thereby breaking neural pathways. This phenomenon of neural change within the brain, known as neuroplasticity, is a relatively recent discovery. For many years it was believed that the neurons in the brain were incapable of forming new connections and growing in response to new inputs. In the late 20th century, however, when scientists discovered that the human brain undergoes constant adaptation to environmental stimuli, there occurred a major shift in the neurosciences, with many studies coming to focus on how neural connections are established and what factors influence their formation and their destruction.

PERCEPTION

To the biologist, the life of animals (including that of humans) consists of seeking stimulation and responding appropriately. A reflex occurs before an individual knows what has happened—for example, what made him or her lift a foot or drop an object. It is biologically correct to be alarmed before one knows the reason. It is only after the immediate and automatic response that the cerebral cortex is involved and conscious perception begins.

Perception comes between simple sensation and complex cognitional behaviour. It is so automatic that people hardly realize that seeing what they see and hearing what they hear is only an interpretation. Each act of perception is a hypothesis based on prior experience; the world is made up of things people expect to see, hear, or smell, and any new sensory event is perceived in relation to what they already know. People perceive trees, not brown upright masses and blotches of green. Once one has learned to understand speech, it is all but impossible to hear words as sibilants and diphthongs, sounds of lower and higher frequencies. In other words, recognizing a thing entails knowing its total shape or pattern. This is usually called by its German name, gestalt.

As well as perception of the external environment, there is perception of oneself. Information about one's position in space, for example, comes from vision, from vestibular receptors, and from somatic receptors in the skin and deep tissues. This information is collected in the vestibular nuclei and passed on to the thalamus. From there it is relayed to the central gyri and the parietal region of the cerebral cortex, where it becomes conscious perception.

General Organization of Perception

Perception relies on the special senses—visual, auditory, gustatory, and olfactory. Each begins with receptors grouped together in sensory end organs, where sensory input is organized before it is sent to the brain. A reorganization of impulses occurs at every synapse on a sensory pathway, so that by the time an input arrives at the thalamus, it is far from being the original input that stimulated the receptors.

The afferent parts of the thalamus fall into two divisions: a medial part, which is afferent but not sensory, and a ventral and lateral part, which is sensory. Nerve impulses reaching the medial part of the thalamus are derived from the reticular formation. This pathway is for emotional and other rapid reactions such as surprise, alarm, vigilance, and the readiness to react. The lateral part of the thalamus is a station on the way to areas of the cerebral cortex that are specific for each kind of sensation.

The cerebral cortex has three somatosensory areas. The primary sensory area occupies the postcentral gyrus immediately behind the motor strip and receives input from the ventrolateral thalamus. The secondary area is above the Sylvian fissure, behind the secondary motor area, and receives somatosensory input from the lateral part of the thalamus and also auditory and visual input from the medial and lateral geniculate nuclei. The primary and secondary areas are reciprocally connected. The supplementary area is in the upper part of the parietal lobe on the medial surface of the hemisphere, just behind the primary area.

The cerebral cortex (and the thalamus as well) is composed of nonspecific and specific sensory areas. Most neurons of the specific regions have small receptive fields in the periphery, respond to only one kind of stimulus, and follow the features of stimulation exactly. Most neurons of the nonspecific regions have large receptive fields and respond to many kinds of stimuli; many do not exactly reproduce the features of the stimulus.

Although different regions of the body are normally represented by specific parts of the somatosensory regions of the cortex, the parts of the body where afferent impulses arrive are not fixed. For example, the leg area is at the top of the postcentral gyrus, but when there is a painful state in the periphery—sciatica, for example—the leg area of the cortex can enlarge and occupy some of the arm area. Furthermore, injury to the peripheral nerves or brain may alter the sensory map of the cortex. These changes in the cortex and similar changes in anatomical function are referred to as plasticity.

From the somatosensory area, nerve fibres run to other regions of the cortex, traditionally called association areas. It is thought that these areas integrate sensory and motor information and that this integration allows objects to be recognized and located in space. With these regions acting upon all their inputs, the brain is carrying out those aspects of neural activity that are commonly labeled mental. It is not known how or where the brain collects messages from sensory receptors and then arranges them to produce a complete representation of the world and of the individual's place in the world.

VISION

The area of the brain concerned with vision makes up the entire occipital lobe and the posterior parts of the temporal and parietal lobes. The primary visual area, also called the striate cortex, is on the medial side of the occipital lobe and is surrounded by the secondary visual area. The visual cortex is sensitive to the position and orientation of edges, the direction and speed of movement of objects in the visual field, and stereoscopic depth, brightness, and colour; these aspects combine to produce visual perception.

The ganglion neurons of the retina are categorized into three functional types: X-, Y-, and W-cells. X-cells have small peripheral fields and are necessary for high-resolution vision. Y-cells are the largest of the three cells, have large peripheral fields, and respond to fast movement. W-cells are the smallest of the three cells, have large peripheral fields, and are sensitive to directional movement. In the retina, 50 to 55 percent of ganglion cells are W-type, 40 percent are X-type, and 5 to 10 percent are Y-type.

As constituent fibres of the optic nerves and optic tracts, X- and Y-cells connect to the lateral geniculate nucleus of the thalamus, while W-cells connect primarily to the superior colliculus of the midbrain. From these regions, input from the X-cells travels mainly to the primary visual area, that from the Y-cells to the secondary visual area, and that from the W-cells to the area surrounding the secondary area. The collicular pathway serves movement detection and direction of gaze. The tract from the lateral geniculate nucleus is the pathway for visual acuity.

The primary area sends fibres back to the lateral geniculate nucleus, the superior colliculus, and the pupillary reflex centre for feedback control of input to the visual areas. It also sends fibres to the secondary area and to the visual area of the temporal lobe. The secondary area sends fibres to the temporal and parietal lobes. Also, fibres cross from visual areas of one cerebral hemisphere to the other in the corpus callosum. This link allows neurons of the two hemispheres with similar visual fields to have direct contact with each other.

Neurons of the striate cortex may form the first step in appreciation of orientation of objects in the visual field. It is thought, however, that excitation of cortical neurons is insufficient to account for orientation and that inhibition of other neurons in the visual cortex is also necessary. Whatever the mechanism, experiments on cats and monkeys have shown that individual neurons are activated by lines at different angles—for example, at 90° to the horizontal or at an angle of 45°.

Most neurons of the deeper layers of striate cortex are movement analyzers. Some are direction analyzers, activated by a line or an edge moving in one direction and silenced when it changes direction (the changed direction then activating other neurons). Some neurons may be excited by a dark line on a bright background and others by a light line on a dark background. Form analyzers are located in other regions of the striate cortex; for example, some are activated by rectangles and others by stars. Position neurons respond strongly to a spot located in a certain position and poorly to stimulation of a larger area; others respond only to simultaneous binocular stimulation. Colour-specific neurons are sensitive to red, green, or blue. Each of these neurons is excited by one colour and inhibited by another.

In the secondary visual area, many neurons respond particularly to the direction of moving objects. Neurons activated by colour are not activated by white light. In the part of this area where there are many neurons responding to colour, the periphery of the visual field is not mapped; this is because the periphery of the retina does not contain colour receptors, called cones. The peripheral field is mapped in an area with neurons that respond to movement—notably in the region of the superior temporal gyrus.

It seems that one function of the pathway from the superior colliculus to the temporal and parietal cortices is as a tracking system, enabling the eyes and head to follow moving objects and keep them in the visual field. The pathway from the geniculate nucleus to the primary visual area may be said to perceive what the object is and also how and in what direction it moves.

Some neurons in the parietal cortex become active when a visual stimulus comes in from the edge of the visual field toward the centre, while others are excited by particular movements of the eyes. Other neurons react with remarkable specificity—for example, only when the visual stimulus approaches from the same direction as a stimulus moving on the skin, or during the act of reaching for an object and tracking it with the hand. These parietal neurons greatly depend on the state of vigilance. In monkeys that are apparently merely waiting for something to happen or that have nothing to which to pay attention, the neurons are inactive or minimally active. But when the animal is looking at a visual target whose change it has to detect in order to obtain a reward, the parietal neurons become active.

A great number of neurons of the middle temporal area are sensitive to the direction of movement of a visual stimulus and to the size of an object. Neurons involved in perceiving shape and colour are located in the inferior temporal area. The neurons of the superior temporal polysensory area respond best to moving stimuli—in particular to movements away from the centre of the visual field. Both these areas are involved with the incorporation of visual stimuli and movement.

HEARING

Much of the knowledge of the neurological organization of hearing has been acquired from studies on the bat, an animal that relies on acoustic information for its livelihood.

In the cochlea (the specialized auditory end organ of the inner ear), the frequency of a pure tone is reported by the location of the reacting neurons in the basilar membrane, and the loudness of the sound is reported by the rate of discharge of nerve impulses. From the cochlea, the auditory input is sent to many auditory nuclei. From there, the auditory input is sent to the medial geniculate nucleus and the inferior colliculus, as with the relay stations of the retina. The auditory input finally goes to the primary and secondary auditory areas of the temporal lobes.

The auditory cortex provides the temporal and spatial frames of reference for the auditory data that it receives. In other words, it is sensitive to aspects of sound more complex than frequency. For instance, there are neurons that react only when a sound starts or stops. Other neurons are sensitive only to particular durations of sound. When a sound is repeated many times, some neurons respond, while others stop responding. Some neurons are sensitive to differences in the intensity and timing of sounds reaching the ears. Certain neurons that never respond to a note of constant frequency respond when the frequency falls or rises. Others respond to the rate of change of frequency, providing information on whether distance from the source of a sound is increasing or decreasing. Some neurons respond to the ipsilateral ear, others to the contralateral, and yet others to both ears.

THEORIES OF PAIN SENSATION

There have always been two theories of the sensation of pain, a quantitative, or intensity, theory and a stimulus-specific theory. According to the former, pain results from excessive stimulation (e.g., excessive heat or cold, excessive damage to the tissues). This theory in its simplest form entails the belief that the same afferent nerve fibres are activated by all of these various stimuli; pain is felt merely when they are conducting far more impulses than usual. But knowledge acquired in the 20th century demonstrated that the quantitative theory—at least in its classic form—was wrong. Peripheral nerve fibres are stimulus-specific; each one is excited by certain forms of energy. The stimulus-specific theory of pain proposes that pain results from interactions between various impulses arriving at the spinal cord and brain, that these impulses travel to the spinal cord in certain nonmyelinated and small myelinated fibres, and that the specific stimuli that excite these nerve fibres are noxious, or harmful.

Certain kinds of nerve fibres in the somatic tissues do not give rise to pain, no matter how many there are or how frequently they are stimulated. Included in this category are mechanoreceptors that report only deformation of the skin and larger afferent nerve fibres of muscles and tendons that form part of the organization of posture and movement. No matter how they are excited, these receptors never give rise to pain. But the smaller fibres from these tissues do cause pain when they are excited mechanically or chemically.

Thermoreceptors of the skin are also stimulus-specific. Warmth fibres are excited by rising temperature and inhibited by falling temperature, and cold fibres respond similarly with cold stimuli. Although pain arises from very hot and very cold stimulation and with intense forms of mechanical stimulation, this occurs only with the activation of afferent nerve fibres that specifically report noxious events. When no noxious events are occurring, these nerve fibres are silent.

In contrast, the quantitative theory of pain seems to apply to the viscera, where afferent nerve fibres used in reflex organization also report events that cause pain. In the heart, rectum, and bladder, pain appears to be due to a summation of impulses in sensory nerve fibres and may not be mediated by a special group of fibres reserved for reporting noxious events. In the heart, for example, the same nerve fibres are excited by mechanical stimulation as are excited by chemical substances formed in the body that cause pain. In the bladder, rectum, and colon, nerve fibres activated by substances that cause pain are the same as those activated by distension and contraction of the viscera. This means that the same nerve fibres are reporting the state that underlies the desire to urinate or defecate and the sensation underlying the pain felt when these organs are strongly contracting in an attempt to evacuate their contents.

EMOTION AND BEHAVIOUR

In order to carry out correct behaviour—that is to say, correct in relation to the survival of the individual—humans have developed innate drives, desires, and emotions and the ability to remember and learn. These fundamental features of living depend on the entire brain, yet there is one part of the brain that organizes metabolism, growth, sexual differentiation, and the desires and drives necessary to achieve these aspects of life. This is the hypothalamus and a region in front of it comprising the septal and preoptic areas. That such basic aspects of life might depend on a small region of the brain was conceived in the 1920s by the Swiss physiologist Walter Rudolph Hess and later amplified by German physiologist Erich von Holst. Hess implanted electrodes in the hypothalamus and in septal and preoptic nuclei of cats, stimulated them, and observed the animals' behaviour. Finally, he made minute lesions by means of these electrodes and again observed the effects on behaviour. With this technique he showed that certain kinds of behaviour were organized essentially by just a few neurons in these regions of the brain. Later, von Holst stimulated electrodes by remote control after placing the animals in various biologically meaningful conditions. This contributed to the realization that the artificial stimulation of certain neurons is accompanied by emotion and by movements expressing that emotion.

The hypothalamus, in company with the pituitary gland, controls the emission of hormones, body temperature, blood pressure and the rate and force of the heartbeat, and water and electrolyte levels. The maintenance of these and other changing events within normal limits is called homeostasis; this includes behaviour aimed at keeping the body in a correct and thus comfortable environment.

The hypothalamus is also the centre for organizing the activity of the two parts of the autonomic system, the parasympathetic and the sympathetic. Above the hypothalamus, regions of the cerebral hemispheres most closely connected to the parasympathetic regions are the orbital surface of the frontal lobes, the insula, and the anterior part of the temporal lobe. The regions most closely connected to the sympathetic regions are the anterior nucleus of the thalamus, the hippocampus, and the nuclei connected to these structures.

In general, the regions of the cerebral hemispheres that are closely related to the hypothalamus are those parts that together constitute the limbic lobe, first considered as a unit and given its name in 1878 by the French anatomist Paul Broca. Together with related nuclei, it is usually called the limbic system, consisting of the cingulate and parahippocampal gyri, the hippocampus, the amygdala, the septal and preoptic nuclei, and their various connections.

The autonomic system also involves the hypothalamus in controlling movement. Emotional expression, which depends greatly on the sympathetic nervous system, is controlled by regions of the cerebral hemispheres above the hypothalamus and by the midbrain below it.

A great deal of human behaviour involves social interaction. Although the whole brain contributes to social activities, certain parts of the cerebral hemispheres are particularly involved. The surgical procedure of leucotomy, cutting through the white matter that connects parts of the frontal lobes with the thalamus, upsets this aspect of behaviour. This procedure, proposed by the Spanish neurologist Egas Moniz, used to be performed for severe depression or obsessional neuroses. After the procedure, patients lacked the usual inhibitions that were socially demanded, appearing to obey the first impulse that occurred to them. They told people what they thought of them without regard for the necessary conventions of civilization.

Which parts of the cerebral hemispheres produce emotion has been learned from patients with epilepsy and from surgical procedures under local anesthesia in which the brain is electrically stimulated. The limbic lobe, including the hippocampus, is particularly important in producing emotion. Stimulating certain regions of the temporal lobes produces an intense feeling of fear or dread; stimulating nearby regions produces a feeling of isolation and loneliness, other regions a feeling of disgust, and yet others intense sorrow, depression, anxiety, ecstasy, and, occasionally, guilt. In addition to these regions of the cerebral cortex and the hypothalamus, regions of the thalamus also contribute to the genesis of emotion. The hypothalamus itself does not initiate behaviour; that is done by the cerebral hemispheres.

When certain neurons of the hypothalamus are excited, an individual either becomes aggressive or flees. These two opposite behaviours are together called the defense reaction, or the fight-or-flight response; both are in the repertoire of all vertebrates. The defense reaction is accompanied by strong sympathetic activity. Aggression is also influenced by the production of androgen hormones.

The total act of copulation is organized in the anterior part of the hypothalamus and the neighbouring septal region. In the male, erection of the penis and the ejaculation of semen are organized in this area, which is adjacent to the area that controls urination. Under normal circumstances, the neurons that organize mating behaviour do so only when they receive relevant hormones in their blood supply. But when the septal region is electrically stimulated in conscious patients, sexual emotions and thoughts are produced. There are visible differences between the male and female sexes in nuclei of the central nervous system related to reproduction. These differences are a form of sexual dimorphism.

Electrical stimulation in cats of regions in and related to the anterior part of the hypothalamus can induce the behaviour of expelling or retaining urine and feces. When electrodes planted in these regions are stimulated by radio waves, the cat stops whatever it is doing and behaves as though it is going to urinate or defecate. It goes through its usual behaviour of digging a hole, squatting, and assuming the correct posture, and then it passes urine or feces. At the end, it even goes through its customary ritual of hiding its excreta.

The eating and drinking centres are in the lateral and ventromedial regions of the hypothalamus, although such basic aspects of living concern most of the brain. If the lateral region is experimentally destroyed, the animal consumes less food or stops eating altogether; if the ventromedial region is destroyed, it eats enormously. When neurons of the lateral region are electrically stimulated, a monkey eats, and when those of the ventromedial area are stimulated, the monkey stops eating. There is an increase in the activity of these neurons when the monkey looks at food, but only when it is hungry. Receptors in the lateral region monitor blood glucose and are stimulated only when blood glucose is low; satiety stops their response.

Hunger does not depend only on these glucose receptors. Severe hunger is associated with contractions of the stomach, which are felt almost as a sensation of pain. Yet neither is this an essential mechanism for feeling hungry, as patients who have had total removal of the stomach still feel hunger. In experiments in rats, it is found that stress may make the animal either increase or reduce the amount it eats. This is probably the same in humans.

When certain neurons in the same regions of the hypothalamus are experimentally destroyed, animals lose the urge to drink, although they continue to eat normally. Stimulation of these neurons causes them to drink excessively. Control of drinking depends on osmoreceptors located throughout the hypothalamus. When receptors detect a minimal increase in the concentration of dissolved substances in the extracellular fluid, which indicates cellular dehydration, the sensation of thirst occurs. A less-important contributor to the sensation of thirst is a reduction in blood volume. Dryness of the mouth can also be a component of thirst, noted by receptors in the mucous membrane. The feeling of having drunk enough depends not only on the hypothalamic neurons but also on receptors in the wall of the stomach, which report when the stomach is full. In addition, both glucose receptors and osmoreceptors are sensitive to the temperature of the passing blood. When the temperature starts to rise, one feels thirsty but not hungry; cooling the blood makes one feel hungry.

To maintain homeostasis, heat production and heat loss must be balanced. This is achieved by both the somatomotor and sympathetic systems. The obvious behavioral way of keeping warm or cool is by moving into a correct environment. The posture of the body is also used to balance heat production and heat loss. When one is hot, the body stretches out—in physiological terms, extends—thus presenting a large surface to the ambient air and losing heat. When one is cold, the body curls itself up—in physiological terms, flexes—thus presenting the smallest area to the ambient temperature.

The sympathetic system is the most important part of the nervous system for controlling body temperature. On a long-term basis, when the climate is cold, the sympathetic system produces heat by its control of certain fat cells called brown adipose tissue. From these cells, fatty acids are released, and heat is produced by their chemical breakdown. Body temperature also fluctuates regularly within 24 hours and in rhythm according to the menstrual cycle in women. During fever, the body temperature is set at a higher point than normal.

In a fundamental discovery made in 1954, Canadian researchers James Olds and Peter Milner found that stimulation of certain regions of the brain of the rat acted as a reward in teaching the animals to run mazes and solve problems. The conclusion from such experiments is that stimulation gives the animals pleasure. The discovery has also been confirmed in humans. These regions are called pleasure, or reward, centres. One important centre is in the septal region, and there are reward centres in the hypothalamus and in the temporal lobes of the cerebral hemispheres as well. When the septal region is stimulated in conscious patients undergoing neurosurgery, they experience feelings of pleasure, optimism, euphoria, and happiness.

Regions of the brain also clearly cause rats distress when electrically stimulated; these are called aversive centres. However, the existence of an aversive centre is less certain than that of a reward centre. Electrodes stimulating neurons or neural pathways may cause an animal to have pain, anxiety, fear, or any unpleasant feeling or emotion. These pathways are not necessarily centres that provide punishment in the sense that a reward centre provides pleasure. Therefore, it is not definitely known that connections to aversive centres punish the animal for biologically wrong behaviour, but it is thought that correct behaviour is rewarded by pleasure provided by neurons of the brain.

Humans have inevitably adapted to the orderly rhythms of the universe. These biological cycles are called circadian rhythms, from the Latin *circa* ("about") and *dies* ("day"). They are essentially endogenous, built into the central nervous system. Circadian activities include sleeping and waking, rest and activity, taking in of fluid, formation of urine, body temperature, cardiac output, oxygen consumption, cell division, and the secreting activity of endocrine glands. Rhythms are upset by shift work and by rapid travel into different time zones. After long journeys it takes several days for the endogenous rhythm generator to become synchronized to the local time.

The alternation of night and day has been important in inducing rhythms affecting many physiological functions. Even in isolation, rhythms related to the time of day are maintained from clues giving information about light and dark. Curiously, the endogenous sleep-wake rhythm deviates slightly from Earth's 24-hour cycle; a bird's endogenous cycle is 23 hours, and the human cycle is 25 hours. In both cases the cycle is corrected by features of the environment called zeitgebers ("time givers"). One zeitgeber is Earth's magnetic field, which changes on a 24-hour cycle as Earth turns on its axis. More obvious and important a zeitgeiber is the alternation of dark and light.

The suprachiasmatic nucleus of the hypothalamus is essential for the rhythms of sleeping, waking, rest, and activity. It is not surprising that this nucleus is adjacent to the incoming fibres from the eye; for this reason, the light-dark cycle appears to be the most important zeitgeber for circadian rhythms. The suprachiasmatic nucleus is most active in light. In experiments on the hamster, when the nucleus is destroyed, the rhythms of general activity, drinking, sleeping, waking, body temperature, and some endocrine secretion are disrupted.

NEUROPLASTICITY

Neuroplasticity is the capacity of neurons and neural networks in the brain to change their connections and behaviour in response to new information, sensory stimulation, development, damage, or dysfunction. Although neural networks also exhibit modularity and carry out specific functions, they retain the capacity to deviate from their usual functions and to reorganize themselves. In fact, for many years, it was considered dogma in the neurosciences that certain functions were hard-wired in specific, localized regions of the brain and that any incidents of brain change or recovery were mere exceptions to the rule. However, since the 1970s and '80s, neuroplasticity has gained wide acceptance throughout the scientific community as a complex, multifaceted, fundamental property of the brain.

Rapid change or reorganization of the brain's cellular or neural networks can take place in many different forms and under many different circumstances. Developmental plasticity occurs when neurons in the young brain rapidly sprout branches and form synapses. Then, as the brain begins to process sensory information, some of these synapses strengthen and others weaken. Eventually, some unused synapses are eliminated completely, a process known as synaptic pruning, which leaves behind efficient networks of neural connections. Other forms of neuroplasticity operate by much the same mechanism but under different circumstances and sometimes only to a limited extent. These circumstances include changes in the body, such as the loss of a limb or sense organ, that subsequently alter the balance of sensory activity received by the brain. In addition, neuroplasticity is employed by the brain during the reinforcement of sensory information through experience, such as in learning and memory, and following actual physical damage to the brain (e.g., caused by stroke), when the brain attempts to compensate for lost activity.

Today it is apparent that the same brain mechanisms—adjustments in the strength or the number of synapses between neurons—operate in all these situations. Sometimes this happens naturally, which can result in positive or negative reorganization, but other times behavioral techniques or brain-machine interfaces can be used to harness the power of neuroplasticity for therapeutic purposes. In some cases, such as stroke recovery, natural adult neurogenesis can also play a role. As a result, neurogenesis has spurred an interest in stem cell research, which could lead to an enhancement of neurogenesis in adults who suffer from stroke, Alzheimer disease, Parkinson disease, or depression.

TYPES OF CORTICAL NEUROPLASTICITY

Developmental plasticity occurs most profoundly in the first few years of life as neurons grow very rapidly and

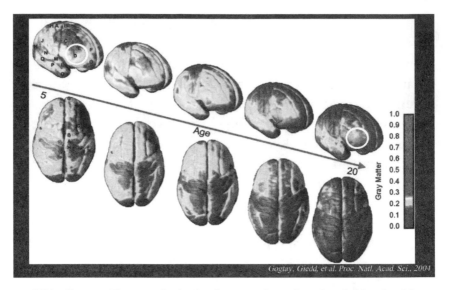

This diagram illustrates brain development through early adulthood, with dark areas indicating the mature state. The prefrontal cortex (white circle), which governs judgment and decision-making functions, is the last part of the brain to develop. National Institutes of Health

send out multiple branches, ultimately forming too many connections. In fact, at birth, each neuron in the cerebral cortex (the highly convoluted outer layer of the cerebrum) has about 2,500 synapses. By the time an infant is two or three years old, the number of synapses is approximately 15,000 per neuron. This amount is about twice that of the average adult brain. The connections that are not reinforced by sensory stimulation eventually weaken, and the connections that are reinforced become stronger. Eventually, efficient pathways of neural connections are carved out. Throughout the life of a human or other mammal, these neural connections are fine-tuned through the organism's interaction with its surroundings. During early childhood, which is known as a critical period of development, the nervous system must receive certain sensory inputs in order to develop properly. Once such a critical period ends, there is a precipitous drop in the number of connections that are maintained, and the ones that do remain are the ones that have been strengthened by the appropriate sensory experiences. This massive "pruning back" of excess synapses often occurs during adolescence.

American neuroscientist Jordan Grafman has identified four other types of neuroplasticity, known as homologous area adaptation, compensatory masquerade, cross-modal reassignment, and map expansion.

Homologous Area Adaptation

Homologous area adaptation occurs during the early critical period of development. If a particular brain module becomes damaged in early life, its normal operations have the ability to shift to brain areas that do not include the affected module. The function is often shifted to a module in the matching, or homologous, area of the opposite brain hemisphere. The downside to this form of neuroplasticity is that it may come at costs to functions that are normally stored in the module but now have to make room for the new functions. An example of this is when the right parietal lobe (the parietal lobe forms the middle region of the cerebral hemispheres) becomes damaged early in life and the left parietal lobe takes over visuospatial functions at the cost of impaired arithmetical functions, which the left parietal lobe usually carries out exclusively. Timing is also a factor in this process, since a child learns how to navigate physical space before he or she learns arithmetic.

Compensatory Masquerade

The second type of neuroplasticity, compensatory masquerade, can simply be described as the brain figuring out an alternative strategy for carrying out a task when the initial strategy cannot be followed due to impairment. One example is when a person attempts to navigate from one location to another. Most people, to a greater or lesser extent, have an intuitive sense of direction and distance that they employ for navigation. However, a person who suffers some form of brain trauma and impaired spatial sense will resort to another strategy for spatial navigation, such as memorizing landmarks. The only change that occurs in the brain is a reorganization of preexisting neuronal networks.

Cross-Modal Reassignment

The third form of neuroplasticity, cross-modal reassignment, entails the introduction of new inputs into a brain area deprived of its main inputs. A classic example of this is the ability of an adult who has been blind since birth to have touch, or somatosensory, input redirected to the visual cortex in the occipital lobe of the brain—specifically, in an area known as V1. Sighted people, however, do not display any V1 activity when presented with similar touch-oriented experiments. This occurs because neurons communicate with one another in the same abstract "language" of electrochemical impulses regardless of sensory modality. Moreover, all the sensory cortices of the brain— visual, auditory, olfactory (smell), gustatory (taste), and somatosensory—have a similar six-layer processing structure. Because of this, the visual cortices of blind people can still carry out the cognitive functions of creating representations of the physical world but base these representations on input from another sense—namely, touch. This is not, however, simply an instance of one area of the brain compensating for a lack of vision; it is a change in the actual functional assignment of a local brain region. Nevertheless, there are limits to this type of neuroplasticity, since some cells such as the colour-processing cells of the visual cortex are so specialized for visual input that there is very little likelihood that they would accept input from other senses.

Map Expansion

Map expansion, the fourth type of neuroplasticity, entails the flexibility of local brain regions that are dedicated to performing one type of function or storing a particular form of information. The arrangement of these local regions in the cerebral cortex is referred to as a "map." When one function is carried out frequently enough through repeated behaviour or stimulus, the region of the cortical map dedicated to this function grows and shrinks as an individual "exercises" this function. This phenomenon usually takes place during the learning and practicing of a skill such as playing a musical instrument. Specifically, the region grows as the individual gains implicit familiarity with the skill and then shrinks to baseline once the learning becomes explicit. (Implicit learning is the passive acquisition of knowledge through exposure to information, whereas explicit learning is the active acquisition of knowledge gained by consciously seeking out information.) But as one continues to develop the skill over repeated practice, the region retains the initial enlargement.

Map expansion neuroplasticity also underlies the phenomenon of phantom limb syndrome. In the 1990s Indian-born American neuroscientist Vilayanur S. Ramachandran discovered that an amputee, when touched on the side of the face with a cotton swab, felt a sensation in his or her phantom arm. Further studies employing advanced imaging technologies revealed that an amputee's face brain map had taken over the adjacent area of the arm and hand brain maps. Ramachandran concluded that after the arm was amputated the arm and hand brain maps were starved for input and sent out growth factors (cell growth-stimulating proteins) that attracted neuronal sprouting from the face map stored in an adjacent area of the brain.

BRAIN-COMPUTER INTERFACE

Some of the earliest applied research in neuroplasticity was carried out in the 1960s, when scientists attempted to develop machines that interface with the brain in order to help blind people. In 1969 American neurobiologist Paul Bach-y-Rita and several of his colleagues published a short article titled "Vision Substitution by Tactile Image Projection," which detailed the workings of such a machine. The machine consisted of a metal plate with 400 vibrating stimulators. The plate was attached to the back of a chair so that the sensors could touch the skin of the patient's back. A camera was placed in front of the patient and connected to the vibrators. The camera acquired images of the room and translated them into patterns of vibration, which represented the physical space of the room and the objects within it. After patients gained some familiarity with the device, their brains were able to construct mental representations of physical spaces and physical objects. Thus, instead of visible light stimulating their retinas and creating a mental representation of the world, vibrating stimulators triggered the skin of their backs to create a representation in their visual cortices. A similar device exists today, only the camera fits inside a pair of glasses and the sensory surface fits on the tongue. The brain can do this because it "speaks" in the same neural "language" of electrochemical signals regardless of what kinds of environmental stimuli are interacting with the body's sense organs.

Today neuroscientists are developing machines that bypass external sense organs and actually interface directly with the brain. For example, researchers implanted a device that monitored neuronal activity in the brain of a female macaque monkey. The monkey used a joystick to move a cursor around a screen, and the computer monitored and compared the movement of the cursor with the activity in the monkey's brain. Once the computer had effectively correlated the monkey's brain signals for speed and direction to the actual movement of the cursor, the computer was able to translate these movement signals from the monkey's brain to the movement of a robot arm in another room. Thus, the monkey became capable of moving a robot arm with its thoughts. However, the major finding of this experiment was that as the monkey learned to move the cursor with its thoughts, the signals in the monkey's motor cortex (the area of the cerebral cortex implicated in the control of muscle movements) became less representative of the movements of the monkey's actual limbs and more representative of the movements of the cursor. This means that the motor cortex does not control the details of limb movement directly but instead controls the abstract parameters of movement, regardless of the connected apparatus that is actually moving. This has also been observed in humans whose motor cortices can easily be manipulated into incorporating a tool or prosthetic limb into the brain's body image through both somatosensory and visual stimuli.

For humans, however, less-invasive forms of brain-computer interfaces are more conducive to clinical application. For example, researchers have demonstrated that real-time visual feedback from fMRI can enable patients to retrain their brains and therefore improve brain functioning. Patients with emotional disorders have been trained to self-regulate a region of the brain known as the amygdala (located deep within the cerebral hemispheres and believed to influence motivational behaviour) by self-inducing sadness and monitoring the activity of the amygdala on a real-time fMRI readout. Stroke victims have been able to reacquire lost functions through self-induced mental practice and mental imagery. This kind of therapy takes advantage of neuroplasticity in order to reactivate damaged areas of the brain or to deactivate overactive areas of the brain. Today researchers are investigating the efficacy of these forms of therapy for individuals who suffer not only from stroke and emotional disorders but also from chronic pain, psychopathy, and social phobia.

CHAPTER 6

NEUROBIOLOGICAL DISORDERS OF DEVELOPMENT AND BEHAVIOUR

Neurobiological disorders are illnesses of the nervous system that arise from abnormalities in biological factors, including defects in genes and in metabolic proteins. These disorders generally affect the brain and include a number of developmental conditions and psychiatric and mental disorders. In fact, many conditions that were traditionally referred to as psychiatric disorders, such as schizophrenia and obsessive-compulsive disorder, are now considered neurobiological disorders because they are associated with known abnormalities in biological entities affecting neuronal function. For example, studies have revealed that many behavioral and mental afflictions involve imbalances in levels of specific neurotransmitters, thereby altering brain function and behaviour. This information has helped scientists to identify the causes of these conditions and to develop diagnostic procedures for their detection. Neurobiological disorders of development and behaviour are extremely diverse in their etiology, and the group as a whole consists of many complex disorders, including autism, depression, and attention-deficit/hyperactivity disorder (ADHD).

NEURAL TUBE DEFECTS

The neural tube, the embryonic structure that develops into the central nervous system, normally closes by the end of the third week of fetal growth; severe deficits result if it fails to close. Examples of neural tube defects include the absence of brain (anencephaly) and a cyst replacing the cerebellum. The spinal canal or cord may also fail to close.

Spina bifida is a neural tube defect that varies in severity. In spina bifida occulta there is only X-ray evidence of damage to the spinal cord. The meningocele form of the disorder is characterized by a meningeal pouch that visibly projects through the skin. Spina bifida meningomyelocele is diagnosed when such a pouch contains elements of the spinal cord or nerve roots. Function of the legs and bladder and bowel control is often severely impaired in individuals with spina bifida. Infants with the defect commonly have hydrocephalus as well.

CEREBRAL PALSY

Cerebral palsy is a neurological disorder characterized by paralysis resulting from abnormal development of or damage to the brain either before birth or during the first years of life. There are four types of cerebral palsy: spastic, athetoid, ataxic, and mixed. In the spastic type, there is a severe paralysis of voluntary movements, with spastic contractions of the extremities either on one side of the body (hemiplegia) or on both sides (diplegia).

In spastic diplegia, spastic contractions and paralysis are usually more prominent in the lower extremities than in the arms and hands (Little diplegia), or only the legs may be affected (paraplegia). The cerebral damage causing spastic cerebral palsy primarily affects the neurons and connections of the cerebral cortex, either of one cerebral hemisphere (contralateral to paralysis), as in infantile hemiplegia, or of both hemispheres, as in diplegia.

In the athetoid type of cerebral palsy, paralysis of voluntary movements may not occur, and spastic contractions may be slight or absent. Instead, there are slow, involuntary spasms of the face, neck, and extremities, either on one side (hemiathetosis) or, more frequently, on both sides (double athetosis), with resulting involuntary movements in the whole body or its parts, facial grimacing, and inarticulate speech (dysarthria)—all of which increase under stress or excitement. Damage to the brain particularly affects the basal ganglia underlying the cerebral cortex.

Ataxic cerebral palsy is a rare form of the condition that is characterized by poor coordination, muscle weakness, an unsteady gait, and difficulty performing rapid or fine movements. If symptoms of two or more types are present, most often spastic and athetoid, an individual is diagnosed with mixed cerebral palsy.

Cerebral palsy does not necessarily include intellectual disability. In fact, many children affected with cerebral palsy are mentally competent. However, any cerebral disorder in early life may result in impairment, sometimes severe, of intellectual and emotional development. Epileptic attacks in the form of convulsive seizures, especially in the parts of the body affected by paralysis, occur in many children with cerebral palsy. In the spastic type of cerebral palsy, intellectual disability and epileptic attacks are particularly frequent. In the athetoid type, the incidence of severe intellectual disability is much lower, and occurrence of convulsive seizures is rare. Children affected with athetoid cerebral palsy may be perceptive and intelligent; however, because of the involuntary movements and dysarthria, they are often unable to communicate by intelligible words or signs.

The causes of cerebral palsy are multiple but basically involve a malfunctioning of the complex neuronal circuits

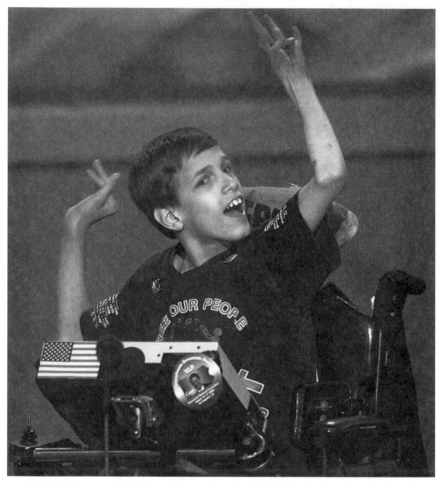

Kyle Golzier, who suffers from cerebral palsy, delivers a speech on patients' rights in Los Angeles, Calif., in August 2000. Paul J. Richards/AFP/ Getty Images

of the basal ganglia and the cerebral cortex. Heredity plays only a small role. It may manifest itself in malformations of neurons, interstitial tissues, or blood vessels of the brain that may produce tumours, or it may express itself in an abnormal chemistry of the brain. More common causes of the condition are fetal diseases and embryonic malformations of the brain. Incompatibility of blood types of the mother and fetus, leading to severe jaundice at birth, may cause brain damage and cerebral palsy. Respiratory problems of the fetus during birth may indicate earlier brain damage. Pediatric infections, severe head injuries, and poisoning are other less common causes of cerebral palsy.

There is no cure for cerebral palsy; treatment includes medications that relax the muscles and prevent seizures. The basic program of treatment aims at the psychological management, education, and training of the child to develop sensory, motor, and intellectual assets, in order to compensate for the physical liabilities of the disorder.

PERVASIVE DEVELOPMENTAL DISORDERS

Pervasive developmental disorders (PDDs) are conditions characterized by early-childhood onset and by varying degrees of impairment of language acquisition, communication, social behaviour, and motor function.

There are five types of PDDs. These include the three known autism spectrum disorders—autism, Asperger syndrome, and pervasive developmental disorder not otherwise specified (PDD-NOS)—as well as childhood disintegrative disorder (CDD) and Rett syndrome. Most PDDs are characterized by deficits in a child's ability to interact socially and by one or more abnormalities of childhood development. For example, children with PDD-NOS typically suffer from an inability to interact with others and from abnormalities in either communication or behaviour patterns and interests. In addition, some PDDs such as Asperger syndrome have little or no adverse effect on intelligence, whereas other PDDs, such as Rett syndrome and autism, can result in severe intellectual disability. Symptoms of autism spectrum disorders and CDD usually first appear around age three. In contrast, symptoms of Rett syndrome can appear before age one.

PDDs affect an estimated 30 in every 10,000 children. However, because the clinical definitions used to diagnose PDDs classified as autism spectrum disorders differ worldwide, the reported incidence of these specific disorders varies significantly. The most commonly occurring PDD is autism, which has been reported to affect as many as one in every 150 children in the United States. The least common PDDs are Rett syndrome and CDD, which appear to have a worldwide incidence of roughly one in 15,000 and one in 50,000–100,000 individuals, respectively. With the exception of Rett syndrome, which primarily affects females, PDDs occur more commonly in males than in females.

There is no curative treatment for PDDs; however, early intervention may alleviate some of the social and behavioral symptoms associated with the disorders. Some examples of treatment approaches include speech therapy, behaviour modification therapy, and medications to reduce depression or anxiety.

AUTISM SPECTRUM DISORDERS

Autism spectrum disorders are characterized by deficits in social interaction and communication and by abnormalities in behaviours, interests, and activities. In 1911 Swiss psychiatrist Eugen Bleuler coined the term *autism* (from the Greek *autos*, meaning "self"), using it to describe the withdrawal into the self that he observed in patients affected by schizophrenic disorders. However, in 1943 Austrian-born American psychiatrist Leo Kanner recognized autism as a disorder distinct from schizophrenia, giving autism its modern description. In the subsequent decades several autismlike disorders also were identified, resulting in the group of conditions known as autism spectrum disorders, or ASDs. The group of ASDs includes three distinct neurobiological disorders: autism (or classic autism), Asperger syndrome, and PDD-NOS.

AUTISM

Autism, also known as classic autism, or autistic disorder, is a developmental disorder affecting physical, social, and language skills, with an onset of symptoms typically before age three.

Incidence

Autism predominates in males, who are affected about three to four times more often than females. The incidence of autism varies significantly between and within countries, which is due in part to differences in the clinical definitions used for diagnosis. For example, in one region of the United Kingdom roughly one in every 185 individuals was found to be affected by an ASD. However, in the same region of the country classic autism was found to range in incidence between one in 250 and one in 400 individuals. In addition, there appears to have been a dramatic increase in the global incidence of autism between the mid-1900s and the early 2000s. However, it is not known whether there has been a true increase in the incidence of the disorder, since the increase could be due to the use of broader diagnostic criteria or other factors.

Causes and Symptoms

The cause of autism remains unclear. Based on sibling studies, the disorder is thought to be highly heritable. Scientists have found that a region on chromosome 15 is deleted or duplicated in some children with autism; defects in and near this region have been implicated in other disorders associated with neurobiological development, including Angelman syndrome, Prader-Willi syndrome, and epilepsy. Another proposed cause of autism emerged in the late 1990s, when a suggested association was made between childhood vaccination and autism. This suggestion quickly developed into a controversial issue between parents and the scientific community. However, the scientific evidence, collected from extensive studies investigating the proposed association, does not support a causal relationship.

The symptoms of autism are variable, ranging from mild to moderate to severe in nature. There are three major categories of symptoms: (1) abnormalities in social interaction; (2) abnormalities in communication; and (3) abnormalities in behaviours, interests, and activities, which are usually restricted and repetitive. Social communication problems include a narrow range of facial expressions, poor eye contact during interactions, and difficulty establishing relationships with peers. This may result in a decreased quality of their relationships and can lead to social avoidance when severely affected. Communication problems include delayed or lack of spoken language, poor conversation skills, lack of appropriate developmental play, and diminished gestures. Repetitive behaviour problems include stereotyped motor mannerisms, such as hand flapping, restricted interests, inflexible adherence to routines, and a preoccupation with parts of objects. For example, a child with autism may play with the wheels of a toy car instead of playing with the car as a vehicle. Some children become obsessed with specific objects such as buttons and sometimes form deep attachments to these objects. In addition, disruption of routines and schedules or familiar surroundings may cause agitation and tantrums.

Neuropathology

One striking feature of many young children with autism is an enlargement of head size. In the 1980s information gathered from autopsies of individuals with autism indicated that the brains of people affected by the disorder weighed more than normal. In the early 2000s it was reported that the head circumference of autistic children increased between ages two and four and that this overgrowth was followed by a period of slowed growth, resulting in a normal head size in older children with autism. In some cases, overgrowth is present as early as one to two months following birth. Scientists have hypothesized that this unusual overgrowth pattern may be due to an enlargement of the brain white matter—the nerve fibres that connect one brain area to another.

Studies of the neuropathology of brain structures in autistic individuals have investigated the hippocampus, an area that is important for learning and memory; the amygdala, an area important for fear and other emotions; the cerebellum, a motor and cognitive brain region; and the anterior cingulate cortex, a part of the cerebral cortex that is important for social and emotional behaviour. In children affected by autism these brain structures often exhibit increased cell density, with reduced cell size. In addition, the cerebellum typically has a reduction in Purkinje cells, which receive and integrate information from sensory and motor neurons.

A large amount of research has focused on the neurotransmitter systems in autism, and many studies have reported involvement of the serotonin (5-HT) and the inhibitory gamma-aminobutyric acid (GABA) systems. Early findings of elevated serotonin in the peripheral blood (hyperserotonemia) in many autistic individuals have led scientists to investigate whether similar abnormalities are found in the brain. Although the mechanisms by which the serotonin and GABA neurotransmitter systems contribute to symptoms of autism remain unclear, much evidence has emerged demonstrating that levels of GABA and GABA receptors are altered in many parts of the autistic brain. Key GABA-synthesizing enzymes known as GAD67 and GAD65 (glutamic acid decarboxylase 67 and 65, respectively) have been shown to be altered in specific cerebellar neurons in autism brains. Studies also have shown that between one-quarter and one-third of adolescents with autism have some type of seizure abnormality; this is suspected to be related to abnormalities in the GABA system.

Treatment

There is no cure for autism, and treatment is mainly directed toward controlling behavioral symptoms. Some children show significant improvements, and the best predictors for future function are typically IQ and language skills, especially in children who acquire language before age five. Early intervention, including promoting language, developing social skills, and regulating behaviour, allow for significant improvement in many children. Pharmacological treatments are directed toward secondary symptoms, such as behavioral problems, anxiety, depression, aggression, and seizures. Selective serotonin reuptake inhibitors (SSRIs), such as fluoxetine (Prozac) and sertraline (Zoloft), have proved successful in helping some individuals overcome secondary symptoms. Clinical trials are being conducted on other drugs that may be useful in the treatment of autism.

ASPERGER SYNDROME

Asperger syndrome is a neurobiological disorder characterized by autism-like abnormalities in social interactions but with normal intelligence and language acquisition. The disorder is named for Austrian physician Hans Asperger, who first described the symptoms in 1944 as belonging to a condition he called autistic psychopathy. Today, Asperger syndrome is considered an autism spectrum disorder.

Asperger syndrome occurs in roughly two in every 10,000 individuals, and the disorder is about three to four times more common in boys than in girls. Symptoms may be apparent after age three, though diagnosis is most frequent in children between ages five and nine. In contrast to patients with autism, individuals with Asperger syndrome usually do not have major cognitive difficulties—their IQ is in the normal or even high range—and they do not exhibit a delay in language acquisition. However, children with Asperger syndrome do display repetitive behaviour patterns similar to those observed in children with autism, and they often avoid eye contact, have poor control over fine motor movements, giving an impression of clumsiness, and have an obsessive interest in a single object, such as a computer or a type of car. This obsession generally manifests as a persistent desire to learn and to speak only about the object. Children with Asperger syndrome may become upset when instructed to focus on a task not related to their obsession and when their day-to-day routines are disrupted even in only minor ways, such as drinking from a cup that differs in colour or texture from the cup the child normally uses. Some individuals with Asperger syndrome also are affected by anxiety and depression in adolescence and adulthood. In many patients symptoms may go unrecognized for years. In the absence of a formal diagnosis, individuals affected by Asperger syndrome may be perceived as simply absent-minded, socially and physically awkward, or highly intelligent.

The cause of Asperger syndrome is unclear; however, neuroimaging studies have demonstrated the presence of structural and neuronal abnormalities in certain areas of the brain in Asperger patients. These abnormalities likely contribute to the unusual thinking patterns and behaviours associated with the disorder. Asperger syndrome is best treated through early intervention methods aimed at improving social skills, physical coordination, and communication. Many people affected by Asperger syndrome improve significantly with effective treatment programs. In addition, because people with Asperger syndrome may develop a high level of expertise in a very specific area or about a single device, many are able to find jobs at which they can be successful.

PERVASIVE DEVELOPMENTAL DISORDER NOT OTHERWISE SPECIFIED

Pervasive developmental disorder not otherwise specified (PDD-NOS; or atypical autism) is a neurobiological disorder characterized by impairment in ability to interact with others and by abnormalities in either communication or behaviour patterns and interests. PDD-NOS is described as atypical autism, because individuals with the disorder exhibit some but not all of the same symptoms associated with autism (sometimes called classic autism). Likewise, "not otherwise specified" indicates that an individual's symptoms are nonspecific, meaning that they differ from symptoms characteristic of other pervasive developmental disorders, such as Rett syndrome and childhood disintegrative disorder.

PDD-NOS affects boys four times more often than girls. The overall prevalence of the disorder remains unclear, because of the varying clinical definitions used for diagnosis. Many children who have only several symptoms of an autismlike condition, which prevents a definitive diagnosis of autism, are often diagnosed instead with PDD-NOS. Symptoms associated with PDD-NOS appear after age three, and the pattern in which symptoms manifest and the behaviours displayed by affected children vary widely. Most children with the disorder appear to develop normally in the first several years of life and then experience an unusual delay in the development of social abilities. It is usually at this point in the child's development when other features of PDD-NOS become apparent. These features may include gaze avoidance, lack of expressive facial responses, irregularities in speech, repetitive and obsessive behaviours, and delayed development of motor skills. The incidence of severe intellectual disability in PDD-NOS patients is low relative to other pervasive developmental disorders.

Although the precise cause of PDD-NOS is unknown, abnormalities in certain structures and in neuronal signaling pathways in the brain have been implicated. Researchers also suspect underlying genetic defects may be involved. Treatment for PDD-NOS consists primarily of behavioral therapy, though some children may require the administration of medications to stabilize mood or behaviour.

CHILDHOOD DISINTEGRATIVE DISORDER

Childhood disintegrative disorder (CDD), also known as Heller syndrome (or disintegrative psychosis), is a rare neurobiological disorder characterized by the deterioration of language and social skills and by the loss of intellectual functioning following normal development throughout at least the initial two years of life. The disorder was first described in 1908 by Austrian educator Thomas Heller. However, because the disorder is rare, occurring in one in every 50,000–100,000 individuals, it was not officially recognized as a developmental disorder until the 1990s. Today, CDD is classified as a pervasive developmental disorder and is known to affect boys more frequently than girls.

Children affected by CDD progress normally in their development at least until age two, acquiring communication, social, and intellectual abilities typical for their age. Symptoms of the disorder often appear between ages three and four, although in some cases symptoms may not be present until age nine or 10. Onset generally occurs over a period of several months to a year. The disorder becomes evident when a child loses the skills that he acquired previously, though this may manifest initially in the form of anxiety or increased, unexplained irritability. Children with CDD regress in motor function and intelligence, and many affected individuals develop symptoms similar to those of autism, including repetitive behaviour patterns, inability to interact with others, and delayed development of speech. In addition, children affected by CDD often lose control over bladder and bowel function and experience seizures.

The cause of CDD is not known. However, it is suspected that an abnormality in a gene or genes involved in the development of the central nervous system contributes to the disorder. Although CDD has been associated with other disorders, such as abnormalities in lipid storage and in immune response, none of these conditions appear to be an underlying cause of CDD. The prognosis of children with CDD is poor, since many individuals experience severe and permanent intellectual disability. Treatment consists of various types of therapies aimed at stabilizing or improving behaviour, communication, and language skills.

RETT SYNDROME

Rett syndrome, also known as cerebroatrophic hyperammonemia, is a rare progressive neurological disorder characterized by severe intellectual disability, autismlike behaviour patterns, and impaired motor function. The disorder was first described in the 1960s by the Austrian physician Andreas Rett. Today Rett syndrome is classified as a pervasive developmental disorder.

In about 1 percent of affected individuals, Rett syndrome arises from an inherited sex-linked defect. The majority of cases, however, arise from sporadic mutations in a gene known as *MECP2* (methyl CpG binding

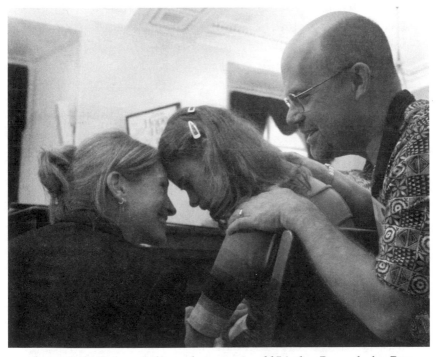

Actress Julia Roberts (left) speaks to 15-year-old Lindsey Ross, who has Rett syndrome, during a news conference on May 9, 2002, in Washington, DC. Rett Syndrome is a debilitating neurological disorder that affects motor skills. Mark Wilson/Getty Images

protein 2). Because this gene is located on the X chromosome, Rett syndrome almost always affects girls; the disorder is relatively rare, occurring in roughly one in every 15,000 females.

Rett syndrome causes progressive disabilities in intellectual and motor development, with the initial onset of symptoms usually appearing in infancy, between the 6th and 18th months of life. Symptoms include compulsive hand movements, reduced muscle tone, difficulties in walking, decreased body weight, failure of the head to grow with age, and increased levels of ammonia in the blood (hyperammonemia).

There is no cure for Rett syndrome. However, some symptoms may be treated through physical therapy, speech therapy, and the administration of medications to control anxiety or to alleviate depression.

MENTAL AND BEHAVIORAL DISORDERS

Mental disorders manifest either in symptoms of emotional distress or in abnormal behaviour. Most mental disorders can be broadly classified as either psychoses or neuroses. Psychoses (e.g., schizophrenia and bipolar disorder) are major mental illnesses characterized by severe symptoms such as delusions, hallucinations, and an inability to evaluate reality in an objective manner. Neuroses are less severe and more treatable and include depression, anxiety, and paranoia as well as obsessive-compulsive disorders and post-traumatic stress disorders. Some mental disorders are clearly caused by organic disease of the brain, but the causes of most others are either unknown or not yet verified.

Neuroses often appear to be caused by psychological factors such as emotional deprivation, frustration, or abuse during childhood, and they may be treated through psychotherapy. Certain neuroses, particularly the anxiety disorders known as phobias, may represent maladaptive responses built up into the human equivalent of conditioned reflexes.

Schizophrenia

Schizophrenia is any of a group of severe disorders that are characterized by a wide array of symptoms, including hallucinations, delusions, blunted emotions, disordered thinking, and a withdrawal from reality. Five main types of schizophrenia, differing in their specific symptomatology as follows, are recognized by some authorities.

1. The simple or undifferentiated type of schizophrenic manifests an insidious and gradual reduction in external relations and interests. The patient's emotions lack depth, and ideation is simple and refers to concrete things. There is a relative absence of mental activity, a progressive lessening in the use of inner resources, and a retreat to simpler or stereotyped forms of behaviour.
2. The hebephrenic or disorganized type of schizophrenic displays shallow and inappropriate emotional responses, foolish or bizarre behaviour, false beliefs (delusions), and false perceptions (hallucinations).
3. The catatonic type is characterized by striking motor behaviour. The patient may remain in a state of almost complete immobility, often assuming statuesque positions. Mutism (inability to talk), extreme compliance, and absence of almost all voluntary actions are also common.

This state of inactivity is at times preceded or interrupted by episodes of excessive motor activity and excitement, generally of an impulsive, unpredictable kind.

4. The paranoid type, which usually arises later in life than the other types, is characterized primarily by delusions of persecution and grandeur combined with unrealistic, illogical thinking, often accompanied by hallucinations.

5. The residual type is typically distinguished by the lack of distinct features that define the other types and is considered a less severe diagnosis. Individuals diagnosed with the residual type generally have a history of schizophrenia but have reduced psychotic symptoms.

These different types of schizophrenia are not mutually exclusive, and schizophrenics may display a mixture of symptoms that defy convenient classification. There may also be a mixture of schizophrenic symptoms with those of other psychoses, notably those of the manic-depressive group.

Stressful life experiences may trigger the disease's initial onset, and symptoms of hallucinations and delusions, although not invariably present, are often conspicuous in schizophrenia. The most common hallucinations are auditory: the patient hears (nonexistent) voices and believes in their reality. Schizophrenics are subject to a wide variety of delusions, including many that are characteristically bizarre or absurd. One symptom common to most schizophrenics is a loosening in their thought processes; this syndrome manifests itself as disorganized or incoherent thinking, illogical trains of mental association, and unclear or incomprehensible speech.

Schizophrenia crosses all socioeconomic, cultural, and racial boundaries. The lifetime risk of developing the illness has been estimated at about 8 per 1,000. Schizophrenia is the single largest cause of admissions to mental hospitals and accounts for an even larger proportion of the permanent populations of such institutions. The illness usually first manifests itself in the teen years or in early adult life, and its subsequent course is extremely variable. About one-third of all schizophrenic patients make a complete and permanent recovery, one-third have recurring episodes of the illness, and one-third deteriorate into chronic schizophrenia with severe disability.

Various theories of the origin of schizophrenia have centred on anatomical, biochemical, psychological, social, genetic, and environmental causes. No single cause of schizophrenia has been established or even identified; however, there is strong evidence that a combination of genetic and environmental factors plays an important role in the development of the disease. Researchers have found that rare inherited gene mutations occur three to four times more frequently in people with schizophrenia compared with healthy people. These mutations typically occur in genes involved in neurodevelopment, of which there are hundreds. In addition, thousands of small-effect genetic variants have been identified on chromosome 6 in persons with schizophrenia. It is believed that the interaction of these variants—many of which occur in a region of the chromosome that contains the major histocompatibility complex, a group of genes associated with regulating responses of the immune system—contributes to some 30 percent of cases of the illness. A similar polygenic pattern, in which many minor genetic variants interact to give rise to disease, has been found in persons with bipolar disorder. This knowledge sheds light on the enormous complexity of mental disorders associated with genetic factors. Today scientists continue to investigate the mechanisms by which genetic mutations give rise to biochemical abnormalities in the brains of people suffering from schizophrenia.

There is no cure for most patients with chronic schizophrenia, but the disease's symptoms can in many cases be effectively treated by antipsychotic drugs given in conjunction with psychotherapy and supportive therapy. For example, therapies involving antipsychotic drugs and estradiol (the most active form of estrogen) have proved effective in reducing certain psychotic symptoms in postmenopausal women with schizophrenia. In addition, there is some evidence that estradiol treatment can reduce psychotic symptoms, such as delusions and hallucinations, in premenopausal women. Hormone therapy has become an important area of schizophrenia research because decreased estrogen levels in women affected by the disease are associated with an increased occurrence of severe psychotic symptoms. In addition, estradiol therapy has the potential to enable doctors to prescribe lower doses of antipsychotics, which can have harmful side effects (e.g., abnormalities in heart function, movement disorders).

DEPRESSION

Depression is a mood or emotional state that is marked by feelings of low self-worth or guilt and a reduced ability to enjoy life. A person who is depressed usually experiences several of the following symptoms: feelings of sadness, hopelessness, or pessimism; lowered self-esteem and heightened self-depreciation; a decrease or loss of ability to take pleasure in ordinary activities; reduced energy and vitality; slowness of thought or action; loss of appetite; and disturbed sleep or insomnia.

Depression differs from simple grief or mourning, which are appropriate emotional responses to the loss of loved persons or objects. Where there are clear grounds for a person's unhappiness, depression is considered to be present if the depressed mood is disproportionately long or severe vis-à-vis the precipitating event. A person who experiences alternating states of depression and mania (abnormal elevation of mood) or hypomania (distinct, though not necessarily abnormal, elevation of mood) is said to suffer from bipolar disorder.

Depression is common and has been described by physicians since before the time of Hippocrates, who called it melancholia. The course of the disorder is extremely variable from person to person; it may be mild or severe, acute or chronic. Untreated, depression may last an average of four months or longer. Depression is twice as prevalent in women than in men. The typical age of onset is in the 20s, but it may occur at any age.

Depression can have many causes. Unfavourable life events can increase a person's vulnerability to depression or trigger a depressive episode. Negative thoughts about oneself and the world are also important in producing and maintaining depressive symptoms. However, both psychosocial and biochemical mechanisms seem to be important causes; the chief biochemical cause appears to be the defective regulation of the release of one or more naturally occurring neurotransmitters in the brain, particularly norepinephrine and serotonin. Reduced quantities or reduced activity of these chemicals in the brain is thought to cause the depressed mood in some sufferers.

Depression is also associated with disordered rapid eye movement (REM) sleep. REM sleep is modulated by a region of the brain known as the amygdala, which is also associated with processing negative thoughts and which may be enlarged or dysfunctional in some depressed persons. Although the significance of these associations are yet to be defined, the link between depression, disordered REM sleep, and abnormalities of the amygdala has led to new avenues of research into the neurobiology and treatment of depression.

There are three main treatments for depression. The two most important—and widespread by far—are psychotherapy and psychotropic medication, specifically antidepressants. Psychotherapy aims to alter the patient's maladaptive cognitive and behavioral responses to stressful life events while also giving emotional support to the patient. Antidepressant medications, by contrast, directly affect the chemistry of the brain and presumably achieve their therapeutic effects by correcting the chemical dysregulation that is causing the depression.

Two types of medications, tricyclic antidepressants and selective serotonin reuptake inhibitors (SSRIs), though chemically different, both serve to prevent the presynaptic reuptake of serotonin (and in the case of tricyclic antidepressants, norepinephrine as well). This results in the buildup or accumulation of neurotransmitters in the brain and allows them to remain in contact with the nerve cell receptors longer, thus helping to elevate the patient's mood. By contrast, the antidepressants known as monoamine oxidase inhibitors (MAO) interfere with the activity of monoamine oxidase, an enzyme that is known to be involved in the breakdown of norepinephrine and serotonin.

In cases of severe depression in which therapeutic results are needed quickly, electroconvulsive therapy (ECT) has sometimes proved helpful. In this procedure, a convulsion is produced by passing an electric current through the person's brain. In many cases of treatment, the best therapeutic results are obtained by using a combination of psychotherapy and antidepressant medication.

Bipolar Disorder

Bipolar disorder, also known as manic-depressive illness, is characterized by severe and recurrent depression or mania with abrupt or gradual onsets and recoveries. The states of mania and depression may alternate cyclically, one mood state may predominate over the other, or they may be mixed or combined with each other. The disorder was first described in antiquity by the 2nd-century Greek physician Aretaeus of Cappadocia and was defined in modern times by the German psychiatrist Emil Kraepelin.

A bipolar person in the depressive phase may be sad, despondent, listless, lacking in energy, and unable to show interest in his or her surroundings or to enjoy oneself and may have a poor appetite and disturbed sleep. The depressive state can be agitated—in which case sustained tension, overactivity, despair, and apprehensive delusions predominate—or it can be retarded—in which case the person's activity is slowed and reduced, he or she is sad and dejected, and he or she suffers from self-depreciatory and self-condemnatory tendencies.

Mania is a mood disturbance that is characterized by abnormally intense excitement, elation, expansiveness, boisterousness, talkativeness, distractibility, and irritability. The manic person talks loudly, rapidly, and continuously and progresses rapidly from one topic to another; is extremely enthusiastic, optimistic, and confident; is highly sociable and gregarious; gesticulates and moves about almost continuously; is easily irritated and easily distracted; is prone to grandiose notions; and shows an inflated sense of self-esteem.

The most extreme manifestations of these two mood disturbances are, in the manic phase, violence against others and, in the depressive, suicide. A bipolar disorder may also feature psychotic symptoms, such as delusions and hallucinations. Depression is the more common symptom, and many patients never develop a genuine manic phase, although they may experience a brief period of overoptimism and mild euphoria while recovering from a depression.

Bipolar disorders of varying severity affect about 1 percent of the general population and account for 10 to 15 percent of readmissions to mental institutions. Statistical studies have suggested a hereditary predisposition to bipolar disorder, and this predisposition has been linked to a defect on a dominant gene located on chromosome 11. In addition, bipolar disorder has been associated with polygenic factors, meaning that multiple, possibly thousands, of small-effect genetic variants can interact to give rise to the disease. Schizophrenia shares a similar polygenic component, suggesting that the two disorders may have a common origin.

In a physiological sense, it is believed that bipolar disorder is caused by the faulty regulation of one or more naturally occurring amines at sites in the brain where the transmission of nerve impulses takes place; a deficiency of the amines results in depression and an excess of them causes mania. The most likely candidates for the suspect amines are norepinephrine, dopamine, and serotonin (5-hydroxytryptamine, or 5-HT). The ingestion of lithium carbonate on a long-term basis has been found effective in alleviating or even eliminating the symptoms of many persons with bipolar disorder.

ANXIETY DISORDERS

Anxiety is characterized as a feeling of dread, fear, or apprehension, often with no clear justification. It is distinguished from fear because the latter arises in response to a clear and actual danger, such as one affecting a person's physical safety. Anxiety, by contrast, arises in response to apparently innocuous situations or is the product of subjective, internal emotional conflicts, the causes of which may not be apparent to the person. Some anxiety inevitably arises in the course of daily life and is considered normal. But persistent, intense, chronic, or recurring anxiety not justified in response to real-life stresses is usually regarded as a sign of an emotional disorder. When such an anxiety is unreasonably evoked by a specific situation or object, it is known as a phobia. A diffuse or persistent anxiety associated with no particular cause or mental concern is called general, or free-floating, anxiety.

There are many causes (and psychiatric explanations) for anxiety. Austrian neurologist Sigmund Freud viewed anxiety as the symptomatic expression of the inner emotional conflict caused when a person suppresses (from conscious awareness) experiences, feelings, or impulses that are too threatening or disturbing to live with. Anxiety is also viewed as arising from threats to an individual's ego or self-esteem, as in the case of inadequate sexual or job performance. Behavioral psychologists view anxiety as a learned response to frightening events in real life; the anxiety produced becomes attached to the surrounding circumstances associated with that event, so that those circumstances come to trigger anxiety in the person independently of any frightening event. Personality and social psychologists have noted that the mere act of evaluating stimuli as threatening or dangerous can produce or maintain anxiety.

An anxiety disorder may develop where anxiety is insufficiently managed, characterized by a continuing or periodic state of anxiety or diffuse fear that is not restricted to definite situations or objects. The tension is frequently expressed in the form of insomnia, outbursts of irritability, agitation, palpitations of the heart, and fears of death or insanity. Fatigue is often experienced as a result of excessive effort expended in managing the distressing fear. Occasionally the anxiety is expressed in a more acute form and results in physiological symptoms such as nausea, diarrhea, urinary frequency, suffocating sensations, dilated pupils, perspiration, or rapid breathing. Similar indications occur in several physiological disorders and in normal situations of stress or fear, but they may be considered neurotic when they occur in the absence of any organic defect or pathology and in situations that most people handle with ease.

Other anxiety disorders include panic disorder, agoraphobia, stress and post-traumatic stress disorders, obsessive-compulsive disorder, and generalized anxiety.

Obsessive-Compulsive Disorder

Obsessive-compulsive disorder is a type of mental disorder in which an individual experiences obsessions or compulsions or both. Either the obsessive thought or the compulsive act may occur singly, or both may appear in sequence.

Obsessions are recurring or persistent thoughts, images, or impulses that, rather than being voluntarily produced, seem to invade a person's consciousness despite attempts to ignore, suppress, or control them. Obsessional thoughts are frequently morbid, shameful, repugnant, or merely tedious; they are usually experienced as being meaningless and are accompanied by anxiety to a varying degree. Common obsessions include thoughts about committing violent acts, worries about contamination (as by shaking hands with someone), and doubt (as in wondering whether one had turned off the stove before leaving the house).

Obsessions are accompanied by compulsions in approximately 80 percent of cases. Compulsions are urges or impulses to commit repetitive acts that are apparently meaningless, stereotyped, or ritualistic. The compulsive person may be driven to perform the act not as an end in itself but as a means to produce or prevent some other situation, although he or she is usually aware that the two bear no logical causal relation to each other. Most compulsive acts are rather simple—such as persistent hand washing, counting, checking (e.g., the turned-off stove), touching, or the repetition of stereotyped words or phrases. Occasionally, however, elaborately formalized and time-consuming ceremonials are necessary. The compulsive person usually knows the act to be performed is meaningless, but his or her failure or refusal to execute it brings on a mounting anxiety that is relieved once the act is performed. Should the sufferer be forcibly or externally prevented from performing the compulsive act, he or she may experience an overwhelming anxiety.

Obsessive-compulsive disorders affect from 2 to 3 percent of the general population, occur equally in males and females, and can first appear at any age. The tricyclic antidepressant drug clomipramine (Anafranil) and the selective serotonin reuptake inhibitor fluoxetine (Prozac) have been found to markedly reduce the symptoms in about 60 percent of cases and have thus become the treatment of choice. Both drugs affect the brain's metabolism of the neurotransmitter serotonin, and this had led researchers to suspect that obsessive-compulsive disorders arise primarily from defects in the brain's neurochemical functioning rather than from purely psychological causes. A drug traditionally used for tuberculosis, d-cycloserine, has also been shown, when used in combination with behavioral therapy, to increase the rate of fear extinction in patients with obsessive-compulsive disorder. The highest rates of the condition occur in high-stress groups, such as those who are young, divorced, or unemployed.

Panic Disorder

Panic disorder is an anxiety disorder characterized by repeated panic attacks that leads to persistent worry and avoidance behaviour in an attempt to prevent situations that could precipitate an attack. Panic attacks are characterized by the unexpected, sudden onset of intense apprehension, fear, or terror and occur without apparent cause. Panic attacks often occur in people with breathing disorders such as asthma and in people experiencing bereavement or separation anxiety. While about 10 percent of people experience a single panic attack in their lifetimes, repeated attacks constituting panic disorder are less common; the disorder occurs in about 1–3 percent of people in developed countries. (The incidence in developing countries is unclear due to a lack of diagnostic resources and patient reporting.) Panic disorder typically occurs in adults, though it can affect children. It is more common in women than men, and it tends to run in families.

The underlying cause of panic disorder appears to arise from a combination of genetic and environmental factors. One of the most significant genetic variations that has been identified in association with panic disorder is mutation of a gene designated *HTR2A* (5-hydroxytryptamine receptor 2A). This gene encodes a receptor protein in the brain that binds serotonin, a neurotransmitter that plays an important role in regulating mood. People who possess this genetic variant may be susceptible to irrational fears or thoughts that have the potential to induce a panic attack.

Environmental and genetic factors also form the basis of the suffocation false alarm theory. This theory postulates that signals about potential suffocation arise from physiological and psychological centres involved in sensing factors associated with suffocation, such as increasing carbon dioxide and lactate levels in the brain. People affected by panic disorder appear to have an increased sensitivity to these alarm signals, which produce a heightened sense of anxiety. This increased sensitivity results in the misinterpretation of nonthreatening situations as terrifying events.

Altered activity of neurotransmitters such as serotonin can give rise to depression. Thus, there exists a close association between panic disorder and depression, and a large percentage of persons suffering from panic disorder go on to experience major depression within the next few years. In addition, about 50 percent of people with panic disorder develop agoraphobia, an abnormal fear of open or public places that are associated with anxiety-inducing situations or events. Panic disorder also may coincide with another anxiety disorder, such as obsessive-compulsive disorder, generalized anxiety disorder, or social phobia.

Because persistent worry and avoidance behaviour are major characteristics of panic disorder, many patients benefit from cognitive therapy. This form of therapy typically consists of developing skills and behaviours that enable a patient to cope with and to prevent panic attacks. Exposure therapy, a type of cognitive therapy in which patients repeatedly confront their fears, becoming desensitized to their fears in the process, can be effective in panic disorder patients who are also affected by agoraphobia. Pharmacotherapy can be used to correct for chemical imbalances in the brain. For example, tricyclic antidepressants, such as imipramine and desipramine, are effective treatments for panic disorder because they increase the concentrations of neurotransmitters at nerve terminals, where the chemicals exert their actions. These agents may also provide effective relief of associated depressive symptoms. Other antidepressants, including benzodiazepines, monoamine oxidase inhibitors, and serotonin reuptake inhibitors, also can be effective in treating both anxiety- and depression-related symptoms.

ATTENTION-DEFICIT/HYPERACTIVITY DISORDER

Attention-deficit/hyperactivity disorder (ADHD) is a behavioral syndrome characterized by inattention and distractibility, restlessness, inability to sit still, and difficulty concentrating on one thing for any period of time. ADHD most commonly occurs in children, though an increasing number of adults are being diagnosed with the disorder. ADHD is three times more common in males than in females and occurs in approximately 3 to 6 percent of all children. Although behaviours characteristic of the syndrome are evident in all cultures, they have garnered the most attention in the United States, where ADHD is the most commonly diagnosed childhood psychiatric disorder.

It was not until the mid-1950s that American physicians began to classify as "mentally deficient" individuals who had difficulty paying attention on demand. Various terms were coined to describe this behaviour, among them *minimal brain damage* and *hyperkinesis*. In 1980 the American Psychiatric Association (APA) replaced these terms with *attention deficit disorder* (ADD). Then in 1987 the APA linked ADD with hyperactivity, a condition that sometimes accompanies attention disorders but may exist independently. The new syndrome was named attention-deficit/hyperactivity disorder, or ADHD.

Symptoms and Treatment

Physicians may distinguish between three subtypes of the disorder: predominantly hyperactive-impulsive, predominantly inattentive, and combined hyperactive-impulsive and inattentive. Children and adults are diagnosed with

ADHD if they persistently show a combination of traits including, among others, forgetfulness, distractibility, fidgeting, restlessness, impatience, difficulty sustaining attention in work, play, or conversation, or difficulty following instructions and completing tasks. According to criteria issued by the APA, at least six of these traits must be present "to a degree that is maladaptive," and these behaviours must cause "impairment" in two or more settings—e.g., at school, work, or at home. Studies have shown that more than a quarter of children with ADHD are held back a grade in school, and a third fail to graduate from high school. The learning difficulties associated with ADHD, however, should not be confused with a deficient intelligence.

The most common medication used to treat ADHD is methylphenidate (Ritalin), a mild form of amphetamine. Amphetamines increase the amount and activity of the neurotransmitter norepinephrine in the brain. Although such drugs act as a stimulant in most people, they have the paradoxical effect of calming, focusing, or "slowing down" people with ADHD. Ritalin was developed in 1955, and the number of children with ADHD taking this and related medications increased steadily in the following decades. Between 1990 and 1996 alone, the number of American children regularly taking Ritalin grew from 500,000 to 1,300,000, according to one study. Another study found that Ritalin prescriptions for adults rose from 217,000 in 1992 to 729,000 in 1997.

The fact that many people diagnosed with ADHD experience fewer problems once they start taking stimulants such as Ritalin may confirm a neurological basis for the condition. Ritalin and similar medications help people with ADHD to concentrate better, which helps them get more work done and, in turn, reduces frustration and increases self-confidence. ADHD may also be treated with a nonstimulant drug known as atomoxetine (Strattera). Atomoxetine works by inhibiting the reuptake of norepinephrine from nerve terminals, thereby increasing the amount of the neurotransmitter available in the brain.

Another form of treatment, often used in conjunction with drug therapy, is cognitive behavioral therapy, which focuses on teaching affected individuals to learn to monitor and control their emotions. Behavioral therapy has proved beneficial in helping patients to establish structured routines and to set and achieve clearly defined goals.

Causes

The cause of ADHD is not known and may be a combination of both inherited and environmental factors. Many theories regarding causation have been abandoned for lack of evidence. Past suspects have included bad parenting; brain damage due to head trauma, infection, or exposure to alcohol or lead; food allergy; and too much sugar. ADHD is thought to be at least partly hereditary. About 40 percent of children with the condition have a parent who has ADHD, and 35 percent have a sibling who is affected.

Using imaging technologies such as positron emission tomography and fMRI, neurobiologists have found subtle differences in the structure and function of the brains of people with and without ADHD. One study, which compared the brains of boys with and without ADHD, found that the corpus callosum, the band of nerve fibres that connects the two hemispheres of the brain, contained slightly less tissue in those with ADHD. A similar study discovered small size discrepancies in the brain structures known as the caudate nuclei. In boys without ADHD, the right caudate nucleus was normally about 3 percent larger than the left caudate nucleus; this asymmetry was absent in boys with ADHD.

Other studies have detected not just anatomic but functional differences between the brains of persons with and without ADHD. One research team observed decreased blood flow through the right caudate nucleus in adults with ADHD. Another study showed that an area of the prefrontal cortex known as the left anterior frontal lobe metabolizes less glucose in adults with ADHD, an indication that this area may be less active than in those without ADHD. Still other research showed higher levels of the neurotransmitter norepinephrine throughout the brains of people with ADHD and lower levels of another substance that inhibits the release of norepinephrine. Metabolites, or broken-down products, of another neurotransmitter, dopamine, have also been found in elevated concentrations in the cerebrospinal fluid of boys with ADHD. Increases in dopamine concentrations may be related to a deficiency of neuronal dopamine receptors and transporters in persons affected by ADHD. Dopamine plays a central role in the reward system in the brain; however, the absence of receptors and transporters prevents cellular uptake of the neurotransmitter, which renders the neural reward circuit dysfunctional. This in turn leads to significant alterations in mood and behaviour.

These anatomic and physiological variations may all affect a sort of "braking system" in the brain. The brain is constantly coursing with many overlapping thoughts, emotions, impulses, and sensory stimuli. Attention can be defined as the ability to focus on one stimulus or task while resisting focus on the extraneous impulses; people with ADHD may have reduced ability to resist focus on these extraneous stimuli. The cortical-striatal-thalamic-cortical circuit, a chain of neurons in the brain that connects the prefrontal cortex, the basal ganglia, and the thalamus in one continuous loop, is thought to be one of the main structures responsible for impulse inhibition.

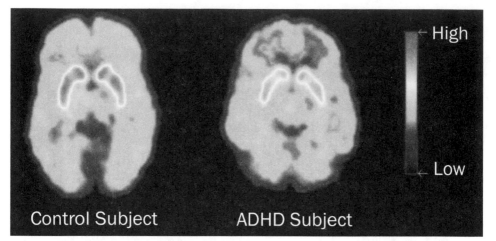

These positron emission tomography (PET) scans show that patients with attention deficit/hyperactivity disorder (ADHD) have lower levels of dopamine transporters in the nucleus accumbens, a part of the brain's reward centre, than control subjects. Courtesy of Brookhaven National Laboratory

The size and activity differences found in the prefrontal cortex and basal ganglia of people with ADHD may be evidence of a delay in the normal growth and development of this inhibitory circuit. If this supposition is true, it would help explain why the symptoms of ADHD sometimes subside with age. The cortical-striatal-thalamic-cortical circuit in the brains of people with ADHD may not fully mature—providing more normal levels of impulse inhibition—until the third decade of life, and it may never do so in some people. This developmental lag may explain why stimulant medications work to enhance attention. In one study, treatment with Ritalin restored average levels of blood flow through the caudate nucleus. In other trials, dopamine levels, which normally decrease with age but remain high in people with ADHD, fell after treatment with Ritalin. The hypothesis would coincide, finally, with observations that the social development of children with ADHD progresses at the same rate as that of their peers but with a lag of two to three years.

CHAPTER 7

NEUROLOGICAL AND NEURODEGENERATIVE DISORDERS AFFECTING THE BRAIN

The function of the nervous system can be altered by a variety of disorders that affect the brain and hence movement, memory, and cognition. For example, genetic defects that manifest late in life underlie a variety of diseases that affect the aging brain, causing memory impairment and unusual patterns of movement. In addition, infectious agents, such as viruses and bacteria, can alter brain function and give rise to neurological disease.

In many cases, infectious conditions can be treated pharmacologically, reversing symptoms and curing the disease. Other disorders of movement and memory, however, sometimes require surgical intervention. The complex and delicate nature of brain tissue makes invasive procedures exceptionally difficult and risky. Thus, despite significant advancements in the diagnosis and understanding of neurological disorders of the brain, there remains no effective treatment for some of these conditions.

DEMENTIA

Dementia is a chronic and usually progressive deterioration of intellectual capacity associated with the widespread loss of nerve cells and the shrinkage of brain tissue. Dementia is most commonly seen in the elderly (senile dementia), though it is not part of the normal aging process and can affect persons of any age.

The most common irreversible dementia is Alzheimer disease. This condition begins with memory loss, which may first appear to be simple absentmindedness or forgetfulness. As dementia progresses, the loss of memory broadens in scope until the individual can no longer remember basic social and survival skills or function independently. Language, spatial or temporal orientation, judgment, or other cognitive capacities may decline, and personality changes may also occur. Dementia is also present in other degenerative brain diseases including Pick disease and Parkinson disease.

The second most common cause of dementia is hypertension (high blood pressure) or other vascular conditions. This type of dementia, called multi-infarct, or vascular, dementia results from a series of small strokes that progressively destroy the brain. Dementia can also be caused by Huntington disease, syphilis, multiple sclerosis, acquired immune deficiency syndrome (AIDS), and some types of encephalitis. Treatable dementias occur in hypothyroidism, other metabolic diseases, and some malignant tumours. Treatment of the underlying disease in these cases may inhibit the progress of dementia but usually does not reverse it.

PICK DISEASE

Pick disease is a form of premature dementia caused by atrophy of the frontal and temporal lobes of the brain. It resembles Alzheimer disease but is much less common. Pick disease is characterized by a progressive deterioration of intellect, judgment, and memory, resulting in increased irritability, inappropriate behaviour, depression, and paranoia. Histologically some cerebral nerve cells are swollen and contain abnormal inclusions called Pick bodies.

The cause of Pick disease is unknown, but in some cases the disease appears to be inherited. Average survival from onset (generally between ages 40 and 60) to death is about 10 years; there is no specific treatment. The disease was first described by the German neurologist Arnold Pick.

ALZHEIMER DISEASE

Alzheimer disease is a degenerative brain disorder that develops in mid- to late-adulthood. It results in a progressive and irreversible decline in memory and a deterioration of various other cognitive abilities. The disease is characterized by the destruction of nerve cells and neural connections in the cerebral cortex of the brain and by a significant loss of brain mass. The disease was first described in 1906 by German neuropathologist Alois Alzheimer.

Stages of Alzheimer Disease

Alzheimer disease is the most common form of dementia. The disease develops differently among individuals, suggesting that more than one pathologic process may lead to the same outcome. The first symptom marking the transition from normal aging to Alzheimer disease is forgetfulness. This transitional stage, known as amnestic mild cognitive impairment (MCI), is characterized by noticeable dysfunction in memory with retention of normal cognitive ability in judgment, reasoning, and perception. As amnestic MCI progresses to Alzheimer disease, memory loss becomes more severe, and language, perceptual, and motor skills deteriorate. Mood becomes unstable, and the individual tends to become irritable and more sensitive to stress and may become intermittently

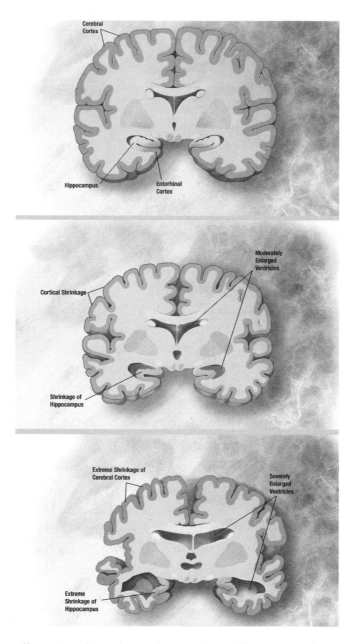

These illustrations show a human brain at three different stages of Alzheimer disease (top to bottom): *preclinical Alzheimer disease, mild Alzheimer disease, and severe Alzheimer disease.* Alzheimer's Disease Education and Referral Center, a service of the National Institute of Aging, National Institutes of Health angry, anxious, or depressed. In advanced stages, the individual becomes unresponsive and loses mobility and control of body functions; death ensues after a disease course lasting from 2 to 20 years.

About 10 percent of those who develop the disease are younger than age 60. These cases, referred to as early-onset familial Alzheimer disease, result from an inherited genetic mutation. The majority of cases of Alzheimer disease, however, develop after age 60 (late-onset); they usually occur sporadically—i.e., in individuals with no family history of the disease—although a genetic factor has been identified that is thought to predispose these individuals to the disorder.

Neuropathology

The presence of neuritic plaques and neurofibrillary tangles in the brain are used to diagnose Alzheimer disease in autopsy. Neuritic plaques—also called senile, dendritic, or amyloid plaques—consist of deteriorating neuronal material surrounding deposits of a sticky protein called beta-amyloid. This protein is derived from a larger molecule called amyloid precursor protein, which is a normal component of nerve cells. Neurofibrillary tangles are twisted protein fibres located within nerve cells. These fibres consist of a protein, called tau, that normally occurs in neurons. When incorrectly processed, tau molecules clump together and form tangles.

Both neuritic plaques and neurofibrillary tangles, which also may be found in smaller amounts in the brains of healthy elderly persons, are thought to interfere in some way with normal cellular functioning. However, it is not known whether the plaques and tangles are a cause or a consequence of the disease. Other features have been noted in the brains of many persons with Alzheimer disease. One of these features is a deficiency of the

neurotransmitter acetylcholine; neurons containing acetylcholine play an important role in memory.

Abnormal insulin signaling in the brain has been
associated with Alzheimer disease. Under normal conditions, insulin binds to insulin receptors, which are
expressed in great numbers on the membranes of neurons, to facilitate neuronal uptake of glucose, which the
brain depends upon to carry out its many functions.
However, neurons in the brains of patients with
Alzheimer disease have very few, if any, insulin receptors
and therefore are resistant to the actions of insulin. As a
result of the inability of insulin to bind to the neurons, it
accumulates in the blood serum, leading to a condition
known as hyperinsulinemia (abnormally high serum levels of insulin). Hyperinsulinemia in the brain is suspected
to stimulate inflammation that in turn stimulates the
formation of neuritic plaques. Abnormal insulin signaling in the brain has also been associated with nerve cell
dysfunction and death, decreased levels of acetylcholine,
and decreased levels of transthyretin, a protein that normally binds to and transports beta-amyloid proteins out
of the brain.

Underlying genetic defects have been identified for
both late- and early-onset cases of Alzheimer disease. A
defect in the gene that codes for amyloid precursor protein may increase the production or deposition of
beta-amyloid, which forms the core of neuritic plaques.
This gene, however, is responsible for only 2 to 3 percent
of all early-onset cases of the disease; the remainder are
attributed to two other genes. A defect in the gene that
directs production of apolipoprotein E (ApoE), which is
involved in cholesterol transport, may be a factor in the
majority of late-onset Alzheimer cases. There are three
forms of this gene—*APOE2*, *APOE3*, and *APOE4*—two

of which, *APOE3* and *APOE4*, are associated with an increased risk of disease and influence the age of onset of disease.

Studies employing fMRI have shown that individuals between ages 20 and 35 who carry the *APOE4* variant frequently have increased activity in the hippocampus of the brain. This region plays a central role in the formation and recall of memories and is involved in the production of emotions. Scientists suspect that in some *APOE4* carriers hyperactivity of the hippocampus early in life leads to this region's later dysfunction, which contributes to the development of Alzheimer disease. Brain imaging using fMRI in young *APOE4* carriers may be useful for identifying those carriers at greatest risk of disease.

Genetic screening to determine the status of a gene known as *TOMM40* (translocase of outer mitochondrial membrane 40 homolog [yeast]) can be used to provide additional information about the risk of Alzheimer disease and to predict the age of onset. There are several forms of this gene, which differ in their length due to variations that influence the number of repeats of a specific base-pair segment within the gene sequence. In persons who have inherited variants of *TOMM40*, the occurrence of a long form of the gene, in conjunction with either *APOE3* or *APOE4*, correlates with onset of the disease before age 80. In contrast, short forms of *TOMM40* were found to correlate with onset of the disease after age 80.

Treatment and Detection

There is no cure for Alzheimer disease; however, there are several therapeutic agents that can be used to slow disease progression or to alleviate symptoms. In roughly 50 percent of patients, the progression of amnestic MCI can be delayed for about one year by drugs called acetyl-cholinesterase inhibitors (or anticholinesterases). These drugs, which include galantamine, donepezil, rivastig-mine, and tacrine (no longer marketed but still available), work by slowing the breakdown of acetylcholine. Common side effects of acetylcholinesterase inhibitors include nausea, vomiting, and diarrhea; a common and serious side effect of tacrine is liver toxicity. Symptoms of Alzheimer disease can be reduced in some patients by the drug memnatine, which decreases abnormal brain activity by blocking the binding of glutamate (an excit-atory neurotransmitter) to certain receptors in the brain. While this drug can improve cognition and enable patients to become more engaged in daily activities, it may cause certain patients to become unusually agitated or delusional. Other treatments aim to control the depression, behavioral problems, and insomnia that often accompany the disease.

There are also a number of experimental drugs for Alzheimer disease in early- and late-stage clinical trials. One drug that has demonstrated some success in prevent-ing cognitive decline in affected patients is tarenflurbil, a gamma-secretase modulator (sometimes referred to as a selective amyloid-beta-42-lowering agent). Tarenflurbil has been shown to reduce levels of amyloid-beta-42 pro-tein, which is thought to be the primary amyloid protein involved in plaque formation. Another drug, methylthio-ninium chloride (Rember), more commonly known as methylene blue (an organic dye), targets the tau protein of neurofibrillary tangles. In clinical trials, methylthionin-ium chloride either stopped or significantly slowed the progression of cognitive decline in patients with Alzheimer disease. It is the first drug capable of dissolv-ing tau protein fibres and preventing the formation of neurofibrillary tangles.

Today, improved detection and treatments for Alzheimer disease are areas of concentrated scientific investigation. Early detection relies on the discovery of biomarkers (physiological changes specific to and indicative of a disease) and on the development of methods sensitive enough to measure these biomarkers. Several detection methods being developed for Alzheimer disease include blood tests to measure increased expression of a protein present in certain white blood cells and positron emission tomography to detect increased levels of an enzyme in cerebrospinal fluid.

ESSENTIAL TREMOR

Essential tremor is a disorder of the nervous system characterized by involuntary oscillating movements that typically affect the muscles of the arms, hands, face, head, and neck. These involuntary movements often make daily tasks, such as writing, eating, or dressing, difficult. The disorder also may affect the voice and, in rare cases, the legs, sometimes causing difficulty with walking. The tremor is usually absent at rest and is not associated with any other primary symptoms, which distinguishes it from the type of tremor that occurs in Parkinson disease.

Essential tremor is common and affects both men and women. Onset most often occurs in people over age 65, although the disorder can appear in people of all ages. The cause of essential tremor is unknown; however, the disorder does tend to run in families. There are several genetic variations that have been identified in association with essential tremor. The best-characterized variation occurs in a gene known as *DRD3* (dopamine receptor 3; formerly designated *ETM1*, or essential tremor 1). The *DRD3* gene encodes a protein called dopamine receptor D3. This receptor binds dopamine and thereby contributes to the regulation of physical movements. However, the variant *DRD3* gene encodes a receptor molecule that alters neuronal response to dopamine, presumably giving rise to the involuntary movements of essential tremor. Variations in a gene called *HS1BP3* (HCLS1 binding protein 3) have been identified in association with essential tremor, although the mechanisms by which these variations give rise to the disorder are unclear.

There is no cure for essential tremor; however, there exist a variety of treatments that can be effective in reducing the severity of involuntary movements. In some patients the symptoms of tremors can be controlled through lifestyle and dietary modifications to eliminate stress and the intake of stimulants such as caffeine. Physical therapy can improve muscle control and coordination in the arms and legs of some patients, and speech therapy can alleviate symptoms of mild voice tremor.

In cases in which tremor interrupts daily tasks and affects quality of life, drugs or surgery may be necessary to control symptoms. Agents known as beta-blockers (e.g., propanolol), which act on the nervous system to reduce neuronal excitation, are effective treatments, particularly for reducing tremors that affect the hands and voice. In addition, the antiepileptic agent primidone, which reduces neuronal excitation in the brain, is effective in suppressing most symptoms of essential tremor. Patients with essential tremor that does not respond to drug therapy may need surgery, such as deep brain stimulation, to relieve debilitating symptoms; however, because there are dangerous risks associated with brain surgery, it is considered a last resort.

PARKINSONISM

Parkinsonism is a group of chronic neurological disorders characterized by progressive loss of motor function resulting from the degeneration of neurons in the area of the brain that controls voluntary movement. It was first described in 1817 by the British physician James Parkinson in his *Essay on the Shaking Palsy*. Various types of the disorder are recognized, but the disease described by Parkinson, called Parkinson disease, is the most common form. Parkinson disease is also called primary parkinsonism, paralysis agitans, or idiopathic parkinsonism, meaning the disease has no identifiable cause. This distinguishes it from secondary parkinsonism, a group of disorders very similar in nature to Parkinson disease but that arise from known or identifiable causes.

All types of parkinsonism are characterized by four main signs, including tremors of resting muscles, particularly of the hands; muscular rigidity of the arms, legs, and neck; difficulty in initiating movement (bradykinesia); and stooped posture (postural instability). A variety of other features may accompany these characteristics, including a lack of facial expression (known as masked face), difficulty in swallowing or speaking, loss of balance, a shuffling gait, depression, and dementia.

Parkinsonism results from the deterioration of neurons in the region of the brain called the substantia nigra. These neurons normally produce the neurotransmitter dopamine, which sends signals to the basal ganglia, a mass of nerve fibres that helps to initiate and control patterns of movement. Dopamine functions in the brain as an inhibitor of nerve impulses and is involved in suppressing unintended movement. When dopamine-producing (dopaminergic) neurons are damaged or destroyed, dopamine levels drop and the normal signaling system is disrupted. In both primary and secondary parkinsonism, the physiological effects of this deterioration do not manifest until roughly 60 to 80 percent of these neurons are destroyed.

While the cause of deterioration of the substantia nigra in primary parkinsonism remains unknown, deterioration in secondary parkinsonism can result from trauma induced by certain drugs, exposure to viruses or toxins, or other factors. For example, a viral infection of the brain that caused a worldwide pandemic of encephalitis lethargica (sleeping sickness) just after World War I resulted in the development of postencephalitic parkinsonism in some survivors. Toxin-induced parkinsonism is caused by carbon monoxide, manganese, or cyanide poisoning. A neurotoxin known as MPTP (1-methyl-4-phenyl-1,2,3,6-tetrahydropyridine), previously found in contaminated heroin, also causes a form of toxin-induced parkinsonism. The ability of this substance to destroy neurons suggests that an environmental toxin similar to MPTP may be responsible for Parkinson disease.

Pugilistic parkinsonism results from head trauma and has affected professional boxers such as Jack Dempsey and Muhammad Ali. The parkinsonism-dementia complex of Guam, which occurs among the Chamorro people of the Pacific Mariana Islands, is also thought to result from an unidentified environmental agent. In some individuals genetic defects are thought to incur susceptibility to the disease. Parkinsonism-plus disease, or multiple-system degenerations, includes diseases in which the main features of parkinsonism are accompanied by other symptoms. Parkinsonism may appear in patients with other neurological disorders such as Huntington disease, Alzheimer disease, and Creutzfeldt-Jakob disease.

Both medical and surgical therapies are used to treat parkinsonism. In primary parkinsonism, the medication levodopa (l-dopa), a precursor of dopamine, is used in conjunction with the medication carbidopa to alleviate symptoms, although this treatment tends to become less effective over time. Other medications used are selegiline, a type of drug that slows the breakdown of dopamine, and bromocriptine and pergolide, two drugs that mimic the effects of dopamine. Surgical procedures are used to treat parkinsonism patients who have failed to respond to medications. Pallidotomy involves destroying a part of the brain structure called the globus pallidus that is involved in motor control. Pallidotomy may improve symptoms such as tremors, rigidity, and bradykinesia. Cryothalamotomy destroys the area of the brain that produces tremors by inserting a probe into the thalamus. Restorative surgery is an experimental technique that replaces the lost dopaminergic neurons of the patient with dopamine-producing fetal brain tissue.

PARKINSON DISEASE

Parkinson disease is a degenerative neurological disorder that is characterized by the onset of tremor, muscle rigidity, bradykinesia, and postural instability. It is believed that, in the majority of cases, Parkinson disease arises from a combination of genetic predisposition and certain environmental factors, such as exposure to pesticides. Although Parkinson disease is rarely inherited, individuals who have first-degree relatives with the disease appear to be at increased risk. In addition, autosomal recessive mutations in a gene called *parkin* have been associated with early-onset Parkinson disease. Mutations in several other genes have been linked to noninherited forms of the disease.

The onset of Parkinson disease typically occurs between ages 60 and 70, although in about 5 to 10 percent of cases onset occurs before age 40. The worldwide incidence of Parkinson disease is estimated to be about 160 per 100,000 persons, with about 16 to 19 new cases per 100,000 persons appearing each year. Men are slightly more affected than women, and there are no apparent racial differences. Parkinson disease often begins with a slight tremor of the thumb and forefinger, sometimes called "pill-rolling," and slowly progresses over a period of 10 to 20 years. Advanced disease is often characterized by loss of facial expression, reduced rate of swallowing leading to drooling, severe depression, dementia, and paralysis.

The hallmark neurobiological feature of Parkinson disease is a decrease in dopamine levels in the brain, primarily in the substantia nigra. The cause of this decrease is unclear. A protein known as alpha synuclein appears to be involved in neuronal degeneration. Alpha synuclein is produced by dopaminergic neurons and is broken down by other proteins, such as parkin and neurosin. Defects in any of the proteins that break down alpha synuclein may lead to its accumulation, resulting in the formation of deposits called Lewy bodies in the substantia nigra. However, other mechanisms affecting the accumulation of alpha synuclein have been identified, and it is not clear whether Lewy bodies are a cause of or occur as a result of the disease. Other findings in people affected by Parkinson disease include mitochondrial dysfunction, leading to increased production of free radicals that cause significant damage to brain cells, and heightened sensitivity of the immune system and neurons to molecules called cytokines, which stimulate inflammation.

The most effective treatment for Parkinson disease is administration of levodopa. Levodopa crosses the blood-brain barrier (a physiological partition blocking the entry of large molecules into the central nervous system) via special transport proteins and is converted to dopamine in the brain, primarily in the region containing the substantia nigra. Although initially beneficial in causing a significant remission of symptoms, levodopa frequently is

Actor Michael J. Fox, who suffers from the neurological condition Parkinson disease, often speaks out to raise funding for the Michael J. Fox Foundation for Parkinson's Research. Michael Buckner/Getty Images

effective for only 5 to 10 years, and serious side effects, including uncontrolled movements, hallucinations, persistent nausea and vomiting, and changes in behaviour and mood, often accompany treatment. Cotreatment with a drug called carbidopa, which inhibits an enzyme that breaks down levodopa prior to crossing the blood-brain barrier, allows higher concentrations of levodopa to reach the brain. Thus, levodopa-carbidopa combination therapy enables lower doses of levodopa to be administered, thereby reducing side effects. This combination therapy has allowed many patients to live reasonably normal lives.

Other drugs used to relieve the symptoms of Parkinson disease include agents that stimulate dopamine production in the brain, such as pergolide and bromocriptine, and agents that slow the degradation of dopamine, such as selegiline. In addition, the antiviral agent amantadine can reduce certain symptoms of the disease. In some cases, surgery may be necessary to alleviate advanced symptoms. For example, a surgical procedure known as deep brain stimulation (DBS) has been successful in decreasing involuntary movements, improving debilitating problems with gait and slowness of movement, and reducing doses of medications. In DBS an electrode is implanted in the brain and is attached via a lead wire to a neurostimulator inserted under the skin, usually near the collarbone. The neurostimulator sends electrical signals to the electrode. These signals work by disrupting the physiological impulses that cause disordered movement.

DYSTONIA

Dystonia is a movement disorder characterized by the involuntary and repetitive contraction of muscle groups, resulting in twisting movements, unusual postures, and possible tremor of the involved muscles. As the disorder persists, movement may affect other muscle groups. Although dystonias may occur in families or sporadically, many are secondary to other disorders as reactions to medications; for example, one of the most common dystonias is induced by levodopa in the treatment of Parkinson disease.

Dystonias may be classified in several ways, one of which is the mode of initiation of the movement; often the dystonia appears only with a specific action, such as the contraction of hand muscles when writing is attempted (writer's cramp). Another means of classification is the extent of muscle involvement: focal, affecting only one muscle group, such as the vocal cords (e.g., spastic dysphonia); segmental, involving two adjacent muscle groups, such as the neck muscles (e.g., spastic torticollis); or general, affecting the entire body.

Treatment varies depending on the cause. In some cases, dystonia may be treated by discontinuing use of the drug that is causing the symptoms. Various medications that act on different parts of the nervous system are often effective in the treatment of dystonias. Surgical therapies also may be used, such as thalamotomy, a procedure that destroys a specific group of cells in the brain, or cutting the nerves that supply the dystonic area. Some dystonias can be treated with botulinum toxin (e.g., Botox, Myobloc, and NeuroBloc). An injection of this potent blocker of nerve transmission produces a temporary chemical denervation of the muscles that may last for several months.

CHOREA

Chorea is a neurological disorder characterized by irregular and involuntary movements of muscle groups in various parts of the body. The principal types of chorea are Sydenham chorea and Huntington disease.

SYDENHAM CHOREA

Sydenham chorea, which is also known as St. Vitus dance (or infectious chorea), is a neurological disorder characterized by irregular and involuntary movements of muscle groups in various parts of the body that follow streptococcal infection. The name St. Vitus dance derives from the late Middle Ages, when persons with the disease attended the chapels of St. Vitus, who was believed to have curative powers. The disorder was first explained by the English physician Thomas Sydenham. Most often a manifestation of rheumatic fever, Sydenham chorea occurs most frequently between ages 5 and 15 and is more common in girls than boys. The disease may occur as an infrequent complication of pregnancy.

The symptoms of Sydenham chorea range in severity from mild to completely incapacitating. A vague deterioration in the ability to perform everyday tasks is replaced by involuntary jerking movements that are most obvious in the extremities and face but are also present in the trunk. Twitching movements are more noticeable on the limbs of one side of the body. The muscles of speech and swallowing may also be affected. Irritability, anxiety, and emotional instability, chiefly episodes of crying initiated by trivial incidents, are also common symptoms.

It is thought that Sydenham chorea is caused by a malfunctioning of the basal ganglia, groups of nerve cells in the brain. There is evidence that both the emotional manifestations and the abnormal movements of the disease are related to changes in the cerebral cortex. Attacks of Sydenham chorea tend to be self-limited, although the duration of each is several weeks; recurrence is frequent. Recovery is usually complete and is accelerated by bedrest. Sedation or the administration of tranquilizers may provide protection from self-injury in severe cases, when the patient is helpless.

HUNTINGTON DISEASE

Huntington disease, also known as Huntington chorea, is a relatively rare, and invariably fatal, hereditary neurological disease that is characterized by irregular and involuntary movements of the muscles and progressive loss of cognitive ability. The disease was first described by the American physician George Huntington in 1872.

Symptoms of Huntington disease usually appear between ages 35 and 50 and worsen over time. They begin with occasional jerking or writhing movements, called choreiform movements, or what appear to be minor problems with coordination; these movements, which are absent during sleep, worsen over the next few years and progress to random, uncontrollable, and often violent twitchings and jerks. Mental deterioration may manifest initially in the form of apathy, fatigue, irritability, restlessness, or moodiness; these symptoms may progress to memory loss, dementia, bipolar disorder, or schizophrenia.

A child of someone with Huntington disease has a 50 percent chance of inheriting the genetic mutation associated with the disease, and all individuals who inherit the mutation will eventually develop the disease. The genetic mutation that causes Huntington disease occurs in a gene known as *HD* (officially named huntingtin [Huntington disease]). This gene, which is located on human chromosome 4, encodes a protein called huntingtin, which is distributed in certain regions of the brain, as well as other tissues of the body. Mutated forms of the *HD* gene contain abnormally repeated segments of DNA (deoxyribonucleic acid) called CAG trinucleotide repeats. These repeated segments result in the synthesis of huntingtin proteins that contain long stretches of molecules of the amino acid glutamine. When these abnormal huntingtin proteins are cut into fragments during processing by cellular enzymes, molecules of glutamine project out from the ends of the protein fragments, causing the fragments to adhere to other proteins. The resulting clumps of proteins have the potential to cause neuron (nerve cell) dysfunction. The formation of abnormal huntingtin proteins leads to the degeneration and eventual death of neurons in the basal ganglia, a pair of nerve clusters deep within the brain that control movement.

The progression and severity of Huntington disease are associated with the length of the CAG trinucleotide repeat region in the *HD* gene. For example, the trinucleotide region in *HD* appears to expand during middle age, coinciding with the onset of symptoms, and may also expand from one generation to the next, causing a form of the disease known as anticipation, in which symptoms develop at an earlier age in the offspring of affected individuals. While a genetic test is available for Huntington disease, no effective therapy or cure is available for the disorder, although choreiform movements may be partially and temporarily suppressed by phenothiazines or other antipsychotic medications.

EPILEPSY

Epilepsy is a chronic neurological disorder characterized by sudden and recurrent seizures that are caused by excessive signaling of nerve cells in the brain. Seizures may include convulsions, momentary lapses of consciousness, strange movements or sensations in parts of the body, odd behaviours, and emotional disturbances. Epileptic seizures typically last one to two minutes but can be followed by weakness, confusion, or unresponsiveness.

Epilepsy is a relatively common disorder affecting about 40 million to 50 million people worldwide; it is slightly more common in males than females. Causes of the disorder include brain defects, head trauma, infectious diseases, stroke, brain tumours, or genetic or developmental abnormalities. Several types of epileptic disorders are hereditary. Cysticercosis, a parasitic infection of the brain, is a common cause of epilepsy in the developing world. About half of epileptic seizures have an unknown cause and are called idiopathic.

PARTIAL SEIZURES

A partial seizure originates in a specific area of the brain. Partial seizures consist of abnormal sensations or movements, and a lapse of consciousness may occur. Epileptic individuals with partial seizures may experience unusual sensations called auras that precede the onset of a seizure. Auras may include unpleasant odours or tastes, the sensation that unfamiliar surroundings seem familiar (déjà vu), and visual or auditory hallucinations that last from a fraction of a second to a few seconds. The individual may also experience intense fear, abdominal pain or discomfort, or an awareness of increased respiration rate or heartbeat. The form of the onset of a seizure is, in most cases, the same from attack to attack. After experiencing the aura, the individual becomes unresponsive but may examine objects closely or walk around.

Jacksonian seizures are partial seizures that begin in one part of the body such as the side of the face, the toes on one foot, or the fingers on one hand. The jerking movements then spread to other muscles on the same side of the body. This type of seizure is associated with a lesion or defect in the area of the cerebral cortex that controls voluntary movement.

Complex partial seizures, also called psychomotor seizures, are characterized by a clouding of consciousness and by strange, repetitious movements called automatisms. On recovery from the seizure, which usually lasts from one to three minutes, the individual has no memory of the attack, except for the aura. Occasionally, frequent mild complex partial seizures may merge into a prolonged period of confusion, which can last for hours or days with fluctuating levels of awareness and strange behaviour. Complex partial attacks may be caused by lesions in the frontal lobe or the temporal lobe.

GENERALIZED SEIZURES

Generalized seizures are the result of abnormal electrical activity in most or all of the brain. This type of seizure is characterized by convulsions, short absences of consciousness, generalized muscle jerks (clonic seizures), and loss of muscle tone (tonic seizures), with falling.

Generalized tonic-clonic seizures, sometimes referred to by the older term *grand mal*, are commonly known as convulsions. A person undergoing a convulsion loses consciousness and falls to the ground. The fall is sometimes preceded by a shrill scream caused by forcible expiration of air as the respiratory and laryngeal muscles suddenly contract. After the fall, the body stiffens because of generalized tonic contraction of the muscles; the lower limbs are usually extended and the upper limbs flexed. During the tonic phase, which lasts less than a minute, respiration stops because of sustained contraction of the respiratory muscles. Following the tonic stage, clonic (jerking) movements occur in the arms and legs. The tongue may be bitten during involuntary contraction of the jaw muscles, and urinary incontinence may occur. Usually, the entire generalized tonic-clonic seizure is over in less than five minutes. Immediately afterward, the individual is usually confused and sleepy and may have a headache but will not remember the seizure.

Studies measuring electric currents in the heart have demonstrated that some patients affected by tonic-clonic seizures experience abnormal cardiac rhythms either during or immediately after a seizure. In some cases the heart may stop beating for several seconds, a condition known as asystole. Asystole has been linked to a phenomenon called sudden unexpected death in epilepsy (SUDEP), which affects more than 8 percent of epilepsy patients and typically occurs in people between ages 20 and 30. The cause of SUDEP is not known with certainty. Scientists suspect that accumulated damage and scarring in cardiac tissue, caused by multiple, recurring seizures, has the potential to interfere with electrical conduction in the heart and thus precipitate SUDEP during a typical tonic clonic seizure. In addition, genetic defects associated with epilepsy and abnormalities in heart function have been identified in families affected by both inherited epilepsy and SUDEP.

Primary generalized, or absence, epilepsy is characterized by repeated lapses of consciousness that generally last less than 15 seconds each and usually occur many times a day. This type of seizure is sometimes referred to by the older term *petit mal*. Minor movements such as blinking may be associated with absence seizures. After the short interruption of consciousness, the individual is mentally clear and able to resume previous activity. Absence seizures occur mainly in children and do not appear initially after age 20; they tend to disappear before or during early adulthood. At times absence seizures can be nearly continuous, and the individual may appear to be in a clouded, partially responsive state for minutes or hours.

DIAGNOSIS AND TREATMENT

A person with recurrent seizures is diagnosed with epilepsy. A complete physical examination, blood tests, and a neurological evaluation may be necessary to identify the cause of the disorder. Electroencephalogram (EEG) monitoring is performed to detect abnormalities in the electrical activity of the brain. Magnetic resonance imaging (MRI), positron emission tomography (PET), single photon emission computed tomography (SPECT), or magnetic resonance spectroscopy (MRS) may be used to locate structural or biochemical brain abnormalities.

Most people with epilepsy have seizures that can be controlled with antiepileptic medications such as valproate, ethosuximide, clonazepam, carbamazepine, and primidone; these medications decrease the amount of neuronal activity in the brain. Brain damage caused by epilepsy usually cannot be reversed. Epileptic seizures that cannot be treated with medication may be reduced by surgery that removes the epileptogenic area of the brain. Other treatment strategies include vagus nerve stimulation, a diet high in fat and low in carbohydrates (ketogenic diet), and behavioral therapy. It may be necessary for epileptic individuals to refrain from driving, operating hazardous machinery, or swimming because of the temporary loss of control that occurs without warning.

Family and friends of an epileptic individual should be aware of what to do if a seizure occurs. During a seizure the clothing should be loosened around the neck, the head should be cushioned with a pillow, and any sharp or hard objects should be removed from the area. An object should never be inserted into the person's mouth during a seizure. After the seizure the head of the individual should be turned to the side to drain secretions from the mouth.

MENINGITIS

Meningitis is an inflammation of the meninges, the membranes covering the brain and spinal cord. Meningitis can be caused by various infectious agents, including viruses, fungi, and protozoa, but bacteria produce the most life-threatening forms. The patient usually experiences fever, headache, vomiting, irritability, anorexia, and stiffness in the neck.

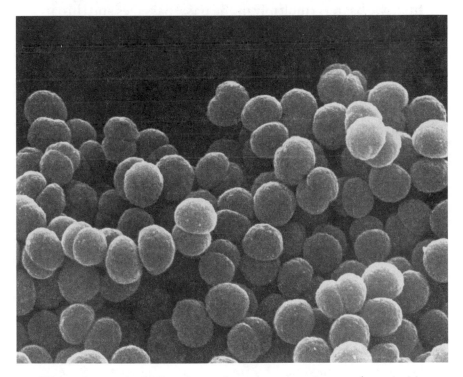

Neisseria meningitidis, *shown here, causes meningococcal meningitis. Infection results from inhalation of the bacteria. Symptoms include severe headache, neck pain, and extreme sensitivity to light and sound.* S. Lowry/ Univ Ulster/Stone/Getty Images

Among the bacteria that can cause meningitis are the meningococcus (*Neisseria meningitidis*), *Haemophilus influenzae*, and various strains of pneumococci, streptococci, or staphylococci. A bacterial infection elsewhere in the body may be carried to the meninges through the bloodstream itself or from an adjacent infected organ, such as the middle ear or the nasal sinuses. The infectious agents multiply in the meninges, where they produce a pus that thickens the cerebrospinal fluid, thereby causing various symptoms and complications such as seizures, deafness, blindness, paralysis, and various degrees of impairment of the intellect.

Bacterial meningitis usually has three main stages. At first, the bacteria multiply in the nasal passages and throat, often causing no painful symptoms. Next, they invade the blood, introducing toxic substances into the circulation and causing fever; if the infection is caused by *N. meningitidis*, a rash may appear and develop into hemorrhagic spots (petechiae and purpura) in severe cases. In the third stage, the bacteria multiply in the meninges, where they produce intense inflammatory changes and an exudate of pus.

A characteristic of meningitis is the rapid onset of symptoms, which may result in death within only a few hours. The first symptom of meningitis is usually vomiting. A severe bursting headache develops when the meninges have become inflamed and the pressure of the cerebrospinal fluid has increased. Stiffness of the neck then develops, due to irritation of the spinal nerves supplying those muscles. Deep tendon reflexes are exaggerated, and convulsions may occur in infants and small children. In more severe cases, the cerebrospinal fluid becomes so thickened by pus that the passages between the ventricles (cavities) of the brain and the spaces in the spinal meninges become blocked, causing fluid to accumulate. The accumulation of fluid in the ventricles may in turn result in hydrocephalus, which causes coma and death unless relieved.

The term *meningitis* is often applied to meningococcal meningitis, which is caused by *N. meningitidis*. Epidemics of this disease occurred at irregular intervals, with death occurring in 40–50 percent of cases, until the use of antibiotic drugs greatly reduced both mortality rates and the incidence of the disease; however, severe epidemics are still seen in parts of Africa. Meningococcal meningitis is worldwide in distribution and more likely to occur in cold weather. It is primarily a disease of youth and especially of children under age 10, though all ages may be affected. The disease is usually acquired by nasal droplet transmission. Vaccines against some types of *N. meningitidis* are available. Another serious cause of meningitis is *H. influenzae*; it occurs in infants and young children but only rarely in older persons, and its course and symptoms resemble those of *N. meningitidis*. The bacterium *Streptococcus pneumoniae* is a common cause of meningitis in adults. In many developing countries, tuberculous meningitis is common.

Diagnosis of meningitis is made by examination and confirmed by the performance of a test called a spinal tap (or lumbar puncture). In this test a needle is inserted into the lower part of the patient's back between two vertebrae (bones of the spinal column) and a small sample of cerebrospinal fluid is removed. If a bacterial, tuberculous, or fungal infection is found, patients will need intensive medical care; appropriate antibiotics must be administered as soon as meningitis is suspected. The mortality and morbidity of the bacterial disease are substantial, even with the prompt use of appropriate antibiotic therapy.

The early diagnosis and prompt treatment of meningitis is particularly important in preventing possible permanent damage to the brain, especially in affected children. Meningococcal meningitis is best treated with penicillin. Cases caused by *H. influenzae* are treated with ampicillin or chloramphenicol. These drugs have reduced mortality rates from bacterial meningitis to less than 5 percent in some areas. A vaccine that gives protection against the type b strain of *H. influenzae* became commercially available in the 1980s and has proved effective in safeguarding infants and children from the disease. To control the spread of meningitis caused by *H. influenzae* or *N. meningitis*, the antibiotic derivative rifampin should be administered to any who have come in contact with the disease.

Various other forms of meningitis are caused by viruses and ordinarily have a short, uncomplicated, self-limited course that does not require specific therapy. Patients usually recover in three to five days, typically without any serious result.

ENCEPHALITIS

Encephalitis is an inflammation of the brain. The name of the condition comes from the Greek words *enkephalos* ("brain") and *itis* ("inflammation"). Inflammation affecting the brain may also involve adjoining structures; encephalomyelitis is inflammation of the brain and spinal cord, and meningoencephalitis is inflammation of the brain and meninges.

Encephalitis is most often caused by an infectious organism and sometimes by noninfective agents, such as the chemicals lead, arsenic, and mercury. Although encephalitis can be produced by many different types of organisms, such as bacteria, protozoans, and helminths (worms), the most frequent causal agents are viruses. The encephalitis-producing viruses are divided into two groups: (1) those that invade the body and produce no damage until they are carried by the bloodstream to the nerve cells of the brain (e.g., the rabies and arthropod-borne viruses) and (2) those that invade the body and first injure nonnervous tissues and then secondarily invade brain cells (e.g., the viruses causing herpes simplex, herpes zoster, dengue, acquired immune deficiency syndrome [AIDS], and yellow fever).

Symptoms common to most types of encephalitis are fever, headache, drowsiness, lethargy, coma, tremors, and a stiff neck and back. Convulsions may occur in patients of any age but are most common in infants. Characteristic neurological signs include uncoordinated and involuntary movements, weakness of the arms, legs, or other parts of the body, or unusual sensitivity of the skin to various types of stimuli. These symptoms and signs and an examination of the cerebrospinal fluid by a lumbar puncture (spinal tap) can usually establish the presence of encephalitis, but they do not necessarily establish the cause, which often remains unknown. This makes specific treatment difficult, and, even when the causative virus is known, there may be no effective treatment. Treatment of encephalitis is therefore largely supportive. Patients require intensive medical care, with continuous monitoring of their heart and respiratory functions and management of their fluid and electrolyte balances. Symptoms remaining after recovery from the acute phase of brain inflammation vary considerably, depending on the type of encephalitis and on the age and general health of the patient. Many individuals are weak and debilitated after an attack but recover with no serious effects. Some encephalitides may cause irreparable brain damage. Prognosis depends upon the specific viral agent that caused the encephalitis; mortality can be as high as 70 percent.

A large number of acute encephalitides are of the type known as demyelinating encephalitis, which may develop in children as a complication of viral diseases, such as measles or chickenpox, or as a result of vaccination against diseases such as smallpox. Damage to the nerve cell body does not occur, but the insulation (myelin sheath) surrounding the nerve fibres is gradually destroyed.

Encephalitis lethargica, or sleeping sickness (to be distinguished from African sleeping sickness, or African trypanosomiasis), occurred in epidemics in Europe and in the United States about the time of World War I but has not been reported since 1930, although certain individuals may rarely exhibit residual symptoms (postencephalitic Parkinsonism).

BRAIN CANCER

Brain cancer is characterized by the uncontrolled growth of cells in the brain. The term *brain cancer* refers to any of a variety of tumours affecting different brain cell types. Depending on the location and cell type, brain cancers may progress rapidly or slowly over a period of many years. Brain cancers are often difficult to treat, and complete cure is often unattainable.

CAUSES AND SYMPTOMS

The causes of different brain cancers remain largely unknown. Unlike many other cancers, brain tumours seem to occur at random in the population and are not usually associated with known risk factors. However, exposure to ionizing radiation, such as during head X-rays, does increase a person's risk of developing certain brain cancers, as does a suppressed immune system or family history of cancer. Symptoms of brain cancer vary widely depending on the location of the tumour. As the tumour grows, it might put pressure on nearby regions of the brain and thereby affect the functions controlled by those regions. Difficulty or changes in speech, hearing, vision, or motor functions can all indicate the presence of a brain tumour. Many brain tumours are initially discovered following chronic headaches, and in some cases seizures are associated with cancers of the brain. Symptoms may also include vomiting, nausea, or numbness in any part of the body.

Diagnosis and Treatment

If a brain tumour is suspected, a neurological exam is conducted to test general brain function. Further diagnosis usually utilizes imaging procedures such as X rays, computed tomography (CT) scans, and MRI. The location and stage of a tumour can also be determined with positron emission tomography (PET) scans. The blood supply feeding a tumour can be assessed by using an X-ray procedure called angiography. A definitive diagnosis usually requires removal of brain tissue for analysis; often this is done during tumour-removal surgery. In other cases, a needle biopsy guided by the images generated by CT scans or MRI may be used to access the tumour.

Brain cancers are usually not diagnosed until symptoms have appeared, and survival rates vary widely, depending on type and location. Some are completely curable. Slow-growing cancers may progress for decades, whereas other types may be fatal within six to eight years. Average survival from some faster-growing tumours, however, no more than one year.

Surgery is the most frequent approach to treating brain tumours. Such surgery may be curative for some cancers, but for others it may only relieve symptoms and prolong survival. In many cases, complete removal of the tumour is not possible. Radiation therapy may be used to cure some brain cancers, but others do not respond to radiotherapy. Radiation generally works best with fast-growing types. Because radiation therapy typically involves X-rays, which pose a risk to healthy brain tissue, it is important to minimize exposure to the normal cells surrounding the tumour. This is accomplished by employing special procedures that focus the radiation. For instance, a device called a gamma knife, which emits a highly controllable beam of radiation, may be used. Even when radiation is localized, however, radiotherapy can cause side effects such as vomiting, diarrhea, or skin irritation. Radiation to the brain may cause scar tissue to form and potentially cause future problems. Memory loss may also occur.

Chemotherapy is used for some brain tumours, but, owing to the brain's protective barrier, many chemotherapeutic agents cannot enter the brain from the bloodstream. Chemotherapy works best on fast-growing tumours, but it is generally not curative and causes side effects similar to radiation therapy. Both radiation therapy and chemotherapy are often used when a person's general health or the location of the tumour prevents surgery. In rare cases where a family history or a personal history of frequent head X rays suggests an increased risk of brain cancer, regular screening by a neurologist may allow developing cancers to be detected earlier. Otherwise, no means of preventing brain tumours are known.

CHAPTER 8

OTHER DISEASES OF THE CENTRAL AND PERIPHERAL NERVOUS SYSTEMS

In addition to neurobiological diseases of development and behaviour and neurological diseases affecting the brain, there are a variety of other diseases that can alter the activity of the central and peripheral nervous systems. The causes of these conditions are diverse and range from blunt trauma to genetic defects to infectious disease. Examples of these diseases include multiple sclerosis, polio, nerve injury, and muscular dystrophy.

DISEASES OF THE BRAINSTEM

Diseases of the brainstem affect the control centres of the brain and therefore tend to disrupt the fundamental neural activities necessary to sustain life. The brainstem can be injured by trauma, tumours, strokes, infections, and demyelination. Complete loss of brainstem function is regarded by some experts as equivalent to brain death.

TRAUMA

The concussive and shearing stresses of head injury may cause concussion, contusion of the brain (most often of the tips of the frontal and temporal lobes, called contre-coup injury), or laceration of the brain tissue. In the last two cases, neurological deficits are detected at the time of injury, and with laceration (as in a depressed fracture of the skull) or bleeding into the brain, posttraumatic epilepsy is possible.

Extradural hematomas, often from tearing of the middle meningeal artery, may result as a complication of a head injury. Arterial blood, pumped into the space between the dura and the inside of the skull, compresses the brain downward through the tentorium or the foramen magnum. Surgical removal of the clot is necessary. Subdural hematomas usually develop more slowly and may sometimes take weeks to form; they follow the rupture of small veins bridging the gap between the surface of the brain and the meninges. Headache, seizures, intellectual decline, and symptoms similar to those of extradural hematomas may occur. Removal of the clot is the usual treatment.

Other complications of head injury include cranial nerve palsies, subarachnoid hemorrhage, thrombosis of a carotid artery, focal deficits, and cerebrospinal fluid leakage, which may lead to intracranial infection. Later consequences include dementia, seizures, irritability, fatigue, headaches, insomnia, loss of concentration, poor memory, and loss of energy. Repeated minor head injuries, which may occur in some boxers, may also lead to dementia and to a Parkinson-like syndrome.

SLEEP DISORDERS

The raphe nuclei of the pons and the locus ceruleus, which mediate sleep, are situated in the brainstem. Sleep consists of two phases: rapid eye movement (REM) sleep and non-REM, or slow-wave, sleep. During non-REM sleep an individual progresses from drowsiness through deeper and deeper levels of relaxation, with decreasing ability to be aroused; progressively slower waveforms appear on an electroencephalogram (EEG) during this phase. Periods of REM sleep, during which dreaming occurs, punctuate slow-wave sleep. Paradoxically, although the individual appears deeply asleep, fast activity occurs on an EEG during this phase, and numerous brief, small-amplitude movements are made by the eyes and the muscles.

Narcolepsy is a genetic disorder in which, with little warning, irresistible sleepiness overcomes a person during the day. One form includes vivid hallucinations on awaking or falling asleep, temporary but profound sleep paralysis on awakening that does not affect breathing, and sudden, brief loss of muscle power in the limbs and trunk during emotional moments such as laughter (cataplexy). Increased sleepiness, or hypersomnia, may be the cause of drowsiness or narcolepsy. Narcolepsy may be described as an intrusion of REM sleep into the waking hours. Treatment of the disorder with stimulants and tricyclic medications is often effective.

BRAIN DEATH

Brain death is synonymous with brainstem death, since the control centres for essential functions such as consciousness, respiration, and blood pressure are located within the brainstem. In many countries strict criteria for diagnosis of brain death have been established by common consent among medical, religious, ethical, and legal experts. Signs of brain death include the presence of deep coma with an established cause, the absence of any brainstem functions such as spontaneous respiration, pupillary reactions, eye movements, and gag and cough reflexes. Electroencephalography (EEG) may be a useful confirmatory test. When brainstem death is confirmed, the heart usually stops beating within a day or two, even when other vital functions are artificially maintained.

DEMYELINATING DISEASES

Demyelinating diseases frequently affect the spinal cord, particularly the corticospinal tracts and dorsal columns. The only features of Devic disease, a variant of multiple sclerosis, are a band of spinal cord inflammation and demyelination and optic nerve involvement. Demyelination frequently affects the cerebellum and its connections. The primary signs of cerebellar disease are nystagmus, ataxia, and scanning speech.

MULTIPLE SCLEROSIS

Multiple sclerosis (MS; also known as disseminated sclerosis) is a progressive disease of the central nervous system and is characterized by the destruction of the myelin sheath surrounding the nerve fibres of the brain, spinal cord, and optic nerves. As a result the transmission of nerve impulses becomes impaired, particularly in pathways involved with vision, sensation, and movement.

MS has a worldwide distribution but is five times more common in temperate regions than in tropical regions. The disease primarily occurs in individuals between ages 20 and 40, and women are affected by the disease more often than men. The onset of MS is usually gradual, with alternating intervals of exacerbation and remission of symptoms. Initial symptoms include numbness or tingling in the extremities or on the side of the face, muscle weakness, dizziness, unsteady gait, and visual disturbances such as blurred or double vision and partial blindness. The intensity of these early symptoms subside in most individuals for months or even years, but, as the disease progresses, remissions usually become shorter. In subsequent recurrences, old symptoms become more severe, and new signs and symptoms appear including abnormal reflexes, difficulty in coordinating and controlling movement, bladder dysfunction, and neuropsychological problems such as depression, memory loss, and emotional instability. Eventually the impairment of motor control can develop into complete paralysis. In about 30 percent of cases, the disease progresses without remission; however, most people with MS have a normal life expectancy.

The cause of MS remains unclear, but in many cases there is evidence of a heritable component. Several genetic variations (called polymorphisms) associated with MS occur in a cluster of genes that make up the major histocompatibility complex (MHC; also called human leukocyte antigen, or HLA, system), which regulates immune function. Some of these variations appear to be associated with environmental factors that precipitate the onset of disease. For example, the risk of MS in northern Europeans who carry a particular MHC variant is exacerbated by vitamin D deficiency, which weakens immune function. Thus, vitamin D supplementation in those people who carry the variation may confer some degree of protection against MS.

There are also variations in genes outside of the MHC that have been identified and associated with MS, including several occurring in genes that encode proteins for signaling molecules known as interleukin receptors. These receptors are expressed on the cell membranes of B and T lymphocytes and play an important role in regulating lymphocyte development. Some variations in interleukin receptor genes are associated with autoimmune diseases, such as type 1 diabetes and Graves disease. There is much evidence suggesting that MS results from an autoimmune reaction in which a malfunctioning immune system produces T cells that react with and damage the body's own cells, specifically the myelin sheath of nerve fibres. The trigger for this autoimmune reaction is not known, but it is suspected to be related to genetic factors, with the interaction of variations in multiple genes, rather than a single gene, being a likely cause. Some scientists believe these changes in immune function could also be the result of exposure to a virus.

There is no cure for MS, but a number of medications, such as corticosteroids, are used to alleviate symptoms. In addition, there are a handful of disease-modifying agents available for MS. These agents can reduce the frequency of relapses and generally slow the progress of the disease. Immunotherapy with different forms of interferon beta, a protein the body normally produces to modulate immune response, is used to reduce the severity and frequency of the exacerbation periods of the disease. Natalizumab (Tysabri), a monoclonal antibody (an antibody clone derived from a single immune cell), is also effective for controlling the severity and frequency of relapses. Natalizumab attaches to molecules on the cell membrane of lymphocytes, preventing them from entering the central nervous system and attacking nerve cells. Another monoclonal antibody, called Alemtuzumab (Campath), which is used to treat chronic lymphocytic leukemia, also binds to the cell membrane of lymphocytes but works by stimulating antibody-mediated destruction of the cells. In clinical trials in patients with early-stage relapsing-remitting MS, this agent not only stopped progression of the disease but also facilitated the restoration of nerve function in some patients. Other disease-modifying agents used to treat MS include glatiramer acetate (Copraxone) and the immunosuppressant drug mitoxantrone (Novantrone).

Another treatment for MS that has been explored in clinical trials is a form of stem cell therapy called autologous (self) hematopoietic stem cell transplant. This therapy has been tested only in patients who have not responded to conventional treatment regimens and therefore elect to undergo immunosuppressive therapy to destroy lymphocytes that have acquired autoimmune characteristics. Prior to the administration of immunosuppressive drugs, hematopoietic stem cells are harvested from the patient's blood or bone marrow. These cells are then frozen and stored for later reinfusion into the patient following immunosuppressive therapy. Because hematopoietic stem cells have the potential to develop into normally functioning lymphocytes, transplant provides the patient's immune system with an opportunity to recover normal activity. This treatment has proved successful in stopping or delaying disease progression in some patients, and, in rare cases, it has even led to the repair of neurological damage. However, significant risks are associated with stem cell therapy, including increased susceptibility to infection and possibility of transplant failure or relapse of disease.

ATAXIA

Ataxia is the inability to coordinate voluntary muscular movements. In common usage, the term describes an unsteady gait. Most hereditary ataxias of neurological origin are caused by degeneration of the spinal cord and cerebellum; other parts of the nervous system are also frequently involved. The most common of these is Friedreich ataxia, named after the German neurologist Nicholaus Friedreich. During the first three to five years of life, only a few physical deformities (e.g., hammertoe) may be present. During adolescence, the gait becomes progressively unsteady—frequently interpreted as clumsiness. The unsteadiness further progresses to a broad-based, lurching gait; sudden turns are extremely difficult without falling. Tremors develop in the upper extremities and in the head.

Speech is slow, slurred, and monotonous. Skeletal deformities and muscle weakness are common.

Although the course of the disease is slow, it is progressive. Spontaneous remissions occur rarely, and there is usually almost complete incapacity by age 20. There is no specific therapy, and death is usually the result of another complicating disease or heart failure.

DISEASES OF THE PERIPHERAL NERVOUS SYSTEM

The peripheral nervous system is most often afflicted by a set of conditions known as neuropathies, which include diseases such as amyotrophic lateral sclerosis (Lou Gehrig disease) and polio. In some cases, neuropathies arise from traumatic injury to nerves. Abnormal functioning of peripheral nerves also is involved in demyelinating diseases, such as myasthenia gravis and muscular dystrophy, as well as diseases of the cranial nerves.

NEUROPATHIES

Neuropathies are disorders of the peripheral nervous system that may be genetic or acquired, progress quickly or slowly, involve motor, sensory, and autonomic nerves, and affect only certain nerves or all of them. A neuropathy can cause pain or loss of sensation, weakness, paralysis, loss of reflexes, muscle atrophy, or, in autonomic neuropathies, disturbances of blood pressure, heart rate, or bladder and bowel control; impotence; and inability to focus the eyes. Some types damage the neuron itself, others the myelin sheath that insulates it. Examples include carpal tunnel syndrome, amyotrophic lateral sclerosis, polio, and shingles. Causes include diseases (e.g., diabetes mellitus,

Lou Gehrig was forced to retire as first baseman for the New York Yankees because he had amyotrophic lateral sclerosis (ALS). Here he is shown at the microphone during Lou Gehrig Appreciation Day at Yankee Stadium on July 4, 1939. Transcendental Graphics/Getty Images

leprosy, syphilis), injury, toxins, and vitamin deficiency (e.g., beriberi).

Amyotrophic Lateral Sclerosis

Amyotrophic lateral sclerosis (ALS), also known as Lou Gehrig disease (or motor neuron disease), is a degenerative neurological disorder that causes muscle atrophy and paralysis. The disease usually occurs after age 40; it affects men more often than women. ALS is frequently called Lou Gehrig disease in memory of the famous baseball player Lou Gehrig, who died from the disease in 1941.

Disease Progression

ALS affects the motor neurons—i.e., those neurons that control muscular movements. The disease is progressive, and muscles innervated by degenerating neurons become weak and eventually atrophy. Early symptoms of ALS typically include weakness in the muscles of the legs or arms and cramping or twitching in the muscles of the feet and hands. Speech may be slurred as well. As the disease advances, speech and swallowing become difficult. Later symptoms include severe muscle weakness, frequent falls, breathing difficulty, persistent fatigue, spasticity, and intense twitching. The affected muscles are eventually paralyzed. Death generally results from atrophy or paralysis of the respiratory muscles. Most patients with ALS survive between three and five years after disease onset.

Two rare subtypes of ALS are progressive muscular atrophy and progressive bulbar palsy. Progressive muscular atrophy is a variety of ALS in which the neuron degeneration is most pronounced in the spinal cord. Symptoms are similar to the common form of ALS, though spasticity is absent and muscle weakness is less severe. In addition, individuals with progressive muscular atrophy generally survive longer than those suffering from typical ALS. Progressive bulbar palsy is caused by degeneration of the cranial nerves and brainstem. Chewing, talking, and swallowing are difficult, and involuntary emotional outbursts of laughing and tongue twitching and atrophy are common. The prognosis is especially grave in this form of ALS.

Hereditary ALS

Although the majority of cases of ALS are sporadic (not inherited), approximately 10 percent of them are hereditary. In fact, mutations occurring in several genes have been associated with familial forms of ALS. Variations in a gene known as *FUS/TLS* are responsible for about 5 percent of all hereditary cases of the disease. Although the mechanism by which variations in this gene give rise to ALS is unclear, it is known that the FUS/TLS protein plays a role in regulating the translation of RNA to protein in motor neurons. This function is similar to a protein encoded by a gene called *TDP43*, in which rare mutations have been associated with inherited ALS. Variations in the *FUS/TLS* and *TDP43* genes cause an accumulation of proteins in the cytoplasm of neurons. This abnormal protein buildup is suspected of contributing to neuronal dysfunction.

Defects in a gene called *SOD1*, which produces an enzyme known as SOD, or superoxide dismutase, also has been linked to some cases of hereditary ALS. SOD eliminates free radicals from the body's cells. Free radicals are molecular by-products of normal cell metabolism that can accumulate in and destroy cells. Variations in *SOD1* cause ineffective production of superoxide dismutase in neutralizing free radicals, which subsequently destroy motor neurons.

Diagnosis and Treatment

Genetic screening can identify carriers of gene mutations in families with a history of ALS. However, in most cases, diagnosis is based primarily on tests that rule out other neurological disorders, particularly in individuals who do not have a family history of the disease. Urine tests and blood analysis are commonly used when attempting to diagnose ALS. Patients also may undergo electromyography, which records the electrical activity of muscle fibres, and nerve conduction studies, which measure the speed of neuronal conduction and the strength of neuronal signaling. In addition, some patients are examined by means of MRI, which can provide information about brain structure and activity.

There is no cure for ALS. However, the progression of the disease can be slowed by treatment with a drug called riluzole. Riluzole is the only drug treatment available specifically for ALS and has been shown to increase survival by about two to three months. A surgical treatment available to patients with advanced disease is tracheostomy, in which an opening is created in the trachea in order to enable connection to a ventilator (breathing machine). Patients also may choose to undergo physical therapy involving exercises to maintain muscle strength. In addition, speech therapy and the use of special computers and speech synthesizers can help maintain or improve communication.

Some persons affected by ALS carry a variation in a gene called *KIFAP3* that appears to slow the rate of progression of the disease. In fact, in those persons with ALS who carry this genetic variant, survival may be extended by as much as 40–50 percent.

Polio

Polio, also known as infantile paralysis, is an acute viral infectious disease of the nervous system that usually begins with general symptoms such as fever, headache, nausea, fatigue, and muscle pains and spasms and is sometimes followed by a more serious and permanent paralysis of muscles in one or more limbs, the throat, or the chest. More than half of all cases of polio occur in children under age five. The paralysis so commonly associated with the disease actually affects fewer than 1 percent of persons infected by the poliovirus. Between 5 and 10 percent of infected persons display only general symptoms, and more than 90 percent show no signs of illness at all.

For those infected by the poliovirus, there is no cure, and in the mid-20th century hundreds of thousands of children were struck by the disease every year. Since the 1960s, thanks to widespread use of polio vaccines, polio has been eliminated from most of the world, and it is now endemic only in several countries of Africa and South Asia.

Although polio has been widely eradicated, people in some parts of the world, like 25-year-old Mohammad Gulzar Safi of India, still fall victim to the disease. Manpreet Romana/AFP/Getty Images

The Course of the Disease

Poliomyelitis means "gray marrow inflammation," referring to the propensity of the poliovirus to attack certain cells in the spinal cord and brainstem. The poliovirus is a picornavirus (family Picornaviridae), a member of a group known as enteroviruses that inhabits the human digestive tract. (Humans are the only known hosts of the poliovirus.) The virus enters the body most often by the so-called fecal–oral route — that is, from fecal matter taken into the mouth through contaminated food or fingers. It can also enter by ingestion of droplets expelled from the throat of an infected person. New victims may become ill about 7 to 14 days after ingesting the virus. Infected persons may shed the virus from their throats for a week, beginning a day or more before suffering any symptoms themselves, and they may continue to shed the virus in their feces for a month or more after their illness.

After the poliovirus is swallowed, it multiplies in lymph nodes of the intestinal tract and spreads through the body via the bloodstream. In some people the virus gets no farther, causing only a vague flulike illness to develop. The most common early symptoms of polio are mild headache, fever, sore throat, nausea, vomiting, diarrhea, restlessness, and drowsiness. Fever peaks in two to three days and then rapidly subsides, and patients recover within three to four days without the development of paralysis.

In some cases, however, the virus begins an assault on the central nervous system, inflaming and destroying motor cells of the spinal cord and brainstem. In these cases, patients become irritable and develop pain in the back and limbs, muscle tenderness, and stiff neck. Many recover at this stage, but approximately 1 in 200 persons with polio develops what is known as flaccid paralysis.

The motor impulses that normally move along the nerve fibres from the spinal cord to muscles are blocked, and, as a result, muscles become limp and cannot contract. The extent of paralysis depends on where the virus strikes and the number of nerve cells that it destroys. Cells that are not severely injured recover their normal function in time; to the extent that they do recover, a corresponding restoration of muscle function may be expected. Cells that are destroyed, however, are not replaced, because nerve cells cannot regenerate. In this case the paralysis is complete and permanent, with associated progressive atrophy of the unused muscles.

In most cases paralytic polio strikes the limb muscles, particularly the legs. Paralysis does not always involve the limbs, however. The abdominal muscles or the muscles of the back may be paralyzed, affecting posture. The neck muscles may become weak, so that the head cannot be raised. Paralysis of the face muscles may cause twisting of the mouth or drooping eyelids. In some types of spinal polio, the virus damages the upper part of the spinal cord, with resulting difficulties in breathing. In bulbar polio the virus attacks the brainstem, and the nerve centres that control swallowing and talking are damaged. Secretions collect in the throat and may lead to suffocation by blocking the airway. Some 5 to 10 percent of persons afflicted with paralytic polio die, usually of respiratory complications.

There seem to be individual differences in the degree of natural susceptibility to the disease. Many persons have acquired antibodies to the poliovirus in their blood without having had any symptoms of infection. It is generally held that a lasting immunity follows recovery from the disease. However, because there are three different serotypes of poliovirus—commonly called types I, II, and III—second attacks can occur. Persons who recover from an infection caused by one type of poliovirus are permanently immune to reinfection by that type but not to infection by the other types. For this reason polio vaccines are trivalent—that is, designed to generate antibodies to all three poliovirus types.

Among as many as one-quarter of former polio victims whose condition has been stabilized for years or even decades, a condition called post-polio syndrome has been recognized. Post-polio syndrome manifests itself as increased weakness, muscle atrophy, or other conditions involving the originally affected muscle groups or a different group of muscles. The cause of the syndrome is not known for certain, but it may arise when nerve branches grown by nerve fibres that survived the original infection begin to deteriorate as the former polio victim passes through middle age. There is no cure for post-polio syndrome.

Treatment and Vaccination

Treatment during the preparalytic stages of polio includes complete bed rest, isolation, and careful observation. If paralysis occurs, passive movement of the limbs can be used to avoid deformities. As muscle strength returns, exercises are increased. Breathing may require mechanical aids such as the positive pressure ventilator, which pumps air into the patient's lungs through an endotracheal tube inserted into the windpipe. Ventilators have largely replaced the "iron lungs" that gave polio such a dreadful image during the 20th century. Formally known as tank respirators, iron lungs were large steel cylinders that enclosed the abdomen or the entire body (except for the head) of a patient lying immobilized on a bed. Through the action of an attached bellows, air pressure inside the cylinder was alternately reduced and restored, forcing the paralyzed patient's lungs to expand and contract.

There are two types of polio vaccine: the inactivated poliovirus vaccine (IPV), also known as the Salk vaccine after its inventor, Jonas Salk; and the oral poliovirus vaccine (OPV), or Sabin vaccine, named for its inventor, Albert Sabin. IPV, based on killed, or inactivated, poliovirus types I, II, and III, was the first vaccine to break the scourge of polio epidemics in the 1950s. It is administered by injection and circulates through the bloodstream, where it causes the generation of antibodies against active, or "wild" (as opposed to vaccine-type), virus. OPV is based on live but weakened, or attenuated, poliovirus. There are two types of OPV: trivalent (tOPV), which contains all three types of live attenuated polioviruses; and monovalent (mOPV), which contains one of the three types of live attenuated polioviruses. Thus, trivalent vaccine is effective against all three types of poliovirus, and monovalent vaccines are effective against a single type of poliovirus. The specificity of mOPVs increases their effectiveness, such that a single dose of mOPV1, which is effective only against poliovirus type I, confers immunity to type I virus in roughly 70 to 80 percent of children, whereas a single dose of tOPV confers immunity to type I virus in about 20 to 40 percent of children.

OPV is administered by drops in the mouth. After the vaccine is swallowed, the attenuated virus multiplies in the small intestine and lymph nodes and causes the generation of antibodies against wild virus. It is also shed through the inoculated person's feces, thus indirectly immunizing other people through the fecal-oral route. OPV became the predominant vaccine after it was introduced in the early 1960s. Both vaccines are given three times, preferably in the first few months of an infant's life and then usually once as a "booster" when the child reaches school age. With these four doses, immunity against polio is almost completely assured.

In rare cases, OPV can give rise to vaccine-derived polioviruses (VDPVs), which are mutated strains of the live attenuated virus contained in the vaccine. There are several different types of VDPVs, including circulating vaccine-derived viruses (cVDPVs), which cause paralysis and occur within populations that have low polio-immunization rates. OPV has also been known to cause rare cases of what is known as vaccine-associated paralytic polio (VAPP) in both vaccine recipients and their contacts. Such cases occur once in every two million or more doses of OPV. VAPP appears to be caused by a reversion mutation of attenuated virus, thereby converting the virus back to an infectious form that subsequently attacks the nervous system. VAPP is more likely to arise in persons whose immune systems are deficient. Because of this risk, OPV was dropped from immunization programs in the United States in 2000 in favour of IPV. However, OPV, particularly mOPV1, which was found to be four times more effective in children than other polio vaccines, continued to be used in countries such as Nigeria, where polio remained a significant problem in the early 21st century.

Nerve Injuries

Nerve injuries function as neuronal neuropathies affecting the axon far from the cell body. Injuries are of three main grades of severity. In neurapraxia there is temporary blockage of impulse conduction, although the axons remain intact. More severe stretch or incision damage interrupts some axons and is called axonotmesis. Injury that actually severs the nerve is called neurotmesis; surgical reattachment of the severed nerve ends is necessary. Neurosurgery does not guarantee a rapid recovery, since new nerve sprouts grow down the nerve framework at the rate of 1 to 2 mm (0.04 to 0.08 inch) per day at most.

Demyelinating Neuropathies

Demyelinating neuropathies are those in which the Schwann cells, which form myelin (the white, insulating sheath on the axon of many nerve fibres), are primarily affected and migrate away from the nerve. This process causes the insulating myelin of axon segments to be lost, and conduction of nerve impulses down the axon is blocked.

Acquired demyelinating neuropathies may arise as complications of diphtheria and diabetes, which, partly because of damage to the smallest blood vessels supplying the nerves, are sometimes accompanied by a variety of motor, sensory, autonomic, or mixed neuropathies. Some of these are extremely painful. If sensation is impaired, minor injuries can lead to severely deformed, but painless, "Charcot" joints. Leprosy (probably the most common cause of neuropathy in the world), metabolic diseases, cancer, and myeloma or other dysproteinemias also cause demyelinating neuropathies.

Charcot-Marie-Tooth disease (also known as peroneal muscular atrophy because of the special involvement of shin muscles) is a genetically acquired demyelinating neuropathy. High foot arches, distal motor weakness and atrophy, and reduced reflexes are the main symptoms; sometimes the nerves are greatly thickened. The condition first appears in childhood, though patients have a normal life span.

Guillain-Barré syndrome is an acute inflammatory neuropathy. In this disease an autoimmune attack upon the myelin sheath of the motor nerves leads to progressive weakness and reflex loss with only slight sensory changes. Weakness rarely may become so severe that the patient needs mechanical help in breathing, but if further complications do not occur, the disease will remit within a few weeks. In severe cases, blood transfusion may speed recovery.

Carpal tunnel syndrome is a common ischemic neuropathy in which the median nerve is compressed at the wrist. Ischemic neuropathies are those disorders in which nerve compression leads to decreased blood supply and subsequent damage to the Schwann cells. The nerve narrows at the site of pressure, although the axon remains intact. Carpal tunnel syndrome causes pain, numbness, tingling, and weakness of the fingers and thumb, especially at night and in the morning. Cubital tunnel syndrome is a similar problem affecting the ulnar nerve at the elbow. Surgical intervention may be necessary to release the entrapped nerve.

Neuropathies of the autonomic nerves may be hereditary, as in Riley-Day syndrome, or acquired, as in complications of partial nerve injuries, diabetes mellitus, tabes dorsalis, Guillain-Barré syndrome, and other toxic or metabolic disorders (among which alcoholism and certain drug therapies are the most common). Damage to the sympathetic or parasympathetic pathways in the hypothalamus or brainstem may produce similar symptoms—for example, faintness due to disordered regulation of blood pressure and heart rate, disturbances of bladder and bowel control, impotence, and impaired visual accommodation. Some relief may be obtained from medications that replace a deficient neurotransmitter, increase the blood volume, or compress the limbs so that blood no longer pools in the veins.

MYASTHENIA GRAVIS

Myasthenia gravis is a chronic autoimmune disorder characterized by muscle weakness and chronic fatigue that is caused by a defect in the transmission of nerve impulses from nerve endings to muscles. The disease can occur at any age, but it most commonly affects women under age 40 and men over age 60. Persons with the disease often have a higher incidence of other autoimmune disorders. Approximately 75 percent of individuals with myasthenia gravis have an abnormal thymus.

Myasthenia gravis primarily affects the muscles of the face, neck, throat, and limbs. The onset of symptoms is usually gradual, with initial manifestations of the disease seen in the muscles governing eye movements and facial expressions. Weakness may remain confined to these areas, or it may extend to other muscles, such as those involved in respiration. Muscular exertion seems to exacerbate symptoms, but rest helps restore strength.

The autoimmune reaction underlying myasthenia gravis results from a malfunction in the immune system in which the body produces autoantibodies that attack specific receptors located on the surface of muscle cells. These receptors are found at the neuromuscular junction, where nerve cells interact with muscle cells. Under normal circumstances, a nerve cell, stimulated by a nerve impulse, releases the neurotransmitter acetylcholine, which crosses the neuromuscular junction and binds to receptors on the muscle cell, thus triggering a muscular contraction. In myasthenia gravis, autoantibodies bind to the receptors, preventing acetylcholine from binding to them and thus preventing the muscle from responding to the nerve signal.

Treatments for myasthenia gravis include anticholinesterase medications, which stimulate the transmission of nerve impulses, and corticosteroids, such as prednisone, which dampen the immune response. Removal of the thymus often results in improvement.

David Freeman, who suffers from muscular dystrophy, sits near a portable generator used to power his respirator in the event of power outages. Justin Sullivan/Getty Images

MUSCULAR DYSTROPHY

Muscular dystrophy is a hereditary disease that causes progressive weakness and degeneration of the skeletal muscles. Of the several types of muscular dystrophy, the more common are Duchenne, facioscapulohumeral, Becker, limb-girdle, and myotonic dystrophy. In all of these there is usually early evidence of degeneration and then regeneration of some muscle fibres. Those fibres that regenerate become larger than normal, and eventually the muscles are totally replaced by fibrous scar tissue and fat.

Duchenne muscular dystrophy is the most common childhood form of the disease; it occurs in one of every 3,300 male births. It is a sex-linked disorder, meaning that it strikes males almost exclusively. The disease is caused by a defective gene on the 23rd, or X, chromosome that results in the failure of the body to produce a functional muscle protein called dystrophin. Most females who carry the genetic defect are unaffected, but they have a 50 percent probability of passing the disease to each of their sons. Early symptoms, which usually occur between the ages of two and six, include a waddling gait, frequent falling, difficulty in getting up from a lying or sitting position, enlargement of the calf muscles, inability to raise the knees, and disappearance of a normal knee or ankle jerk; symptoms become more obvious as the child ages. Stairs eventually become impossible to climb, and by early adolescence the child is unable to walk. Muscle wasting progresses upward from the legs, and the arms are eventually affected. Ultimately, muscle wasting affects the muscles of the diaphragm, and breathing becomes shallow. Life-threatening pulmonary infections or respiratory failure usually occurs before the age of 20. Genetic testing can reliably detect the Duchenne gene in female carriers and in affected male fetuses.

Becker muscular dystrophy has symptoms similar to Duchenne but begins in later childhood or adolescence and progresses more slowly. It is also a sex-linked disorder that is caused by a defective gene on the X chromosome; however, some functional dystrophin is produced. Individuals with this form of muscular dystrophy may function well into adult life, with certain limitations.

Limb-girdle dystrophy (dystrophy of the pelvic or shoulder muscles) affects both sexes. The first symptoms are manifest in the pelvic region, starting in late childhood. Muscular weakness eventually progresses to the arms and legs. Symptoms include frequent falling, difficulty in climbing, and a waddling gait.

Facioscapulohumeral dystrophy (dystrophy related to the face, the shoulder blade, and the upper arm) starts in adolescence and affects both sexes. The first symptom may be difficulty in raising the arms. Later symptoms may include weakness of the legs and pelvic girdle, forward sloping of the shoulders, and difficulty in closing the eyes. This form of muscular dystrophy can range in severity; individuals with facioscapulohumeral dystrophy may be mildly affected or totally disabled.

Myotonic muscular dystrophy is the most common form of the disease affecting adults. The primary symptom is myotonia, a stiffening of the muscles after use. Myotonic muscular dystrophy may also affect the central nervous system, heart, gastrointestinal tract, eyes, and endocrine glands. Because of the possibility of serious cardiac complications, individuals with this form of muscular dystrophy may require a pacemaker. Myotonic muscular dystrophy type 1 and myotonic muscular dystrophy type 2 are both caused by a genetic mutation, albeit on different chromosomes, that results in defective RNA, the molecule that translates DNA into proteins. Genetic testing can detect these mutations in persons suspected to have the disease.

There is no specific cure or treatment for muscular dystrophy. Physical therapy, exercises, splints, braces, and corrective surgery may help relieve some of the symptoms. Corticosteroid medications may slow the progression of the disease.

CONGENITAL MYOPATHY

Congenital myopathies cause weakness and poor muscle development in the early years of life, but generally they are not progressive. Diagnosis is determined by muscle biopsy. Lipid storage myopathies are associated with disorders of the metabolism of carnitine, a substance that muscle cells use to convert fatty acids into energy. In these conditions severe muscle weakness progresses slowly. A muscle biopsy shows accumulation of fat in the fibres. In the glycogen storage diseases glycogen accumulates in muscle fibre, because of a deficiency of an enzyme that helps degrade glycogen into lactic acid for the production of energy. Beginning in childhood, fatigue, pain, and occasional severe muscle cramps during exercise are common. Diagnosis is determined by demonstrating that the exercising muscles do not produce lactic acid as they should.

OTHER INHERITED MUSCLE DISEASES

Myoglobinuria is a condition in which myoglobin, a substance that stores oxygen within the muscles, spills into the blood and urine. Myoglobin may accumulate in the tubules of the kidney and cause renal failure. This condition, which primarily occurs as a result of muscle damage, can also occur as an inherited metabolic defect or may follow heavy exercise, injury, or toxic damage from drugs or chemicals.

Malignant hyperthermia is a metabolic muscle disease characterized by high fever and extreme rigidity of muscles, usually caused by certain anesthetics or muscle-relaxant medications given during surgery. Rapid cooling of the patient, correction of the accumulation of lactic acid in the blood (the result of intense muscle contraction), and administration of dantrolene sodium to relax the muscles is necessary for treatment.

In familial periodic paralyses episodes of weakness occur in association with abnormally high or low blood levels of potassium. Some attacks are caused by a period of rest following heavy exercise, others are caused by carbohydrate or alcohol consumption. Depending on the type of paralysis, treatment includes the administration of potassium, glucose, and diuretics.

DISEASES OF THE CRANIAL NERVES

Cranial nerves extend to a number of receptors that are involved in sensations such as smell, taste, sight, and hearing. As a result, when these nerves are afflicted by disease, a variety of sensory abnormalities may arise. In addition, the loss of feeling in muscles innervated by cranial nerves may accompany diseases of certain nerves. There are many different causes of cranial nerve diseases. For example, they may result from inherited mutations or from exposure to chemicals in the environment. In some cases, they occur secondary to a preexisting disease.

Damage to the olfactory nerve can occur from a head injury, local nasal disease, or pressure from a tumour and may result in reduced sensitivity to smell or a complete loss (anosmia) on the side supplied by the nerve. Damage to the nerve may also result in a loss of flavour perception. Hallucinations of smell may occur in brain disorders such as epilepsy, with the presence of a tumour, or in depressive illnesses.

Disorders of the optic nerve or of the pathways traveling to the occipital lobe cause visual loss in the affected eye. In the early stages of disease, when the optic process is irritating the nerve rather than decreasing its conducting ability, phenomena such as streaks of light may be seen. When the optic pathways are affected within the brain, the precise location of the disease can be determined by testing the pattern of visual loss affecting both eyes. Pain in the eyes is sometimes due to neuritis of the optic nerves, but it is usually caused by ocular disease. Optic neuritis causes a total or partial loss of vision. It is a condition that is occasionally inherited, but it may also occur because of infection, drug or chemical toxicity, ischemia, or demyelinating disease. Compression of the nerve by a tumour or aneurysm may eventually cause demyelination, which results in optic atrophy. Papilledema is a condition characterized by a swelling of the nerve head with fluid as a result of raised intracranial pressure.

Compression of the oculomotor, trochlear, or abducens nerves may be caused by lesions, diabetes, vascular disease, head injury, infection, or neuropathy. In the brainstem, multiple sclerosis, stroke, Wernicke disease, and tumours are possible causes of compression. Double vision is the primary symptom; if the oculomotor nerve is affected, the pupil may be enlarged as well. In Horner syndrome, interruption of the long sympathetic fibres passing from the brainstem to the pupil causes drooping of the eyelid and a small pupil.

Argyll Robertson pupils, small and irregular pupils that do not react to light but constrict on accommodation to close vision, may be associated with syphilis or other brainstem diseases. Adie pupils constrict very slowly in light and dilate slowly when the light is removed. In progressive external ophthalmoplegia, a disorder of the central nervous system mechanisms controlling gaze, the eyes may fail to move in one or another direction. Other neurological problems, such as parkinsonism, dementia, or neuropathy, may be associated with this condition. Local lesions of the brainstem may also cause paralysis of eye movement, as may severe myasthenia and myopathies affecting the eye muscles.

The jerky eye movements of nystagmus usually signify brainstem, vestibular, or cerebellar disease, but they may also be complications of very poor eyesight or may occur as a congenital defect. When any of the three oculomotor nerves are affected, the axes of the eyes are not able to remain parallel, so light falls on different parts of the two retinas and double vision results.

Numbness of the face is commonly due to compression of the trigeminal nerve caused by a tumour in the cranial cavity or nasopharynx or by a brainstem disorder. Trigeminal neuralgia, also called tic douloureux, is an intense, repetitive, pain felt in the lower half of one side of the face. It occurs primarily in people over age 55. Symptoms may be relieved by medications such as carbamazepine, diphenylhydantoin, or baclofen or by surgical removal of a loop of normal artery where it impinges upon the nerve at its exit from the brainstem.

The facial nerve is damaged most commonly by swelling within the facial canal in the temporal bone that results from viral infection. This causes Bell palsy, an abrupt weakness of all the facial muscles on one side of the face that is often accompanied by pain around the ear, unusual loudness of sounds on the same side, and loss of taste on the front of the tongue. Facial palsy can also be caused by infection with herpes simplex virus, lesions of the brainstem and of the angle between the cerebellum and pons, middle-ear infections, skull fractures, diseases affecting the parotid gland, and Guillain-Barré syndrome. The facial nerve is also affected in hemifacial spasm, a repetitive twitching of one side of the face. Irritation of the facial nerve as it leaves the brainstem appears to be the cause, and in many cases relief is obtained through surgical decompression.

When both divisions of the vestibulocochlear nerve are affected by disease, symptoms may include ringing in the ear (tinnitus), a sensation of spinning (vertigo), and other symptoms such as deafness. Deafness, if not caused by middle-ear disease, suggests damage to the cochlear portion of the nerve. Compression of the nerve at the cerebellopontine angle by a tumour, an aneurysm, a meningioma, certain systemic diseases, drug toxicity, small strokes, or Ménière disease may cause hearing loss. In Ménière disease an accumulation of fluid in the inner ear produces increasing deafness, tinnitus, and vertigo.

Benign postural vertigo is characterized by brief severe attacks of vertigo induced by movement, especially turning in bed. The condition is less persistent than vestibular neuronitis, in which severe vertigo persists for days, probably as a result of viral infection of the inner ear or vestibular nerve.

Damage to the 9th through 12th cranial nerves, the bulbar nerves, causes impairment of swallowing and speech and weakness of the neck muscles. (In this context, the term *bulbar* refers to the medulla oblongata, which looks like a swelling, or bulb, at the top of the spinal cord.) These paralyses often lead to choking and asphyxia due to inhalation of saliva and food and inability to swallow or clear the airway of secretions that may be aspirated into the lungs. A nasal tone to the voice and weakness of coughing are early signs of damage to these nerves. Causes of bulbar palsy include motor neuropathies, such as diphtheria, polio, and botulism, motor neuron diseases, myasthenia gravis, certain muscle diseases, and compression of the nerves by tumours.

NEUROBLASTOMA

Neuroblastoma is a tumour of the sympathetic nervous system (the branch of the autonomic nervous system that is best known for producing the fight-or-flight response) that affects young children. It is the most common pediatric solid tumour that occurs outside the brain, with an annual incidence of about 11 cases per 1 million children between ages 4 and 15 and 30 cases per 1 million children under age 4. Neuroblastoma often arises in the abdomen, usually within the adrenaline-producing adrenal gland, which is located immediately above the kidney. Other common sites of tumour formation include the chest and along the spinal column in the neck or pelvis. Disease may be extensive and metastatic (spreading to other areas of the body) at diagnosis, with cancerous cells typically found throughout the bones and in the bone marrow. Neuroblastoma is unique to pediatric tumours in its genetic and clinical heterogeneity; tumours of infants may spontaneously regress without any therapy, whereas tumours of older children are very difficult to cure. Much is known about the genetics and biology of neuroblastoma, and the development of therapies targeting the underlying biological mechanisms responsible for tumour growth is promising.

DIAGNOSIS

Children are diagnosed with neuroblastoma usually after presenting with symptoms related to the location of the tumour. Children with localized disease in their abdomen may have symptoms such as belly pain, constipation, or diarrhea, whereas patients with metastatic disease may have fever, malaise, weight loss, leg and arm pain, or difficulty walking. In some cases, a clinician can feel the tumour in a child's abdomen during routine physical examination. However, given the nonspecific symptoms of neuroblastoma, it often takes weeks or months for children to be diagnosed with the disease. Diagnostic imaging such as computerized axial tomography can usually identify a tumour. A pathologist confirms the diagnosis through surgical biopsy and histological examination of tumour tissue.

Small molecules called metabolites that are secreted by neuroblastoma cells are usually found in the urine of children with the disease. Although analyzing urine for these molecules in asymptomatic young children was an attractive prospect for early detection, numerous screening studies have shown that this test was not an effective clinical tool. It routinely identified children with neuroblastoma that was destined for spontaneous regression, and it was not associated with a decrease in mortality for older children diagnosed with aggressive forms of the disease. As a result, urine metabolite analysis is used only to aid diagnosis and monitor disease status.

BIOLOGICAL AND GENETIC FACTORS

More than 30 years of neuroblastoma research has demonstrated that there are several important biological and genetic markers that define aggressive disease. Children under 18 months or with tumours that have not disseminated (spread) tend to have a better prognosis and thus require relatively mild forms of therapy compared with children with aggressive disease. Tumours associated with genetic abnormalities, such as amplification of an oncogene (a cancer-inducing gene) known as *MYCN* on chromosome 2 or loss of a part of chromosome 1 or 11, have been correlated with poor prognosis compared with tumours without these genetic changes. It is thought that these abnormalities are responsible, at least in part, for the development and progression of neuroblastoma.

In 2005 data from 8,800 neuroblastoma patients was analyzed to develop a comprehensive classification system based on age, extent of disease (or stage), *MYCN* status, and several other biological and genetic factors. This classification system allows clinicians to predict the progression and risk of relapse of neuroblastoma and to tailor therapy to individual patients.

TREATMENT AND DEVELOPMENT OF TARGETED THERAPIES

Traditional treatment for high-risk (aggressive) neuroblastoma includes intensive, high-dose chemotherapy, surgery, and radiotherapy. Children receive up to six treatments with multidrug chemotherapy regimens. The side effects of these treatments include hair loss, nausea, vomiting, and a decrease in blood cells produced by the bone marrow. Although red blood cells (erythrocytes) and platelets can be replaced by blood transfusion, the infection-fighting white blood cells (leukocytes) cannot, and their loss leads to the risk of serious and even life-threatening infections. Surgery is usually delayed until several cycles of chemotherapy have been completed in order to allow for the tumour to shrink.

Patients often benefit from receiving high-dose chemotherapy treatments followed by bone marrow transplant using their own stem cells, which are isolated and stored prior to undergoing chemotherapy. After recovery from the stem cell transplant, patients are treated with radiation, followed by administration of 13-cis retinoic acid, an agent that is capable of differentiating neuroblastoma cells and therefore of preventing the cells' ability to form tumours. Despite this aggressive approach to treatment, more than half of all children with high-risk neuroblastoma will eventually die from their disease. Children with low- and intermediate-risk neuroblastoma tend to fare much better with surgery alone or with surgery and moderate-dose chemotherapy. Some infants with small localized tumours do not need surgical removal of their tumour, since these tumours usually spontaneously regress.

Traditional chemotherapy targets general cellular mechanisms, affecting normal cells as well as tumour cells. However, emerging therapies for neuroblastoma are designed to target the tumour cells specifically. A molecule called meta-iodobenzylguanidine (MIBG) is selectively internalized by neuroblastoma cells, and when combined with radiolabeled iodine (iodine-131), MIBG can be used to kill tumour cells. Immunotherapy using antibodies that are directed against neuroblastoma cells also have been tested in clinical trials. Other forms of therapy include synthetic retinoids such as fenretinide, which is known to induce neuroblastoma cell death. Drugs that specifically inhibit abnormally activated cellular pathways and blood vessel formation, or angiogenesis, in neuroblastoma have been tested in early-phase clinical studies. In addition, a specific mutation in a gene known as *ALK* (anaplastic lymphoma kinase) was identified in a small subset of patients with neuroblastoma. Therapies designed to target the abnormal gene products of *ALK* have been developed. The incorporation of these targeted treatments into the traditional therapeutic paradigms for neuroblastoma represents an important advance toward improving cure rates.

CONCLUSION

Scientists have only recently come to understand the complexities of the neurons and neurotransmitters that underlie the activity and function of the human nervous system. In the 20th century, advancements in neuroimaging techniques, molecular biology, and genetics enabled scientists to piece together complex details about the function of nerves in health and in disease, ultimately giving rise to the collection of information about the brain and nervous system that exists today. Yet, although scientists can generate images of the living brain and can alter the function of neurons and neurotransmitters with pharmacological agents, they still are unable to provide answers to questions concerning the complex role of neural biochemistry in disorders such as epilepsy and autism.

The modern study of the human nervous system is broad and is based primarily on research into human perception and brain activities that affect movement, behaviour, and memory and on investigations of disease, including neurobiological disorders, cancer, and autoimmune conditions. These studies are supported by the development of novel drugs that alter nervous system activity. Indeed, the emergence of agents capable of inhibiting or stimulating neuronal activity have important roles not only in the treatment of disease but also in basic neuroscience research. For example, drugs that alter neurotransmitter levels have provided key insights into the roles these substances play in maintaining neuronal function.

An important area of modern neuroscience is the study of neuron regeneration in the central nervous system following traumatic injury to the brain or spinal cord. Whereas peripheral neurons frequently are able to regenerate after injury, neurons in the central nervous system are far less adaptable. The two primary lines of research into facilitating recovery from brain or spinal cord injury include devising ways to stimulate neuroprotective mechanisms that prevent excessive neuron death and degeneration and finding ways to stimulate axon regeneration to restore motor function. Scientists are also investigating the use of neural stem cells in the treatment of neurodegenerative conditions, including Parkinson disease. Although these stem cells can grow and differentiate into mature neurons, it remains unclear whether they are able to assume the same functions of the damaged neurons they replace.

An area of neuroscience that is of tremendous value in expanding scientists' understanding of the basic functions of the human brain involves the investigation of neural molecular components that influence human behaviour and that give rise to thoughts, memories, emotions, and dreams. Our perceptions of the world and the cognitive processes associated with these perceptions have long been studied by philosophers, and in the 20th century neuroscientists uncovered a wealth of information that significantly advanced the understanding of the brain and consciousness. Neuroimaging was especially important, because it enabled scientists to associate particular regions of the brain with specific activities; for example, certain areas of the frontal lobe are involved in language acquisition, planning, and speech, whereas the amygdala, located deep within the brain, is involved in processing negative thoughts. It is also known that neurons respond to chemicals and environmental stimuli without our awareness that they are doing so. However, very little is known about how these signals contribute to conscious activities, and uncovering how such processes influence human behaviour is one of the most intriguing challenges facing neuroscientists in the 21st century.

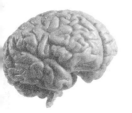
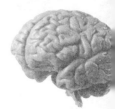

GLOSSARY

afferent Transmitting impulses to the central nervous system.

axon Nerve fibre that connects to other neurons or cells and transports impulses away from the cell body.

caudal Located in the posterior region.

contralateral Corresponding to or coordinated with a part on the opposite side of the body.

cutaneous Related or pertaining to the skin.

cytochemical Related to the chemical makeup of cells.

decussation The crossing of nerve fibres from one side of the nervous system to the other.

dendrite Part of a neuron that typically transports impulses toward a cell body.

diencephalon Portion of the forebrain containing the epithalamus, thalamus, hypothalamus, and subthalamus.

efferent Transmitting impulses away from the central nervous system.

fight-or-flight response Reaction of the sympathetic nervous system that prepares a human or other animal to either take action or retreat when confronted with an external stress and that is characterized by the release of epinephrine, increased heart rate, and other physiological responses.

foramen A small opening.

ganglion Mass of neuron cell bodies located outside the central nervous system.

gestalt The integration of disparate parts into a recognizable unit.

gyrus A ridge on the brain's surface.

homeostasis The maintenance in equilibrium of hormone emission, body temperature, blood pressure, and other bodily functions as the body adjusts to environmental changes.

innervate To provide an organ with nerves; to stimulate a nerve into action.

invaginated Folded or turned inward.

ipsilateral Corresponding to or coordinated with a part on the same side of the body.

kinesthesia Perception of movement by receptors in the joints.

lamina Thin layer.

medial Located in or related to the middle.

myelin White, insulating sheath made up of of fatty materials, protein, and water that covers the axon of many neurons.

neural tube Layer of embryonic tissue that, during development, becomes the brain and spinal cord.

neuron Nerve cell that serves as the basic component of tissue in the nervous system.

phylogenetic Pertaining to evolutionary development.

plexus A network of nerves.

psychogenic Of the mind or emotions.

rostral Located in the anterior (front) area or toward the nose and mouth region.

soma Body of a nerve cell that contains the nucleus but excludes the axons and dendrites.

somatic Pertaining to the wall of the body, including a cell body, skeletal muscle, and the skin surface.

stereotyped Exhibiting repetitive or patterned behaviour.

sulcus A fissure on the brain's surface located between two convolutions (gyri).

synapse The site at which one neuron sends an impulse to another neuron.

telencephalon Portion of the forebrain containing the cerebral hemispheres and related parts of the cerebrum.

tonotopic Arranged such that different sound frequencies are transmitted over different parts of a structure.

ventral Located in the lower or anterior area.

vestibular Pertaining to the detection of movement by the body.

viscera Internal organs of the body.

BIBLIOGRAPHY

General overviews are provided by Malcolm B. Carpenter, *Core Text of Neuroanatomy*, 4th ed. (1991), a popular medical-student text with excellent drawings, photographs, and teaching diagrams; André Parent and Malcolm B. Carpenter, *Carpenter's Human Neuroanatomy*, 9th ed. (1996), a complete, well-documented sourcebook with a coloured atlas; Frank H. Netter (comp.), *Nervous System*, rev. and up-to-date ed., edited by Regina V. Dingle, Alister Brass, and H. Royden Jones, 2 vol. in 1 (1983–86), a work that contributes greatly to three-dimensional concepts; vol. 1 of *The Ciba Collection of Medical Illustrations*, a superb collection of instructive, authoritative colour drawings of the central, peripheral, and autonomic nervous systems as well as diseases of the brain and spinal cord; Stephen G. Waxman, *Correlative Neuroanatomy*, 24th ed. (2000); and Christopher M. Filley, *Neurobehavioral Anatomy* (1995), a discussion of the anatomy of the brain and its functions.

The development of the human nervous system is discussed by Keith L. Moore and T.V.N. Persaud, *The Developing Human: Clinically Oriented Embryology*, 6th ed. (1998), a popular standard book presenting a synopsis of the embryonic development of the nervous system along with relevant clinical information and congenital malformations; Charles R. Noback, Norman L. Strominger, and Robert J. Demarest, *The Human Nervous System: Introduction and Review*, 4th ed. (1991), a general account of the development of the nervous system from its inception through old age, augmented with clinically significant information and appropriate illustrations; and T.W. Sadler and Jan Langman, *Langman's Medical Embryology*, 8th ed.

(2000), a well-known work on human embryology with concise text, excellent illustrations and charts, and numerous points of clinical significance.

Explorations of the central nervous system include Stephen J. DeArmond, Madeline M. Fusco, and Maynard M. Dewey, *Structure of the Human Brain*, 3rd ed. (1989), a photographic atlas of brain sections; Duane E. Haines, *Neuroanatomy: An Atlas of Structures, Sections, and Systems*, 5th ed. (2000), an atlas of brain photographs and vascular supply, with teaching diagrams; and R. Nieuwenhuys, J. Voogd, and Chr. van Huijzen, *The Human Central Nervous System: A Synopsis and Atlas*, 3rd rev. ed. (1988), a well-illustrated, readable text.

Descriptions of the peripheral nervous system—the spinal and cranial nerves—are included in the work by Haines and in the general overviews cited above and in a standard anatomy reference work available in two editions: Henry Gray, *Anatomy of the Human Body*, 30th American ed., edited by Carmine D. Clemente (1985); and *Gray's Anatomy*, 38th (British) ed., edited by Peter L. Williams et al. (1995).

The anatomy of the autonomic nervous system is dealt with in Louis Sanford Goodman and Alfred Gilman, *Goodman & Gilman's The Pharmacological Basis of Therapeutics*, 11th ed., edited by Joel G. Hardman, Lee E. Limbird, and Alfred Goodman Gilman (2005), a text that also provides extensive information on drugs that affect neurotransmission.

General summaries of the functions of the human nervous system are provided by Peter Nathan, *The Nervous System*, 4th ed. (1997), a complete account of the anatomy, physiology, and psychology of the nervous system of humans and other animals, written for readers without an extensive background in biology; and Eric R. Kandel, James H. Schwartz, and Thomas M. Jessel (eds.),

Principles of Neural Science, 4th ed. (2000), an authoritative introduction.

The vestibular system and its functions are the subject of Robert W. Baloh and Vincente Honrubia, *Clinical Neurophysiology of the Vestibular System*, 2nd ed. (1990), a review of the vestibular system in relation to disease states. Discussions of various aspects of the autonomic nervous system include Arthur D. Loewy and K. Michael Spyer (eds.), *Central Regulation of Autonomic Functions* (1990), a review of the brain mechanisms involved in regulating the autonomic nervous system; and Leonard R. Johnson (ed.), *Physiology of the Gastrointestinal Tract*, 3rd ed., 2 vol. (1994), a series of comprehensive reviews on the tract's anatomy, physiology, and pathophysiology.

The following works deal with other functions of the human nervous system: on pain, Ronald Melzack and Patrick D. Wall, *The Challenge of Pain*, updated 2nd ed. (1996); and on vision, Richard L. Gregory, *Eye and Brain: The Psychology of Seeing*, 5th ed. (1997). Also useful is Richard L. Gregory and O.L. Zangwill (eds.), *The Oxford Companion to the Mind* (1987, reissued 1998).

Cerebral functions are described in Alan Baddeley, *Your Memory: A User's Guide*, 2nd ed. (1993); Muriel Deutsch Lezak, *Neuropsychological Assessment*, 3rd ed. (1995); Kenneth M. Heilman and Edward Valenstein, *Clinical Neuropsychology*, 3rd ed. (1993); Bryan Kolb and Ian Q. Whishaw, *Fundamentals of Human Neuropsychology*, 4th ed. (1996); Sally P. Springer and Georg Deutsch, *Left Brain, Right Brain: Perspectives from Cognitive Neuroscience*, 5th ed. (1998); Susan Allport, *Explorers of the Black Box: The Search for the Cellular Basis of Memory* (1986); D. Frank Benson, *The Neurology of Thinking* (1994); Taketoshi Ono et al. (eds.), *Brain Mechanisms of Perception and Memory: From Neuron to Behavior* (1993); and Kevin Walsh and

David Darby, *Neuropsychology: A Clinical Approach*, 4th ed. (1999). I.P. Pavlov, *Conditioned Reflexes: An Investigation of the Physiological Activity of the Cerebral Cortex*, trans. and ed. by G.V. Anrep (1927, reissued 1960; originally published in Russian, 1923), describes the classic experiments and studies of cerebral function in response to signals and reflex behaviour as carried out in dogs and their application to humans.

Sources on the pathology, diagnosis, and treatment of nervous diseases and disorders include *Clinical Neurology on CD-ROM* (2000); H. Houston Merritt, *Merritt's Neurology*, 10th ed., ed. by Lewis P. Rowland (2000); Maurice Victor, Allan H. Ropper, and Raymond D. Adams, *Adams and Victor's Principles of Neurology*, 7th ed. (2001); W. Russell Brain, *Brain's Diseases of the Nervous System*, 11th ed., ed. by Michael Donaghy (2001); Mayo Clinic Department of Neurology, *Mayo Clinic Examinations in Neurology*, 7th ed. (1998); M.-Marsel Mesulam (ed.), *Principles of Behavioral and Cognitive Neurology*, 2nd ed. (2000); Oliver Sacks, *The Man Who Mistook His Wife for a Hat and Other Clinical Tales* (1970, reissued 1998); and William E.M. Pryse-Phillips and T.J. Murray, *Essential Neurology*, 4th ed. (1992).

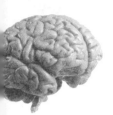
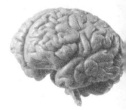

INDEX